THE
REFLECTIVE SPIN

Case Studies of Teachers in
Higher Education Transforming Action

THE
REFLECTIVE SPIN

Case Studies of Teachers in
Higher Education Transforming Action

Edited by

Ai-Yen Chen

National Institute of Education,
Nanyang Technological University, Singapore

John Van Maanen

Sloan School of Management,
Massachusetts Institute of Technology, USA

World Scientific
Singapore • New Jersey • London • Hong Kong

Published by

World Scientific Publishing Co. Pte. Ltd.
P O Box 128, Farrer Road, Singapore 912805
USA office: Suite 1B, 1060 Main Street, River Edge, NJ 07661
UK office: 57 Shelton Street, Covent Garden, London WC2H 9HE

British Library Cataloguing-in-Publication Data
A catalogue record for this book is available from the British Library.

THE REFLECTIVE SPIN
Case Studies of Teachers in Higher Education Transforming Action

ISBN 981-02-4185-2
ISBN 981-02-4186-0 (pbk)

Printed in Singapore by Uto-Print

This book is dedicated to
the late Professor Donald Schon
Massachusetts Institute of Technology, U.S.A.

Contents

Acknowledgements

This book has been an experience in collaboration between two university teachers working together across the Pacific Ocean with about two dozen university colleagues throughout the four corners of the world. Collaboration has been through face-to-face dialogue, infrequent meetings with all the writers including the key leader in reflective practice at the Massachusetts Institute of Technology (MIT), namely Donald Schon, before his untimely death in 1997, computer links, mail and telephone calls. Editing and writing this book have taught both of us much about the nature of long distance virtual collaboration, its agony and joy.

This project would not have been launched without the support of the Sloan School of Management and the Nanyang Business School in funding with a generous research grant in 1994, which facilitated the Reflective Spin project and enabled the organization of two case seminars, one at Sloan, MIT, U.S.A. and the other at the National Institute of Education, Singapore in 1995. The seminars drew more than four dozen scholars from Australia, Britain, Hong Kong, Malaysia, Singapore, and the United States — all committed to the use of case studies as a means of sharing university teaching improvement experiences. Our special thanks therefore go to Alan White and Eleanor Chin of the Sloan School of Management and Tan Teck Meng and Leong Kwong Sin of the School of Accountancy and Business, Nanyang Technological University (NTU) for making our collaboration possible.

Last but not least, our special thanks to Professor Leo Tan, Director, National Institute of Education, Nanyang Technological University, Singapore and the Dean of Education, Professor S. Gopinathan for their encouragement and support throughout the project. Special thanks must be extended to

Joyce James and Tan Boey Geok for their editorial assistance, Emily Ng for her graphic design as well as Cheng Kok Hua and Kenny Ng for their technical support and efficiency in formatting the manuscripts for publication.

We are also grateful to Canadian artist, Pamela Todds Jeffrey, for the cover page painting on *Reflection*.

Preface to The Reflective Spin

S. Gopinathan

National Institute of Education
Nanyang Technological University
Singapore

In spite of the many advances made in our understanding of educational processes in the last fifty years, and in particular the contributions made by the social sciences to such understanding, an enduring problem continues to confront educators, that of developing adequate models for professional education. The necessity for well grounded theories based on the knowledge represented by the social sciences and on the insights, stories and understandings of those individuals and groups in professions has now become urgent. As the century and millennium draw to a close, complex problems such as environment degradation, poverty, malignant diseases, vicious prejudice as represented by "ethnic cleansings" face societies and states around a shrinking globe. It was earlier expected that the professions with their claim to expert knowledge would be equal to these challenges but many are sceptical of such claims. In profession after profession the consequences of an over abundance of knowledge accompanied by a lack of wisdom are apparent. Centres for professional preparation, and universities are but one site, faced with a crucial issue. Many would accept that it is their responsibility to instill in their students both a capacity, and if possible, a disposition to reflect on their experience and learning. However, universities are faced with dynamic change, even turbulence. Capacity for change management and strengthening the organization's ability to learn will be crucial.

This volume represents a modest but impressive effort to tackle the major issue of professional education and the potential for reflective practice within that education. The case studies represented in this volume are the product of a fruitful 3-year Nanyang Technological University–Massachusetts Institute of Technology collaboration inspired by the seminal work of Donald Schon. It represents in twenty chapters the experiences of teachers of professionals who have wrestled with the issues involved in developing educational processes that would create contexts, conditions and opportunities for reflection. What distinguishes the volume is the credible effort to take account of and acknowledge the significance of difference, of norms, values and traditions that colour and shape understanding. The writers and the cases and experiences they talk about do not remain at the level of technique. Importantly, these accounts move the reader to a consideration not only of the purpose of reflection and reflective practice but also of its potential for empowering the individual, and through him/her the collegial communities he/she work with.

The editors, Chen Ai Yen and John Van Maanen are to be congratulated on their devotion to a project which has been long and sometimes taxing. The result, for our benefit, is this handsome volume. That this is a volume bursting with energy and ideas is seen in Schein's use of his Foreword to advance the idea of dialogue, or reflection in a group. I am confident that this book will contribute to the dialogue just begun.

Dialogue: How to Reflect in a Group

Edgar H. Schein

Sloan School of Management
Massachusetts Institute of Technology
United States of America

I would like to take the opportunity in this Foreword to reflect on reflection. It seems to me that there are many calls from various pundits that learning will occur if we learn to reflect, but there is remarkably little advice or even analysis of what might be involved in this process of "reflection." Don Schon showed us brilliantly what this process looks like in reflective practitioners and professionals. I would like to add a small voice to his on what this process looks like if we consider reflection to be a process that occurs within groups as well as within a given individual and if we take the concept of culture seriously, especially if we extend the concept of culture to organizations and occupational communities (Schein, 1992, 1999a).

My basic point is that reflection implies some self-understanding but that in a group how people may understand themselves does not necessarily guarantee that they will understand each other. In fact, if group members come from different organizations or occupational communities, the odds are very high that they will not understand each other because they will have particular ways of interpreting words and concepts based on their histories. Yet they may fall into the trap of thinking they understand each other if the basic language they speak is the same. The problem then is how to uncover this dilemma, confront it together, and do something to overcome it.

Let me give an example. The words "organizational learning" have been very widely used lately by managers, consultants, and academics. Yet one would be hard put to find any kind of common definition that they might agree on. If one looked at the words individually we would find that the word "organization" means different things to different people, and the word "learning" is all over the map in terms of what associations we have to it. Then add the connotation that organizations have to "unlearn" something before they can learn something new and we have a semantic mess. The result of this mess is that we have advocates suggesting all kinds of solutions to how organizations can learn without realizing that they are not talking to each other in any meaningful way. If we take this issue into the domain of "teaching" we find the same complexities. Is teaching science the same thing as teaching history as teaching soccer? Can there be a single theory of teaching? If teachers get together to learn from each other, to reflect together, how can they get past the fact that their language and thought are all different and individual.

The answer to this dilemma lies in finding a new way for people to converse with each other, a way that acknowledges at the outset their different occupational and organizational culture roots, a way that begins to build a new set of concepts and a new set of meanings for old words that are shared, Bill Isaacs in his book on Dialogue (1999) calls it "the art of thinking together," and I think this is a very appropriate concept. How can individual thoughts based on different culture roots come together? Is there a form of conversation that will begin to make this possible? I believe that the way Isaacs conceptualizes Dialogue may provide one avenue. Let me describe briefly my own version of Dialogue based on his seminal work (Schein, 1999b).

We must begin with some motivation to reflect together, to have a conversation that leads to the uncovering of our own assumptions and thought patterns. Dialogue as a form of conversation cannot induce such motivation, but once one gets involved, the rewards in terms of personal insights and mutual understanding keep the process going. Getting involved means the suspension of several norms of conversation that have come to be taken for granted. First, we sit in as nearly a circle as possible. Second, we agree that we are each talking to the group as a whole which can be behaviorally symbolized by talking to a hypothetical campfire in the center of the circle. The point is we do not maintain eye contact, contrary to many "rules" of communication. Third, we begin by "checking in" which means that everyone in the group contributes something before we engage in any kind of exploration. During the check-in we do not ask for clarification or interrupt in any way until everyone is "in." Fourth, we suspend the norm that if we are asked a question, we must answer it, and we try to catch ourselves before we ask a question or voice a disagreement.

For me these are the minimum requirements to get a dialogue started and the purpose of all of these suspensions is to open up my own mind to my own thought processes. The goal is to become conscious of and reflect on what I say and what I think and what my impulses are. If I get in touch with my own assumptions, filters, biases, and impulses, I can begin to listen for these in the contributions of others to the conversation. And as we struggle collectively to listen more to ourselves and each other we are actually building a common framework from which to build joint reflection. The topic is not important, and there need not even be a topic. If we want to be more reflective we just have to begin and see where the process leads us. As you read the fascinating tales in this volume, get together with others who have also read it and begin to reflect together in a dialogic manner. Have Fun.

References

Isaacs, W. (1999). *Dialogue and the art of thinking together*. New York: Doubleday.

Schein, E. H. (1999). *Process consultation revisited: Building the helping relationship*. Reading, MA: Addison-Wesley-Longman.

Schein, E. H. (1992). *Organization culture and leadership*. 2nd Ed. San Francisco, CA: Jossey Bass.

Schein, E. H. (1999). *The corporate culture survival guide*. San Francisco: Jossey Bass.

PROLOGUE

Landscaping the Reflective Spin

Ai-Yen Chen

National Institute of Education
Nanyang Technological University
Singapore

Recent
writings on
reflective practices
by teachers and researchers
*are as diverse as the **landscape** of the Earth.*
It seems apt for those of us who believe in
***critically** and **creatively** thinking about our practices,*
our beliefs, knowledge, competence along with an ethic of care
*will eventually generate **changes in learning:***
***field** and **system-wide changes** in*
how** people **teach** people **how to learn
*in different **disciplines** and **professions.***
*These **changes** can be **evolutionary** or **dramatic***
depending on our mountain-top and valley,
plateau and canyon, or desert and at sea experiences.
*Each **change** is significant because of our*
Reflection** upon the **problem** and the **multiple contexts,
*our **Recognition** of the crux of the problem,*
*our **Realization** that we can **contribute to the solution,***
*our **Response** to the situations*
*and our **Resolve** to*
make a
difference
!

Landscaping the Reflective Spin
Ai-Yen Chen

The new millennium brings with it new challenges and possibilities. A globalised world in which education is going to be the key for cross-national relationships necessitates an understanding, a fundamental understanding, of the ways in which education is practised in different cultures across geographies. The Reflective Spin represents a collection of essays and cases which are going to have an increasing relevance in the world of tomorrow's educational practices as they bring together different perspectives with each their own frames and insights. When the idea for such a book was mooted, few of us realised just how critical the whole education enterprise would be; today we are convinced that the different engagements herewith contained offer a rich resource for educators everywhere. And especially for those of us who are preparing professionals of the future, The Reflective Spin is timely as it allows our students and colleagues to get a handle on those newer and more exciting potentials offered by the new millennium's globalised impact.

To begin with, this collection of cases on reflective practices is a spin-off from my conversations with Donald Schon during my sabbatical leave at the Massachusetts Institute of Technology in 1994. As teachers of professionals, Don in the field of urban planning and I in teacher education, we quite naturally focussed our discussion on reflective practices among teachers of professionals. In our reflection on the relationship between theory and action in a teacher's life, we discussed the focus, cycle and stages of reflection. Don was insistent on focussing on content or professional knowledge in a learning-teaching situation. He firmly believed in the impact of the triadic interaction of the learner, the teacher and the content in understanding a puzzle, confronting a dilemma or solving a problem of a subject. I believe that while content or professional knowledge may be the focus of learning and teaching, the multiple-layered context of learning is crucial in transforming our understanding and beliefs, subsequently changing our actions and professional practices.

On hearing about our conversation, John Van Maanen, Chair of Organisational Studies at the Sloan School of Management, MIT, joined the lively intellectual dialogue. He noted that as there are many different perspectives and ways of analysing the development of reflective practices, the case method would be most appropriate to capture some of the dilemmas and contextual peculiarities. Alan White, the Director of International Studies at Sloan felt that my study on the reflective practices of teachers of professionals is worth sharing among a larger international audience and Sloan was happy to fund the research. His suggestion prompted my journey not only to visit and to observe the different interesting practices of professionals working and teaching in different social and cultural settings but also to invite a number of teachers of professionals in the world to reflect and write about their own practices. John graciously agreed to be my co-editor of the collection of cases while Don consented to comment on their reflections. To generate a collegial setting and negotiate a common framework, we organised two case seminars, one with Don and the MIT writers in Cambridge, another with writers from Asia, Australia, Britain, New Zealand, the United States in Singapore in 1995.

This book is the result of such a prolonged period of reflecting, sharing, and negotiating as the writers faded in and faded out because of their busy schedules and personal commitments. Don Schon's illness in recent months and his untimely death was a tremendous blow to me as he could not fulfil his commitment to critique the cases. However, I greatly believe that the cases in hand offer such valuable insights into the learning of reflective teacher-practitioners that they should be published even without Schon's comments. Schon's zeal and passion for reflective practices have been such an inspiration to me and many other educators that this collection of cases must be dedicated to him for all his educative leadership in this area.

This unique collection of essays and cases focuses on the content, method and contexts of reflective practices by twenty tertiary teachers of professionals from six countries in the East and West. Though writing in different styles and in different contexts, and using different theoretical frameworks and inquiry approaches, they share a great many ideas, values and principles about learning and teaching in higher education. They do not only believe in the role of the individual and the group in active learning and collaborative inquiry into some academic topics and thorny issues, they practice what they believe based on the ethic of care and concern for the individual, the community, their disciplines and professions. Their beliefs and practices seem to spiral in an over-lapping yet very distinct manner in their own disciplinary, social and cultural contexts.

To them, learning and thinking are inseparable. Doing always involves problem-solving. Teaching is most effective when there is a right balance of will, heart, mind and spirit. The writers are knowledgeable and experts in their own fields, yet humble and ready to confess their troubles and toils. They are eager to reflect on their past experiences, joys and failures, extend their capacities and faculties by learning from others, by experimenting with new ideas and technologies, and by discussing with others in their fields. Most of the writers are in their mid-career. A few of them are quite mature in age though not necessarily set and fixed in their ideas. Surprisingly perhaps, they are the most adventurous in trying out new methods and technologies to extend human thought and action, to improve understanding and performance.

So diverse and wide-ranging are their reflections and practices that the use of the *landscape* and *camera lens* metaphors seem to be the most apt to describe the perspectives and organize the cases for easier reading and better understanding of their stories. Two eminent Canadian teacher educators whose recent book on the Teachers' Professional Knowledge Landscapes (Clandinin and Connelly, 1996) and their use of the *landscape* metaphor for the professional knowledge and experience of professionals seem to be an appropriate imagery to set the scene. What follows after scene setting is to find an appropriate method to present the accounts and narratives of the reflective practices and the contexts that transform learning.

How Can Reflective Practices be Framed?

Section One introduces the various perspectives and contexts of reflection. To Richard Pring, Professor of Educational Studies at the University of Oxford, the importance of reflection among practitioners in a learning community must be highlighted particularly in a teacher education programme. His critical comments span across the entire landscape of teacher education from the East and West as he examines the seven teacher educators' cases and shows how their research inform or even change practices in their universities. In the tradition of Lawrence Stenhouse and John Elliot of the University of East Anglia, Pring strongly argues for teachers as researchers or co-researchers of their practices. By so doing, they would reflect, learn from and improve on their practices. By sharing their findings from whichever perspective: content, method or context, they contribute to the shaping of a vibrant learning community in the university or the workplace.

To set the studies within a theoretical and methodological framework, the three dimensions of reflection: the content, the method and the contexts are first presented. Clandinin and Connelly's use of narrative and stories for presenting human reflections serve as a good introduction to the knowledge landscape of human experiences. They believe in creating *safe* places for the expression of the desires of storytelling of professional experiences, of relationship, of reflection. They have created such a *safe* place for their students to reflect in an alternative teacher education programme. As a matter of fact, these *safe* places can be in the classrooms, in schools and universities. They may exist in actual physical spaces, in the minds or hearts of professionals, or in an electronic telecommunication system. Safe places become educative because of the opportunities for telling stories, sharing and reflecting on professional experiences, and building relations in a socio-political context.

John Van Maanen, the eminent sociologist of Sloan School of Management, has been engaged in some major sociological studies, for example, on the London Police Force and Disneyland, justifies the use of the case method for research into the varied and particular nature of reflective practices. Van Maanen's justification for the use of the case method in his essay on 'Case Studies: Why Now, More Than Ever, Cases are Important' in presenting reflective practices can be likened to the human eye focussing on the landscape by using different camera lenses, sometimes clearly focussed in an intimately subjective close-up, sometimes captured in a wide-angle shot, appearing to be distant and objective. The human eye can sometimes zoom-in, sometimes zoom-out, as we think, learn, reflect, and remember people, places and events of the past that will serve as lessons for the present and the future. There are diverse approaches to the use of the case method for sharing knowledge and experience. Some representational, some exemplary, some bottom-up, when the concepts are grounded in the case itself and what the case is about is discovered while doing the research and some are top down, that is, the case is selected to illustrate a general concept.

Ai-Yen Chen and Joyce James reflect upon the multi-layered perspectives of context. Learning and teaching take place in multiple textual, intellectual, emotional, social, cultural, institutional, media and technological, and political contexts. Our understanding and thinking shift and change according to the landscape changes in the physical, disciplinary and institutional settings, not to mention the different lenses through which we perceive and affect changes. There are multiple responses to the different circumstances. These are peculiar and particular to the time and place. They are effective but not necessarily generalisable. Even the changes are positive and transferable, replication of the efforts may be unwise and should not be insisted upon.

The fourteen cases can be categorised into three main perspectives of reflective practices. First, Reflecting On Self and Text; Second, Learning In Community; and third, Educating the Larger Life.

Can Reflective Practice Be Initiated by Direct Reflection On Self and the Text?

Five writers share their personal reflection in disclosing very candidly about themselves, their experiences in teaching in Section Two: *Reflecting on self and text.* Louis Schmier, a history professor at Voldosta ruminates about his teaching at the Georgian university and takes a dramatic turn because of a critical personal event in his life. He confesses that he has not been as student-centred in his teaching as he has wished. He calls himself "a talking addict" that overwhelmed his students with ideas, concepts and questions but seldom addressed the questions to himself. After realising the nub of his teaching problem, he reorganises his curriculum and changes his teaching style. He tries to engage his students in discussion and collaborative inquiry. He learns to listen rather than talk incessantly. Best of all, he makes teaching his life mission rather than just a lifelong career.

In a different vein, Alan Watson of the University of New South Wales, Australia, writes about teacher knowledge in the context of a Sydney classroom. He collaborates in an action research with an exemplary 6th Grade teacher by using mainly classroom observation and interview techniques framed by a series of teaching episodes. In each of the episodes, the teacher shares his dilemma in teaching by focussing on a question or questions, or a practical problem which the teaching procedure sought to address. For example, the question "How can individual spelling lists be taught in the class context?" is addressed alongside the question "How can cheating be discouraged?" The teacher reflects upon these two issues and discusses them with Alan, the researcher-writer. No solutions are offered but the individual and collaborative reflective process is valuable in generating a deeper insight into the complexity of classroom practice even though the teacher is experienced and exemplary, no neat solution to problems are found.

Soh-Loi Loi and Jack Teo of the Nanyang Business School, Nanyang Technological University, Singapore, propose the use of the key ideas in two Chinese classical texts to help their business students reflect on their dilemmas and solve problems. They embed the strategies of Sun Tze in *The Art of War* and the *Book of Change* to plan their business administration lessons, prepare teaching materials, learning activities and assessment modes to enliven their students' learning and stimulate creative and critical thinking about business practices. They reflect on their use of the seven sets of strategies in their classroom and feel that the art of warfare can be used in teaching as they are also grounded in human psychology and can be employed to solve problems in times of rapid changes. By embedding Chinese classical teaching in their course, they hope to enable their students to be more aware of the new contexts in doing business in Asia.

Kirpal Singh's sharing of his experience in teaching the reading of Shakespearean plays such as King Lear, to Singapore student teachers shows the need for multiple readings. This is necessary because of the students' multiple cultural backgrounds and learning contexts existing in a multi-racial, multi-religious and multi-lingual society. A classical text in English has richer meaning for a readership in Singapore if the teachers were knowledgeable and skilful in guiding the discussion so that learning literature becomes truly enjoyable, creative and educative as readers think about what is universal and what is particular or individual response, and how such readings open our mental horizon and deepen our feelings for different levels of relationships.

Will Learning In Community be More Effective and Extensive?

Section Three with five cases about teachers learning in community is introduced by Christine Bennett of Indiana University in the United States. In her study on Teacher Perspectives: As A Tool For Reflection, Partnerships and Professional Growth, she inquires into the classroom practices of her own pre-service middle and secondary school teachers in the Teachers as Decision Maker Program (TADMP). She recognises the importance of knowledge about one's own beliefs about teaching and learning for student teachers to becoming an effective teacher. She describes the tools she used to map the student teachers' perspectives such as interviews, concept mapping, classroom observations with video-taping of lessons, and follow-up interviews. Her use of a colour wheel to analyse, categorise and describe the varied perspectives is vividly innovative. The result is a color wheel representing eight perspectives of teacher beliefs: teacher as a scholar, as a psychologist, as an inculcator, as a facilitator, as an empowerer, as a nurturer and as a pedagogue.

Employing a different approach, Ora Kwo of Hong Kong University helps her pre-service students to reflect on their classroom practices by writing journals, analysing data collected and doing action research into their own teaching experience during their Practicum. Her students are guided to examine their pedagogical knowledge and skills in the teaching of the English language. They are to reflect on their skills in planning and curriculum design, teaching in particular the use of textbooks and material development, and evaluation of the pupils' learning. From the data collected, the student teachers are to draw some conclusion regarding their learning experiences, their development of personal knowledge about teaching and their actual development in classroom practice.

From the National Institute of Education, Singapore, Christine Lee and Maureen Ng's case study of a geography teacher's instructional innovation in her class yields further insights about the teacher's problems in initiating such a process in a secondary school. Cooperative learning groups are organised by the teacher to bring about deeper understanding of certain geographic concepts and skills in a secondary classroom and to improve the academic performance and attitudes of children toward learning and their classmates. However, problems and tensions emerge in the process as most of the girl students preferred a teacher-centred approach.

> "They wait for the teacher to provide them with information. They do not think for themselves and also do not trust themselves to learn on their own".

Even after the students learn to be more independent and co-operative learners in a collaborative environment, the momentum fails to sustain when the students move to classes with competitive or alienating environments. The dilemma is whether the efforts should be sustained.

At the university level, Ziqi Liao and Ai-Yen Chen presents his Group Learning Model for Doing Case Studies in an Engineering and Technology Management Course in the School of Accountancy and Business at the Nanyang Technological University, Singapore. The Model systematically structures a learning process into three phases: establishment, preparation and class. It involves rule setting, group formulation, individual study, group discussion, random group sharing, presentation and reflection. By following the process the students are encouraged to actively participate in group discussion. Both students and their teacher learn to reflect collaboratively and improve on each other's thinking and problem solving skills in complex fuzzy situations. In solving real life problems, they improve their learning about the fast developing technological management field where students have to learn to confront new challenges and solve new problems everyday.

In New Zealand, the reflection of teaching practices takes place at a Masters in Education degree level. Mollie Neville of Massey University, a course lecturer and two participants use work diaries to reflect on their practice in the tradition of the Schonian idea of reflection-in-action which was elaborated by Chen's Cyclical Model of Reflection (1993). As mature practitioners, the three are able to practice reflection before, during and after an event, and the revised or new action. In other words, reflecting on the theory as content as well as the process and the outcome. Mollie Neville is able to draw some conclusion regarding the use of the theoretical framework to guide reflection on and the development of practice. All three learned a great deal from each others' reflections and are deeply satisfied with the experience of joy and sorrows, failures and successes during the programme.

The last case in the section is written by Marnie O'Neill who reflects on a range of practices by lecturers in a Western Australian university. Marnie uses a number of video clips to stimulate the analysis of lecturers about their own knowledge and teaching and others who would like to learn from their honest reflections. How can this knowledge and expertise be transferred from the experts to the novices? What are some of the methods to be used to develop teaching competence in the university? Does knowledge only reside in the cognition of teachers and in their interaction, or does it span over cyberspace? These are some of the research questions posed by Marnie O'Neill of the University of Western Australia in her reflection on university practices. In attempting to answer these questions, a number of multimedia packages have been produced using the computer. Tertiary teachers from diverse disciplinary backgrounds in the university are interviewed to evaluate their learning from such a medium.

Is Reflection A Key Educative Tool or Medium for Higher-Order Education?

Section Four of the book is entitled Educating the Larger Life — the title of the chapter by Lori Breslow of Sloan School of Management (MIT). Lori opens this section by posing the all important question about the purpose of education — to stimulate and guide self-development, particularly the importance of communicating responsibly and sensitively. She narrates an incident in her multinational MBA class that deals with the relationship between men and women in the workplace. A presenter during the course did so in a way that was offensive to some of the women students. The situation during and after the class was tension-saturated but the instructor-researcher tried to use incidents such as this one as an opportunity to teach real-life and workplace communication issues and how they can be treated responsibly and sensitively.

Lum-Peng Lim, a dental professor at the Faculty of Dentistry, National University of Singapore, adopts Chen's 5-R Reflective Thinking and Collaborative Inquiry Framework (1995) in examining her own teaching based on the problem-based learning approach and project work. The framework guides her thinking about the learning strategies introduced. Upon reflection, several problems of the dental course are identified. These include a lack of integration of the basic sciences into clinical dentistry and also across disciplines, the saturated curriculum and the teacher-centred approach in teaching. Her recognition of the specific problems enables her to realise that she could be the solution by changing the teaching approach and assessment mode, hence the creation of a problem-based learning module and the use of project work to assess the students' learning. From the experience of the module, she feels that certain improvements are required and shares her thoughts of what can be done.

What constitutes a fair assessment system usually poses problems for teachers in universities. Fred Kofman, a Sloan professor for the MIT Leaders for Manufacturing programme, which integrates engineering and management, is confronted with this problem in his Accounting for Manufacturing course. His radical change of the curriculum and the grading system is meant to bring real life situations into the classroom. His reflection on the process of the change and the result is extremely insightful. He summarises his action research by concluding that "Most things don't work like they are supposed to work." (P. Crosby, 1979, p. 132) and how this realisation promotes strategic thinking and improved solution.

Howard Mehlinger rounds up Section Four with his reflection on 44 years of teaching. In recollecting his career as a history teacher, a university professor of education, a dean of the School of Education in Indiana University, and the current director of the Center for Excellence in Education, he highlighted his struggles and efforts to find answers to two questions in his teaching: 1) Do I know enough about the subject I am teaching that I can fulfil the role of teacher? 2) Are my students learning what they need to know? The two questions have universal significance and application for every teacher. Mehlinger believes that the first question looms much larger in the initial years of one's teaching career. The second question assumes greater importance as the teacher matures in his profession. In times of rapid change and knowledge and technology explosion, it is extremely important for all teachers, particularly teachers of professionals, to make the right assessment and judgement about what their students need to know. Teachers of professionals have the important role of being change agents themselves. As they learn, they also model learning how to learn, even about deliberately changing mind sets, habits and attitudes as well as more specific learning to learn strategies.

All the writers of the fourteen cases in the Book consciously or unconsciously follow a reflective thinking-learning process. They may use different perspectives, languages and tools to express their thoughts and feelings. However, their thinking falls quite naturally into a pattern and stages that resemble Chen's 5-R Reflective Thinking and Collaborative Inquiry Framework (1995): Reflection, Recognition, Realisation, Response and Resolution.

Their reflection usually starts with a significant happening that is contextualised within time and space, be it a classroom or an institution in a particular setting. It is usually problematic from the learner or teacher's point of view. When the "problem" is subjected to some critical scrutiny, the "real problem" seems to emerge and is recognised as a puzzle, a dilemma or *the* problem. Sometimes the reflective process skips a step and arrives at a deeper understanding of "self" as part of or the solution to the problem. The teacher-researcher realises his/her possible contribution to improve the learning process or situation. S/he responds with some worthwhile and dynamic action, and resolves to continue the effort until the results are evident.

In all the cases, thought and action work hand-in-hand to bring about changes and improvement. The action is continuous and sustained. The positive impact and results are visible and the influence could be quite extensive, class-wise or institution-wise, even though it starts on a small scale and in a focussed manner. The teachers of professionals make a difference to their student professionals' learning. They manage to do so by reflecting on their practices and acting upon their reflections using concrete pedagogical and assessment measures. They certainly reflect-in-action and reflect-on-action as Schon has always advocated in his exposition on the Reflective Practitioner (1983, 1987). This Book is about the reflective spin-off actions of these teacher professionals. In their journey uphill and down-dale and traversing across the *knowledge and thought landscape*, they have sustained their efforts to improve their practices, to transform learning, and to educate for the larger life.

References

Argyris, C. & Schon, D. A. (1974). *Theory in practice: Increasing professional effectiveness*. San Francisco: Jossey Bass.

Chen, A. Y. & Seng, S. H. (1992). Reflection and its relations to reflective practice and teaching competence. Chapter in *Reflection: Theories and Practices*. Kuala Lumpur: Dewan Bahasa Pustaka.

Chen, A. Y. (1992). Student teachers' reflection on classroom practice. Paper presented at the annual conference of the Educational Research Association, Singapore. September 1992.

Chen, A. Y. (1993). Experience and student teachers' reflection on classroom practice, *Educational Research Perspectives*, Vol. 20, No. 2, 24–36.

Chen, A. Y. (1995). Enhancing Teachers of Professionals in Their Reflective Practices. Paper presented at the annual meeting of the American Educational Research Association, San Francisco, 1995.

Chen, A. Y. (1996). Towards Exemplary Teaching Through Collaborative Inquiry. Abstract of Proceeding of the 16 Annual Conference on Teaching and Learning in Higher Education, Ottawa, Canada, 12–15 June 1996, p. 16.

Clandinin, D. J. & Connelly, F. M. (1995). *Teachers' Professional Knowledge Landscape*. In *Advances in Contemprorary Educational Thought Series*, J. F. Soltis (Ed.), New York: Columbia Teacher College.

Schon, D. A. (1983). *The Reflective Practitioner: How professionals think in action*. New York: Basic Books.

Schon, D. A. (1987). *Educating the Reflective Practitioner: Towards a new design for teaching and learning in the professions*. San Francisco: Jossey Bass.

Section
ONE

*Perspectives
and
Contexts of Reflection*

Reflecting On The Reflective Practitioners

Richard Pring

Department of Educational Studies
University of Oxford
England

Synopsis

In this article Richard Pring makes a case for the "reflective practitioner" as exemplified by the seven teacher educators in the book.

Much educational research which is initiated at university level, and often at some expense has little impact in the classroom in terms of teaching and learning — either because the issues researched on are too broad or they are too theoretical.

The solution is that teachers themselves, the practitioners, become the researchers. They can do this by reflecting systematically on what goes on in the classroom and, to raise these reflections to the level of objectivity, to subject them to the critical scrutiny of others

Out of such reflections, though unique to individual researchers, can come "insightful accounts of processes which go beyond the particular story itself".

Reflecting on the Reflective Practitioners

Richard Pring

The seven teacher educators' contributions to this book demonstrate in their respective ways how teachers might engage directly in research into their own practice. Most of the studies are detailed and represent an approach to research which, in terms of its popularity, is relatively recent but which has gained much support in university departments of education across the world — as is reflected in the range of countries from which these contributions come: Singapore, Hong Kong, Australia, New Zealand and United States. Whether or not it has yet gained support outside the universities — particularly amongst those who make decisions about education or who sponsor research — is a different and more controversial matter, which I shall touch upon later.

Furthermore, in illustrating a rather distinctive approach, the case studies frequently refer to certain well-known authorities with whom they share a common interest in the "reflective practitioner" — particularly Schon (1983, 1987) and Shulman (1986, 1987) whose work has done so much to transform educational research and the further professional development of teachers.

The significance of this is not hard to find. It is argued in many countries that, despite much money being spent on educational research, the impact upon practice is slight indeed. Educational research, and the university departments developing it, have so often been dominated either by broader policy matters (such as "why are girls doing less well at science?" or "what are the causes of failure amongst working class children?" or "how might one overcome racist attitudes in schools?") or by a research

4

model which seeks to measure and quantify and generalise. Either way, the teacher often feels left out; the central concern, viz what happens in this or that classroom or between the teacher and the learner, seems to be of little importance. As Christine Lee and Maureen Ng point out, in their fascinating study of a teacher trying to introduce more co-operative learning in her classroom, the most important problem in changing education as in most social reforms is the neglect of how teachers "actually experience change as distinct from how it might have been intended" (what Fullan, 1991, refers to as "the neglect of the phenomenology of change"). Similarly the neglect of the students' perceptions: Kirpal Singh, in his report on the study of King Lear in a cross-cultural setting, argues that

> the globalisation of our world means, in part at least, giving each individual
> a valid voice in terms of intellectual understanding.

Politically that is beginning to matter. Those whose job it is both to improve the educational service and yet at the same time to make sure that limited funds are well spent, question the value and utility of so much educational research which pays scant attention to the details of the classroom and seems so irrelevant, therefore, to teacher improvement. It is not clear, for instance, how the 2800 lecturers in education, declared in the recent United Kingdom universities' Research Assessment Exercise to be active educational researchers, have had much impact upon the daily practice of teachers. The link between so much research, on the one hand, and, on the other, school improvement or professional development, is questioned. Why pay people to do research which has so little effect? For that reason in the United Kingdom there is an emphasis by the Teacher Training Council to promote a more teacher-centred form of research, to some extent by-passing the universities which are perceived to have failed in this respect. University initiated research, either because of its main interest or because of the way it has been conducted, has failed to have an impact upon the teachers. There remains a gulf between theory and practice, between those who theorise or research and those who practise or teach.

On the other hand, there is the danger that, in attempting to bridge this gulf, the politicians sponsor the kind of research which will produce a "technology of teaching" — the belief that if only we were to conduct the right kind of research rigorously enough, then we would have a science of teaching which could, through courses or books, be applied or taught to others. Research would demonstrate how reading should be taught, or groups organised, or fractions illustrated. Teacher development would lie in learning the results of that research and then applying them to practice.

As these case studies illustrate, there is something very wrong with this simplistic understanding of the relation between theory and practice — between the research community and the teachers. The reality of the classroom is complex in the extreme; there are countless interactions between teacher and learner and between learner and learner such that it would be impossible to reduce the many interactions to a set of generalisations, or to generalise from one situation to another. Furthermore, the language and accounts of the researcher, seeking as they often do to provide a more theoretical understanding, might well go unrecognised by the teacher — a game being played at their expense by people who are more concerned with the obscurities of theory than they are with the articulation and improvement of practice.

The solution which some (exemplified by the contributions to this book) have found to this problem is that of seeing those who practise as the main theorisers — the teachers as the ones who, from their privileged position, are able to make sense of the complicated practice of teaching in a way that no one else can. The teachers themselves have to be the researchers. In Britain, this was first most effectively argued by Lawrence Stenhouse (1972) whose book *Introduction to Curriculum Theory and Instruction* started a now well established tradition of teacher research, subsequently developed by those such as John Elliot (1993) who had worked closely with Stenhouse at the Centre for Applied Research in Education at the University of East Anglia.

There is now much written about the teacher as the researcher. He or she alone has full access to what happens in the classroom. Of course, the teacher will not normally be actively engaged in research — nigh impossible where there is a demanding and practical job to be done. But the teacher can be trained to reflect systematically upon practice, to subject such reflections to critical scrutiny, to hypothesise and to test out the hypotheses against relevant experience. The teacher can be assisted in getting to a deeper understanding both of the situation in which he or she is teaching and of the particular episodes which occur in the classroom. Practice improves through the more systematic reflection upon practice — testing out the assumptions which so often go unquestioned, subjecting those assumptions to critical examination, considering alternative ways of understanding and approaching the practical problems which the teacher daily faces. And the question, therefore, is how can one make the thinking of the teacher more objective than it was before.

By "being more objective" is meant taking the steps which are more likely than otherwise to get at the truth. What is the evidence which is relevant to the judgement being made? How might these judgements be tested against experience? How far might the understandings and judgements be subjected to the critical scrutiny of others?

The contributions to this book illustrate in different ways what this might mean in practice. Across them all is a common philosophy reflected in the frequent reference to the *tacit knowledge* of the teacher which surpasses any explicit account, the *wisdom of practice* which is enshrined within this tacit knowledge, the *craft or pedagogic knowledge* which cannot be articulated in the propositional accounts of the theorisers, the *reflective practice* which leads to *self-directed learning*, *deliberation* about the goals and values of practice already engaged in, *naturalistic enquiry*, *narrative* or *telling a story* as it is felt and seen by the practitioners themselves. The purpose is frequently seen as *making sense of* experience prior to further action.

In effect, these case studies are premised on two principles, one ethical, the other epistemological. In the first case, there is a profound respect for teachers and their perception of what is occurring in the classroom (a respect not often given by researchers who have tended to look *at* teachers and to fit them into the researchers' categories, not those of the teachers themselves). The voices of the teachers must find a place in our exploration of how children learn and what will enable them to learn more effectively. In the second case, any science or claim to knowledge must pay attention to the complexity of the subject matter being studied. In this case, the subject matter must be what happens in the classroom or wherever the complex interactions take place between teacher and learner. Essential to those interactions are the perceptions, the motives, the assumptions, the aspirations, the doubts, the values of the teacher. Ignore those and the researcher is not addressing the reality of the school or classroom.

But, one might ask, why should this be seen as research — this "telling a story", this "gathering of teachers' perceptions", these worthy but necessarily limited "reflections" of the teacher? Interesting, perhaps, but why "research"? It is difficult to generalise from the individual case studies — indeed, the more intensive the case studies, the less generalisable they seem to become. Once one starts listening to the authentic voice of the teachers, then it seems less likely that one can reach any general conclusion.

The case studies provide two kinds of answer.

The first lies in the approach — the methodology, if you like — adopted. Research would seem to entail at least this, the systematic gathering of information with a view to answering certain questions and the subjection of that information to objective or public scrutiny and questioning. Obviously, the gathering of that information must be appropriate to the problems being raised. The case studies reflect a certain unity in the gathering of information and the corroboration of this within a critical context. Even what might appear to be the most "subjective" of the studies, that by Clandinin and Connelly on *Storying and Restorying Ourselves: Narrative and Reflection* speaks of the importance of the telling of the story to an audience which can subject that story to a degree of questioning. It is a matter of "trying to understand" and of realising that understanding must be set against the attempts of the teachers themselves to make sense of even a small episode within the context of a human story of hopes and disappointments and aspirations. "Stories of professional practice are stories of relationship and they are stories of thinking again".

Nonetheless, there is much more to the research than that. This is best captured in the account given by Marnie O'Neill in her account of a project aimed at promoting reflective teaching practice amongst lecturers in higher education. The programme was based on the following assumptions:

(i) *realistic settings*: "demonstrations of pedagogical skills are more likely to be helpful if they are illustrated in holistic classroom settings enabling users to become involved in typical student-student and teacher-student interactions".

(ii) *participants' explanations*: "understanding of teacher behaviour in classroom interactions will be enhanced if observers have access to the teachers' explanation of his or her decision-making process".

(iii) *diversity of opinion*: "there is usually more than one effective way of dealing with a problem, so it is useful to access to a diversity of opinion in which to locate reflections on one's own teaching practices".

(iv) *client opinions*: "students, being expert teacher-watchers and clientele can offer valuable advice on the ways in which they experience classroom interactions, and their expectation of teaching and learning situations".

(v) *context specific*: "research findings are sometimes contradictory, depending on the specific contexts in which the research was conducted, and cannot be regarded as absolute guidelines; instead they provide a context in which the users of the program can reflect on their own classroom practices, and pursue congruent research findings".

This might be summed up in the statement of the academic registrar who was engaged in the process of self evaluation, identified by Mollie Neville in her report of the evaluation of a new Masters Course in Administration

> The key to success will be reflection, consciously thinking over each activity and evaluating how and why I performed in the way I did and consider whether it could have been performed better or performed at all.

And then, drawing upon the work of Chen (1993), Neville shows how this reflection *on* action, following upon the reflection *in* and *for* action (to develop distinctions made by Schon), can be developed in a cyclical and interactive process.

In pursuing this kind of research — in developing systematic reflection, in subjecting that reflection to the critical scrutiny of others including the "clients", in welcoming a diversity of judgements, in contextualising the conclusions drawn as these arise from those reflections — so particular methods of data gathering and analysis are applied. The teachers' regular and critical reflections are captured in diaries; an observer keeps notes of what is observed; perceptions of what has occurred are shared between teacher and observer with a view to understanding differences of perception and judgement; underlying assumptions are revealed through probing interrogation; semi-structured interviews are held; video or tape recordings of interactions or interviews are examined. This "trying to make sense of" with a view to more intelligent planning, decision-making and further practice is undertaken in the light of evidence which can be revisited and in the light of others' critical scrutiny of that evidence. That is what raises it to the level of objectivity. Assumptions and implicit beliefs are made "objective" — open to public viewing and criticism, which can thus be pursued in the light of the evidence produced by those, the teachers, most able to gather that evidence.

The second kind of answer provided by the case studies to the question, "Why is this research?", is as follows. In many of the cases, hypotheses are formed in the light of previous research and are put to the test, or a theoretical perspective, tentative maybe, helps to sift the data as it is revealed through observation or self-report. Of course, it is difficult to generalise with any degree of certainty or to conceptualise in too formal and definite a manner — the main lesson to be learnt from case studies is the uniqueness in many ways of each case and the constant need to reconceptualise if sense is to be made of experience. But there is never uniqueness in *every* respect. The experiences of academic staff concerned about the problems of teaching, described by Marnie O'Neill in her paper, "Reflecting on University Teaching Practices", are unique to their own distinctive context in some respects, but they "ring a bell" to many others who have taught in other places and in other conditions. Hence, in promoting reflective teaching practices through multimedia packages, O'Neill proposes that,

> if these are encouraged, the long-term effects of the instructional packages would be greater than that of a set of decontextualised exemplars of "best practice".

Furthermore, this particular case study illustrates the interaction between the exploration of the present set of instances and episodes, with all their complexity, and previous research on similar issues. The literature illuminates the exploration rather than tells what should be the case. In fact, the exposure to other accounts, as revealed in the research literature, becomes in some of the case studies an integral part of the deliberations. As O'Neill explains, "The expectation is that users will relate them to their own teaching practices." Or again, as Alan Watson argues in the case study of an outstanding teacher examining the assumptions and reasons behind specific teaching episodes,

> The teaching behaviour is always particular to that teacher, that class and even that specific moment. The subtle differences of teaching style and student needs and personality mean that even the best knowledge must undergo a transformation if it is to be used by another in another situation...Nevertheless, the teachers' actions provide a valuable starting point for ... teachers to discuss the issue and to think of other approaches which are likely to suit their teaching style and situation.

Moreover, Christine Bennett in her study of "teachers' perspectives as a tool for reflection, partnerships and professional growth", provides a clear set of categories through which teachers might be encouraged to perceive their own teaching and

> to explore ways of helping teachers make explicit their assumptions about teaching, to identify multiple perspectives from which teaching might be viewed, to consider how their teaching might be enhanced....

Therefore, with few exceptions, such studies do not eschew a theoretical perspective normally associated with research.

These studies, therefore, illustrate an important and growing tradition of research in education — *important* because such research penetrates the complexity of the classroom relationship between teacher and learner which too often has been ignored, *research* because it endeavours to do so in as objective and systematic way as the subject-matter will allow. Indeed, since the *professional* knowledge of the teacher necessarily goes beyond that which can be clearly articulated in theory or anticipated in generalisations about teaching, then, as Ora Kwo argues in her case studies of Hong Kong student teachers, there must be an integration of theoretical understanding with the practice within the teachers themselves, achieved through what she refers to as the "action research" of the teachers. *They* have to achieve the integration; no one can do it for them. And this is well illustrated in Kwo's choice of "critical incidents", which become the focal point of enabling her students how to learn how to teach. The "data-sets" of the fifteen students included written reviews of learning experiences, action research assignments, video tapes of critical incidents, the elaboration of the students' perspectives — and then the "triangulation" of these different sorts of data. In this way, there emerged changing understandings of teaching, now based upon evidence and criticism rather than upon unchallenged preconceptions.

There are, however, reasons for concern. The uniqueness of the case can be stressed to the exclusion of relevance elsewhere. If the story is unique, the reader might understandably ask "so what?" Indeed, it is questionable that government or private sponsors should feel in any way motivated to fund research, the significance of which does not go beyond the individual case. Does any bit of one's life story qualify for public exposure in the name of research? If not, how does one select? Why is one bit of the narrative significant to educational understanding and others not? The narrative is an area of research which is attracting much more interest — the understanding of the episode or issue against a richer background of the life story. But much more needs to be said about the ways in which such narrative are to be conducted if they are to be distinguished as research — if they are to be seen as insightful accounts of processes which go beyond the particular story itself. And, indeed, Kwo attempts precisely that — the "real life story of a teacher's struggles" is partly elicited by a series of open ended questions guiding both journal writing and interviews.

This is an important book. Its main argument is that if there is to be school and teacher improvement, then there must be respect for the professional knowledge of the teacher. The question is therefore how might one gain access to that knowledge — or, more importantly, how might the teachers themselves gain access to the insights which are implicit in their own practice but too often unrecognised, unquestioned and uncriticised. There is much theorising about the "reflective practitioner". What are needed are more examples of the reflective practitioner in action. And these case studies provide those examples.

References

Chen Ai-Yen (1996). Towards Exemplary Teaching Through Collaborative Inquiry. Paper presented at the 16 Annual Conference on Teaching and Learning in Higher Education, Ottawa, Canada, 12–15 June 1996.

Elliot, J. (1993). *Action Research: Theory and Practice.*

Fullan, M. (1991). *The New Meaning of Educational Change.* Toronto: OISE Press.

Schon, D. A. (1983). *The Reflective Practitioner.* New York: Basic Books.

Schon, D. A. (1987). *Educating the Reflective Practitioner.* San Francisco: Jossey Bass.

Shulman, L. S. (1986). "Those who understand: Knowledge growth in teaching", *Educational Researcher*, February.

Shulman, L. S. (1987). "Knowledge and teaching: Foundations of the new reform", *Harvard Educational Review*, 57(1).

Stenhouse, L. (1972). Introduction to Curriculum Theory and Instruction. London: RKP.

Storying and Restorying Ourselves: Narrative and Reflection

D. J. Clandinin

Centre for Research for Teacher Education and
Development
University of Alberta
Canada

F. M. Connelly

Joint Centre for Teacher Development
Ontario Institute for Studies in Education
University of Toronto
Canada

Synopsis

Human beings have three desires: to story tell, to relate to others, and to reflect on their actions and thoughts.

Story telling is a relational act. A relationship is created between teller and responder. In the process of telling and re-telling our stories we reflect on our experiences and learn new and different lessons from them each time. Therefore, story telling through the process of reflection is educative.

Story telling is the most basic way human beings make meaning of their experiences.

Storying and Restorying Ourselves: Narrative and Reflection

D. Jean Clandinin and F. Michael Connelly

In our most recent book (Clandinin and Connelly, 1995) Michael Connelly and I write about what we call three human desires: the desire to story tell, the desire for relationship and the desire to think again, to reflect upon actions taken and things thought.

In other places (Connelly and Clandinin, 1990) we have stated that in our view humans are storytelling organisms who, individually and socially, lead storied lives and tell stories of those lives. In our research with others and in reflection on our own lives, we see that teachers must, of necessity, tell stories. It is a way, perhaps the most basic way, humans make meaning of their experience.

As we reflect on our own storied lives as teachers and as teachers of teachers, we see how our desire to tell stories is our way of making meaning of our experiences. But we also see a second interconnected desire, that is, the desire for relationship. It is interconnected because storytelling is a relational act. Stories are told to others. Furthermore, we believe that there is an inevitability of response which parallels the inevitability of story telling. Human connections are made between teller and responder. There is a reciprocity in telling and responding which is relational.

Story tellers are influenced by the telling of their own stories. Active construction and telling of a story is educative: the story teller learns through the act of story telling. This is why the writing of a story for oneself as audience is an educative act. But our interest here is not on the writing of stories for self but on their telling in relationship. And that, we believe, is doubly educative. It is an education that goes beyond writing for the self because it has a responsive audience and that audience has both an imagined response as far as the story teller is concerned and an actual response when the response is made. These possibilities, the imagining of the response and the response, are telling for the storyteller. The possibilities are telling in an educative way because the meaning of the story is reshaped and, so too, is the meaning of the world to which the story refers.

The third desire, that is, the desire to think again is a commonplace in educational studies made so by John Dewey's work on education and experience (Dewey, 1938). Reflection, thinking again, is a basic human drive for Dewey. One lives, looks backward and forward, and then lives again. It is this desire, more so than the desire to know, which, for Dewey, drove human experience and which, for him, was the source of education.

The stories we have heard in our research, and which we tell of ourselves, are stories of reflection on practice. In Schon's (1992) terms, they are stories of reflective practice. We believe that story telling is a reflective act. Stories are not icons to be learned but are inquiries in which further inquiry takes place through their telling and through response to them. In this way, thinking again, relationship, and story telling are interrelated. Stories of professional practice are stories of relationship and they are stories of thinking again.

In order to try to make this clear, we are going to tell a series of stories in which we see these desires at work. And then we look at the professional knowledge landscape from the position of teacher education students and of teacher education teachers. The first story is told around a session with a pre-service teacher education student.

Bill's Story

"Jean, can I talk with you after seminar for a few minutes?",
asked Bill after one of our small group in-school teacher education partnership seminars.
"Sure, Bill, what's up?"

"I'll wait on the couch in the entrance. Finish talking to everyone else first. I'll wait."

I puzzled about Bill as I talked to the others and gathered up my briefcase and papers. He had been withdrawing for a month or more now, actually missing a university seminar without letting me know beforehand and, when he was there, he let me know he was disinterested, bored and thought what we were doing was irrelevant to his teaching. It had been at least two months since he had shared his journal for response. What was he going to say to me now, I thought, as I headed for the entranceway.

He was seated on the couch· in the small foyer to the main school office. He stared straight ahead as I sat down beside him, turning towards him so we could talk.

"Jean, you know in the last couple of months, I don't think I've been getting all I can out of this partnership. There's so much to learn and what you've been doing in the university seminars has been really good. I just haven't been getting all I can out of it. I wrote about it in my journal but I wanted to tell you about it now."

> And then Bill launched into a story, his eyes occasionally connecting with my gaze.
> "Remember that Tuesday I missed coming to the university?"
> "Yeah", I said, "I do".

"Well, I went to the outdoor-centre for an overnight camping trip with the year 5/6 kids. We worked really hard on planning lots of things, interesting things for the class to do. But there was this one boy who said, right away when I was trying to introduce something, that it was boring. He said he didn't want to do it, it was dumb. I told him he hadn't tried yet but he kept on nagging and whining about it. I was really frustrated and I kept on insisting he try what we were doing. Well, after the 2-day camp, I got really sick and I had to stay home for a week by myself. And, being there, I started to think and to write in my journal about what happened ...."

And there was a long pause, and he looked at me, tears welling up in his eyes and in mine.

"And I realized that that boy was me. I've been just like that whenever I've been at the university or in seminars for the past while. I haven't given anyone a chance. I've just wanted to stay at my school and not be involved in any university things. And there's been some really good things happening that I need to learn about and I've missed them. I've figured out I still have a lot to learn. And it happened because I realized I was that boy whining and saying it isn't interesting. And I do have my journal and I'm giving it to you now because I've missed you."

And with that he stood and said "I know I've still got a lot to learn".

I smiled and said "I know. I have a lot to learn too .... now maybe I'll get you back for graduate studies so we can both do some more learning".

He grinned down at me as he said "Maybe you will. I never thought I'd say that".

Jean's Story

As a teacher of teachers, moments like this overwhelm me with the power of story. Bill's story of seeing himself living out his resistant student's story caught me off guard. Storying himself, in relationship, thinking again, had led him to an awakening. He was awakened to his learning to teach that he now knew had just begun for him.

But I, too, am a teacher and for me to make meaning of this situation, I too, needed to tell stories of that lived story. As Bill had with me I sought out a safe place for the expression of my human desires of story telling, of relationship and of thinking again.

I hummed to myself as I drove back to the university. Even as I drove, I composed a story, really, several versions of a story. One telling along the plot line, I suppose, of the prodigal son returned to the family. Another telling with a more mystical plot line. Still another along a plot line of the power of relationship to create safe places for restorying. I began to imagine responses. And, as I drove, I began to wonder what restorying would come out of my stories of these events.

I knew I was happy. I felt like a teacher being part of a moment of learning so intense it felt electrified. But as I began the storytelling to that imagined audience in my car, I knew this had the possibility for being educative for me.

As I drove I began to think about the professional knowledge landscape (Clandinin and Connelly, 1995) at the university. Where were the safe places for my telling, for response that would allow me to make meaning?

If I tell it to a colleague I stop in the hall, will she have time to hear? If she does, will she think I am only bragging, telling a success story in which I am teacher/heroine? Will she murmur "that's nice" as she hurries away? Will she begin to tell of one of her encounters in teaching/learning and, through the expression of her human desires, we can begin our conversation.

But, as usually happens, I hurried in to hallways of closed faculty offices. I was prepared for the silence of the hallways. Our universities create a knowledge landscape where stories of teaching are rarely heard. When they are told, they are stories in which university teachers portray themselves as experts delivering knowledge to those without knowledge. Expert knowledge comes from research and with expert knowledge comes authority (Connelly and Clandinin, 1994). In our hallways, sometimes university teacher educators gather to discuss research but rarely do we gather to discuss teaching. And when we do, the landscape is a "landscape in which we portray expertise in delivering knowledge to students," not "a landscape in which to show confusion, uncertainty, improvisation," the stuff of teaching that was bubbling up in me as I hurried down the hallway.

I was on my way to my computer with its electronic mail message system in search of a place to write my story and to receive response.

Jean and Michael's Story

As Bill had sought me out, I sought out my friend and colleague Michael in order to engage in storytelling, in relationship and in thinking again. The first time I told the story, a version around the plot line of the prodigal son, Michael responded with thoughts about learning about teaching from teaching. In order to have figured out what he had about teaching, Bill needed to have the experience of teaching. Michael mused that the experience that awakened Bill to a new story of learning to teach had been his teaching. Perhaps, he said, it was the structure of the teacher education partnership that allowed that space. We began a conversation about how teacher education programs were structured. I wrote of the long, almost 2 year relationship Bill and I had; of how it would have been impossible for that awakening to have occurred in an 8 or 12 week practicum; of how our relationship allowed him to feel safe enough to tell that story.

As we began to write this paper several weeks later, I again told the story and this time Michael responded to the sense of hope he had heard me express, the hope I had felt driving back in the car. He had not heard the hope in my first telling of the story. He connected the hope in my story to a television show where, in the context of a story, a physicist had tried to figure out one of his moments of euphoria and hopefulness. Michael's response led into a conversation about how I had been feeling about the partnership. When I first told my story of Bill and we had discussed the partnership, I described the barrage of critique there had been about the program. At that time, I was discouraged about sustaining the partnership. I realized that when I heard Michael's response to my retelling of the story of my encounter with Bill that I had now restoried it around a theme of hope.

However, as with many things, as I storied and restoried, things became more complex. In my second retelling of the story with Michael, I had restoried around a more hopeful plot line. As I reflected on this, I shared an early version of this paper with my colleagues at the table in the Centre for Research for Teacher Education. Their response helped me understand the hopeful plot line in two ways. As I drove back after the initial encounter with Bill, I was hopeful — hopeful about Bill and I and our teaching/learning relationship; hopeful about Bill's awakening to a new story of learning to teach. The hope in my telling was about Bill and his learning to teach and about our relationship.

But in the later retelling I was restorying around a hopeful plot line for the possibility of sustaining a teacher education program with a dialectical view of the "relation of theory and practice" rather than around the "theory-driven practice" view that we have characterized as having the quality of a, sacred story. I realized I was now feeling hopeful about the partnership and about telling my teacher education stories. Recently a group of Centre participants, Myer Horowitz, Joy Ruth Mickelson, Hedy Bach and Linda Schulz have been engaged in a research project on the partnership. Now, frequently when I walk into the Centre they are engaged in lively discussions of the partnership as a way of restorying teacher education. They know the participants and I can join them in a conversation about the junior and senior teaching partners, about seminars and classes, about negotiations of collaboration. This recently constructed space for a teacher education conversation in which I tell and retell my stories helps me make new sense of my teacher education work. It also makes me hopeful about restorying the professional knowledge landscape on which I live. I can now understand more clearly why Michael heard a hopeful theme in my restorying.

Summary

As we reflected on our positioning as teacher educators and the positioning of student teachers on the professional knowledge landscape, we wondered about where the safe places, the educative places, were for the expression of the desires of storytelling, of relationship, of reflection. For Bill and Jean, they had created such a space for themselves in the midst of an alternative program. For Jean and Michael, they had created such a place in an electronic telecommunication system. For Jean in the Centre, the researchers working with the partnership had made such a space.

For us, these safe places are educative places. As we examine these places it becomes evident that the telling of stories in such places of relationship goes beyond the mere telling of stories to their retelling and reliving. Storytelling can be noneducative, an end in itself, merely a pleasurable activity. But the stories told and retold in these safe places, at least in our experience, are educative.

Reference

Clandinin, D. J. & Connelly, F. M. (1995). *Teachers Professional Knowledge Landscapes*. New York: Teachers College Press.

Connelly, F. M. & Clandinin, D. J. (1990). Stories of experience and narrative inquiry. *Educational Researcher*, 19(5), 2–14.

Schon, D. A. (1992). A conversation with F. M. Connelly and D. J. Clandinin. *Orbit*, 23(4), 2–5.

Dewey, J. (1938). *Experience and education*. New York: Collier Books.

Connelly, F. M. & Clandinin, D. J. (1994). The promise of collaborative research in the political context. In S. Hollingsworth and H. Sockett (Eds.), *Teacher research and educational reform*. Chicago: University of Chicago Press.

Case Studies: Why Now, More Than Ever, Cases Are Important

John Van Maanen

Sloan School of Management
Massachusetts Institute of Technology
United States of America

Synopsis

John Van Maanen argues for the use of case studies to describe, analyse, interpret, sometimes even predict possible outcomes of developments of reflective practices in the complex real world of work. He demonstrates that case studies can be macro or micro, qualitative or quantitative, cross-sectional or longitudinal, historical or contemporary, singular or comparative. And, as each case study tells a story, it is full of human interest content that grasps attention, demands deep thinking and compels action.

Case Studies: Why Now, More than Ever, Cases are Important

John Van Maanen

This paper began as a speech given on the eve of the Chinese New Year in 1995 in Singapore and was intended to more or less celebrate the charm, eloquence, beauty and learning potential of the well done case study — a form of social science research that I think is again on the upswing partly as a response to the turbulence and change that mark the so-called postmodern world. It is a form I am most familiar with through the reading and writing of ethnographies, the varied cultural stories or "tales of the field" told by anthropologists and sociologists. This of course puts me in the position of acting as something of a literary strumpet whose job it seems is to teach myself as a stand-up (at the moment, a sit-down) living, breathing, talking, typing case study. But, as a singularity specified by situation and biography, I will try nonetheless to locate some of the global in the local and find a bit of the general in the particular.

A good deal of the local and particular however slips away as a necessarily contextualized talk becomes a written text. A speech is a live performance: "a mingling," as Goffman (1981, p. 164) says, "of the living with the read." As words are spoken aloud, an audience can judge the stance of the speaker as sincere or cynical, as a believer or an opportunist. There is a freshness associated with a talk — never mind that a speaker may have written most of it down and the audience may even have read a good deal of it before entering the hall — that is impossible to recreate in print. In Singapore, for example, I took liberties with my words that I dare not take here. From the podium, I felt free to embellish, to exaggerate, to improvise, to tell a joke or two, to pun around and ramble without great concern for the niceties of written and too often stilted communication on the belief — perhaps mistaken — that my listeners would take away the spirit of my remarks more so than my words. And given that my talk was limited to a half-hour (I ran over) this last point is surely of some importance.

Nonetheless, a speech is not a paper and therefore a good deal of editing and elaboration has gone into this ink-stained production. I have tried however to preserve some of the spirit of my verbal performance in the body of the paper and not, for example, force on readers a set of my grim but beloved footnotes or press my points with bracketed string cites to all those authorities who have said similar things to what I say. The form is loose; necessarily brief if not breathless, subject to conjecture and interpretation and put forth more with the intention of opening up our ideas as to what case studies are about than to closing them off. My view of case studies and the affinity of narrative, detail and ambiguity they display may make some nervous for it is anti-foundational and suspect of all types of essentialism.

The spectre of post-modernism lurks then in the background of this paper. It is kept at bay only by my assumption that there is something of a structure to the writing, reading, teaching and learning from case studies. Moreover, I must assume that this is a structure that can be captured by language, put forth in a talk delivered to a cross-disciplinary, multicultural audience, considered in print by a similar but (hopefully) larger audience, and that doing so is a reasonable and worthy thing to do. But, dear reader, keep in mind this is just a claim. Structure may not be so easy to locate in these changing times and mere words may not shelter us from the wind.

What is a Case Study?

Getting down to cases means exploring what we take them to be. This can be a troublesome matter because definitions of case studies differ and sometimes differ spectacularly. What they represent and where I think such a representation fits in our learning of the social world is what I shall first try to convey. By cases, I mean simply in-depth investigations of some particular social setting with a focus on the events that occur in and over time in that arena. From my perspective, the more strictly bounded yet broadly and comparatively located the setting, the closer the writer to the events that occur in that domain, the more detailed and linked the elements of the descriptive work, the higher the quality of the case. Creating high church cases are no easy matter. Most cases are not well done. A typical business school case, for instance, usually falls at the low end of the quality (and status) scale since it most often rests on a flying visit of short duration by a case writing team invited to a self-selecting organization to interview several managers as to their handling of a particular problematic matter. Documents are collected, interviews conducted, scenes visited swiftly and the team flies home to write it all up according to plan and boilerplate as a matter to puzzle and challenge students who presumably may someday move in to similar situations.

Certainly there are a smattering of fine business school cases such as the so-called classics created, taught and marketed by a number of business schools and thus taken up again and again by waves of managers in training. However most cases in the business school libraries — and perhaps most cases of all sorts — are quickly forgotten and shelved as superficial if not fictive versions of events chronicled for no apparent reason. It is their ad hoc and careless character, their lack of analytic bite or interest, their single perspective, their failure to properly situate the case by similarity or difference to broader matters, their anonymity, their formulaic language and format that make them so intellectually vapid, dispensable and easy to satirize (e.g., "Leaning back from his cluttered desk and rubbing his temples, Richard Preston, head of Acme's New Product Development Division, closed his eyes and pondered what he had done to get himself into this mess ...")

Going somewhat up-scale, consider similar genre writings but of higher standards. Examples that come quickly to mind are those succinct and well-crafted case studies that appear each month in the *Harvard Business Review* and have appended to them four or five commentaries written by interested but distinctly outside observers who attempt to locate the specific case materials comparatively (usually by dint of their own experiences). With greater and lesser success and style, these commentators decipher what the case in question signifies to them and what it might mean to readers. Here we have something approaching a polyvocal work that may be based on little more fieldwork than attends to a typical business school case but is put forward in a fashion that begins to personalize, question, open up and reflect on the context that both produces and surrounds a particular case.

Moving up another notch or two on the quality scale are the various sorts of case studies produced by social scientists (and some journalists as well) where the author by intention seeks to extend a reader's field of acquaintance with a particular setting and the social processes that take place there. The aim and function of such work is basic: to familiarize readers with the complex cases of the world. This writing is rarely quantitative, exacting or theoretically explicit but it is precise, explicitly located and takes readers where they have not been before. Such cases constitute what Kenneth Boulding (1958, p. 5) calls "travel over a field of study." Students of organizations, for example, who have never been in a military unit, a research lab, a direct sales organization, an executive suite, a Japanese assembly plant, a police department, a French civil service agency or a mental hospital have presumably missed something such that whatever generalizations they are apt to make of organizational life will be based on too restricted a field. Cases that provide readers with a broader view of their respective areas of interest presumably help to prompt reflection and curb conceits.

Pushing the case envelopes another level we find of course those scholarly monographs rich in local detail, social history, member perspectives, scholarly musings, temporal and spatial grounding, apt analogies and comparative moorings with conclusions of a narrative sort not easily detached or decontextualized from the story told. Dorinne Kondo's *Crafting Selves* (1990), Gideon Kunda's *Engineering Culture* (1992) and Diane Vaughan's *The Challenger Launch Decision* (1996) are recent examples and current favorites of mine. They are indeed case studies but they are about as far as one can get from those on the lower rungs in my presumptive quality scale.

Here is where ethnography and the various arts of social representation based perhaps on living with and living like those studied may take hold and provide value. Whether it is the strange being made familiar to readers or the familiar being made strange, new ways of regarding the world (and one's own situation) are made possible and hence new lines of possible action can be considered. These are cases that lead long lives and thus anchor the high end of the case study trade.

This said, I can now offer a definition, albeit cryptic, for the kinds of case studies I find so valuable. They are, in short, close readings — put in writing — of certain, tightly located social setting and mix descriptive (representational) and analytic (interpretive) elements into the stories told. The world of cases is a world of temporal sequences, of context, of ambiguity, of particular people in particular places doing particular things. It is not a world ruled by abstract social forces, covering laws or universal principles of either thought or action. Methodological restrictions are difficult to fathom for the best of case studies use a variety of methods – interviews, library work, documentary analysis, fieldwork of an extensive sort, social surveys and so forth. Case studies of quality are then based on a variety and wealth of empirical materials and inevitably cross levels of analysis without great worry. Some are comparative, some are singular. Schools, societies, states, communities, families, individuals, industries, organizations, occupations, work groups, classrooms, laboratories, courtrooms can all serve as settings for case studies whose defining features are located more by time and space than subject matter.

From this standpoint, the proper definitional question to be asked is not "what is a case study?" but, as Ragin and Becker (1992) would have it, "what is a given case study about?" Here, of course, we discover that it is not always easy to formulate a straightforward and convincing answer, for even the best of cases can be quite slippery, both to authors and to readers. Definitional claims can be disputed. Take, for example, the social survey, a form of research not ordinarily thought of as falling under the rubric of case studies. Hypothetically but more concretely, take survey data gathered by, say, questionnaires completed in the fall of 1998 by a sample of adults of working age in Singapore. Such material can provide a basis for a set of statements about individual Singaporeans or about Singapore as a whole as well as statements about a variety of possible in-between units of analysis such as residential neighborhoods, males and females, occupational groups, social class categories and so forth. The survey could be seen then as an intensive study of many individual cases, of several in-between cases, or an intensive look at one case.

If we take Singapore as a single case, more questions arise for the survey results might be taken as a representative of any (or all) of the following: an industrially advanced society, a multicultural Asian society, an urban city-state, and so forth. The possibilities are dependent more on the imagination and persuasive powers of the case writer than on the data per se. The same data could be classified also as a result of some historical process such as the progressive implementation of meritocratic principles or as the result of the workings of a political economy marked by strong centralized state planning and control. More artfully perhaps, the results could simply stand as a portrait of an intrinsically intriguing cultural entity in and of itself. How the data are eventually cut, framed and put forward may be conventional but there are more than a few conventions from which to choose. The choice is of course a writer's to make but there are no guarantees that all readers will go along.

Such an example suggests that it is a mistake to regard the case study as simply a kind of small-scale descriptive study of an identifiable group put forth in a qualitative manner. It is not uncommon however for us to think of case studies in just such a way. This is unfortunate and has led to a good deal of misunderstanding between (and among) social researchers and their respective audiences. Case studies can be macro or micro, qualitative or quantitative, cross-sectional or longitudinal, historical or contemporary, singular or comparative. In some sense, any social research project is a case study simply because it involves the analysis and interpretation of data that are always specific to a given place and time. By blurring the genres of social research and pushing the notion of a case study to the limit I am of course being a little facetious for if all products of social research are case studies, the category itself is drained of meaning. To avoid this trap requires looking past settings, methods and topics as defining characteristics and looking instead to the rhetorical practices, analytic styles and textual features on which case studies, as written products, rest.

From this perspective, case studies are the narratives — non-fiction division — of social science. They link events to events and thus provide historically situated tales of real people, doing real things, in real places and at real times. The more ambitious a case, the more likely an interpretation for the narrative events is put forth in the text for why some things happened and other things did not. The specificity, historical character and interpretive features of the narrative mark the case study as distinctive in social science. In this fashion, case studies stand apart from reports of experimental and survey work, from demographic portraits, from empirical tests of theoretical models. Generally speaking, they contrast most starkly with the ahistorical and non-event framework associated with most forms of variable analysis.

Case studies tell a story. They tell of what happened to whom, when, where and why. There are many flavors. A case can be primarily representational when the author places the story in a domain that is said to be ordinary or typical of a given class of actors, events or situations. A case can be extreme when it explores the ends of some continuum such as deviant cases that examine violations of the accepted (or expected) standards of place and time or exemplary cases that tell of the best of places and times. While some cases are explicitly comparative, all cases are at least implicitly comparative if only by virtue of the claims authors make for how their materials are to be located and read.

Cases also can be constructed from the bottom-up or the top-down. A bottom-up case finds its concepts and explanatory slants in the case materials themselves and what the case is about is discovered while doing the research. A top-down case is one in which the case setting is strategically selected in anticipation of illustrating a presumably general concept or process identified prior to undertaking the research. Methodological self-consciousness about such matters is on the rise these days and case writers are increasingly appearing as figures in their own narratives as readers are given accounts for how a given case was put together. Physiocracy is rarely a problem for case study writers since they are little interested in isolating or precisely measuring (so-called) causal variables. Nor are frequencies of great importance to them beyond helping to situate a particular narrative. A case is not a sample.

The end result of a well-constructed case on readers is that they come to know precisely what the case is about to the author and why it may or may not have relevance for matters with which they are concerned. Ideally, readers are both alert to the novelty put forth by a good case as well as intrigued, enlightened and perhaps persuaded by the explanation offered by a case writer. What it means to impress readers of a case writer's good sense is however a matter of some importance but one that cannot be fully appreciated without attending — however briefly — to the up, down and up again history of case studies in social science.

A Case of Case Studies

Case studies have a fairly long and certainly distinguished history in the social sciences. Indeed, case studies, notably of the comparative sort, played an almost exclusive role in sociology, political science, economics and anthropology until the mid-twentieth century when cases, except in anthropology, went into a profound and prolonged slump from which they are now recovering. This slump corresponds of course to the rise of variable analysis.

In telegraphic style and looking primarily at social research in the United States, the increasing prominence of variable studies in the social sciences — taking off in the 1960s — has been tied to administrative needs of the state and other large organizations for reliable data on individuals and groups (as citizens, consumers, employees, etc.) and the disciplinary advances of statistics coupled with the use of sophisticated number-crunching techniques (e.g., Platt, 1995; Harvey, 1987). Tight experimental designs, rigorous statistical sampling and the creation of large data sets went with the formulation of operationally defined and hence measurable variables that could be yoked to a model and tested as to their explanatory power. By

so doing, social researchers sought to place human studies on the same
level as the more prestigious natural and physical sciences thus jettisoning
soft, squishy, qualitative studies with highly contextualized conclusions for
hard, focused, numerical studies with detachable conclusions.

In short, narrative moved out of the mainstream of social science and
variable analysis moved in. Case studies were marginalized. Whatever
value they retained as castaways was limited to that of precursors for
"more serious" studies (legitimate only as pilot or preliminary studies), low
status teaching tools, examples to be exploited and tucked into theoretical
discourse, or merely raw data in need of cooking (i.e., coding, counting
and classifying). The idea that single cases were indispensable to social
science became strange. In many settings, the questions surrounds case
studies became polemic and evaluative, issued with the intent of belittling
anyone who did such work — "you still doing case studies?" or "who
studies cases anymore?" (e.g., Gusfield, 1990).

This did not occur without protest of course. An early alarm and still
one of the best in organization studies was issued by Kenneth Boulding
(1958) who, in a remarkably prophetic review of the first two volumes of
the then new journal *Administrative Science Quarterly* had this to say of
case studies:

> It would be a great pity if a morbid fear of being "unscientific" were ever
> to lead to a suppression of this type of writing. The thing that distinguishes
> social systems from physical or even biological systems is their incomparable
> (and embarrassing) richness in special cases. Generalizations in the social
> sciences are mere pathways which lead through a riotous forest of individual
> trees, each a species unto itself. The social scientist who loses this sense
> of the essential individuality and uniqueness of each case is all too likely
> to make a solemn scientific ass of himself, especially if he (sic) thinks that
> his faceless generalizations are the equivalents of the rich variety in the
> world. I am not arguing that we should cease to make generalizations; this
> would be to abandon science altogether. I am merely urging that we should
> not believe them. (14-5)

Whether or not blame rests fully on the morbid fear carried by solemn
scientific asses, it is true that at least some of Boulding's anticipatory

anxiety was warranted. In *ASQ*, as well as a good many other mainstream social science journals holding an interest in organizations, case studies (and qualitative work in general) suffered a precipitous decline (Van Maanen, 1998).

A number of accounts can be put forward to explain this shift of emphasis in the most prestigious research journals. One story holds that the editors (and referees) of any given period are always (and simply) doing their jobs and while, for example, they may see many case studies, most are without merit, poorly constructed, uninteresting and thus rightfully rejected. Another story, equally plausible, is that relatively few case studies appear during a period because few are submitted. Case studies may dry up during particular periods as scholarly attention turns to other forms of research. A third account has it that case study authors turn away from all journals — by choice or necessity — and look instead to publish their work in monograph form or as chapters in edited books, a strategic move that allows for the presentation of lengthier and more discursive narratives than can be stuffed into journal length articles.

Each of these stories carries, no doubt, some truth. But none address directly the temporal question of why case studies fell out of favor so suddenly during the late 1960s and 1970s. Some finer grained accounts are required. To again take organizational studies as an illustrative field, several historical particulars appear critical. Of importance to the field in this period is the appearance of several influential large-sample structural studies based on organizations as units of analysis — notably, the Aston studies of the late 1960s (e.g., Pugh et al., 1969). In the same period comes the "discovery" of the environment as both an independent and dependent variable in the modeling of organizations and hence the popularity of contingency models of organizational form and behavior. These empirical studies of structure promise to put organizational studies firmly on the scientific map. Not coincidentally, this is also the time when the IBM 360 computer comes along with a standard and user friendly (for the period) statistical software package. The technically sophisticated analysis of data sets both big and small now becomes considerably easier and more convenient for students of organization than ever before. This is also a period of explosive growth of enrollment in American colleges and universities. An enlarged supply of freshly minted Ph.D.s is needed to staff the new teaching and research positions opened up. Jobs are plentiful. In this world, time-consuming, old fashioned qualitative case analysis and writing may well have fallen from grace and favor among those pursuing research careers in organizational studies (and, no doubt, elsewhere).

All this is of course something of a speculative "just so" story. It certainly fits my own career experiences that began as graduate student at the University of California, Irvine in 1965. But, alas, the rise of variable analysis remains a case to be written and there will be no doubt considerable variation in the stories told across fields and subfields, across settings, across countries and across particular research cultures. What does seem clear in retrospect is that the claim of victory for variable analysis over case studies was a trifle premature. As all those who follow the literature in virtually any of the social sciences today are now aware, cases, narrative, history, ethnography and qualitative studies of all sorts are back and back with a vengeance. A concern for meaning, rhetoric, language and the context and politics of research crowd the bookshelves, course reading lists, conference workshops and research journals these days. A good part of this is due to the slow but spreading recognition that variable analysis is failing to accomplish the aims on which its future depends.

In policy studies, for example, variable analysis plays a central role. Critically, a large, policy-minded audience beyond the research community is seemingly under its sway. The upshot is that regression coefficients become parameters of public policy since they are taken by researchers and users alike to provide scientific evidence of just who (or what) is doing well and who (or what) is doing poorly and just what causal forces might exist to explain such outcomes. The view arises among decision-makers and political figures that if the levels of particular input variables are pushed up or down, then, like clockwork, output variables will change in some desirable way. The rub is that there may be few if any cases or familiar stories to support such a view. Sociologist Andrew Abbot (1992) provides a revealing tale in this regard:

Anybody who knew the typical stories of organizations under great stress would never have believed that breaking up AT&T (American Telephone and Telegraph) would result in a highly profitable firm and a cheaper overall phone service. But policy-makers saw economists' equations proving that profit equaled so many parts research plus so many parts resources plus so many parts market competition and so on. No one bothered to ask whether one could tell a real story that led from AT&T as of 1983 to the vision they had in mind. In fact there wasn't one. And so the phone bills that were to get cheaper got both more expensive and less comprehensible, the research laboratory that was to invent wonderful new devises was dismantled, and the firm achieves its current (short-run) profits by laying off the very scientists who policymakers thought were the foundation for the future. (79-80)

The variable approach is precisely the kind of social science that said this would not happen to AT&T and its customers. But it did. And today, I might add, it has all the elements of a great case.

Case Studies Today

While, to be sure, case studies were marginalized for a time — perhaps 15 or 20 years — in the social sciences, they never really went away. Some case studies were smuggled into variable research since illustrations were needed to animate the relationships uncovered by the analysis. Some turned up in publications outside the disciplinary mainstreams. Indeed, many case studies went to new journals (of relatively low visibility) founded in part to make room for such writing. In American sociology, for example, case studies — particularly ethnographic ones — appeared in journals such as *Qualitative Sociology*, *Symbolic Interactionism*, and the *Journal of Contemporary Ethnography*, all established in the 1970s. And, currently, at least some mainstream journals are welcoming back case studies (e.g., Firebaugh, 1997). Even *ASQ* appears to have relaxed its fixation on variable studies as cases and others forms of qualitative work return to the journal (Van Maanen, 1998).

More critically perhaps, scholarly monographs have long been the keepers of the case study flame. A cursory glance at the best selling lists of social science monographs over the years attests to the prominent place of case studies in the social sciences. In sociology, for instance, Clemens et al. (1995) classify over half of the books nominated for awards by the American Sociological Association in 1988–89 as qualitative studies. Not all of these works are case studies of course but, by my rough count, around 30 percent of the nominations cited went to works that I would call case studies. On the monograph front, case studies are — and have been — well represented in the social science literatures.

This is not to suggest that case studies have remained the same over the years. As many have pointed out, over the years they have grown more sophisticated, both theoretically and methodologically (e.g., Fine, 1995; Feagin, 1991). No longer are would-be case writers told to just do it — to simply go "out there" and act like a reporter by "writing up" what they find as were novitiate fieldworkers in the so-called Golden Age of Chicago School sociology (Bulmer, 1984). Description has become linked with interpretation and cases are increasingly explicit as to the theory that informs the construction of the narrative as well as the theory that is advanced by the work. A landmark publication in the analytic domain is no doubt *The Discovery of Grounded Theory* published by Glaser and Strauss in 1967. As to the methodological domain, jesters in the trade like Marcus (1994) suggest (tongue only partially in cheek) that advice now overwhelms practice; that the number of publications put out in the last five to ten years to guide, critique or otherwise inform fieldwork (for casework) might well equal or exceed the number of published substantive studies. Methodological self-consciousness, for better or worse, must surely be at an all-time high.

Just why case studies seem to have recaptured our attention these days requires some passing (and closing) comments. I have four accounts in mind. All are intertwined. First, consider the sorry state of unifying theories. Across the social sciences, from psychology to economics, the very idea of discovering and validating highly general covering laws or general systems theories is slip-sliding away (and fast). Postmodernism (and all its post-toasty variants such as post-structuralism, post-Marxism, post-realism, post-colonialism, post-positivism and so forth) has put grand narratives on the run. Modernism stresses coherence and order, postmodernism emphasizes competing perspectives, contests of meaning, contextual modifiers and the uncertain processes of signification. To the extent that paradigms are out and cases are in, it will do us well to make sure that the cases we do have are good ones, composed with patience and skill. Cases, for example, try often to tell readers what it is like to be someone else and this is — as we have learned from the various crises in anthropology and its related fields — a highly problematic matter, accomplished, if at all, on the epistemological high wire. Case studies of the careful and trustworthy sort in this domain must treat theory lightly (borrowing as much as building) and make few (and usually tentative) generalizing claims for a given analysis may not travel very far. In the wake of conceptual imperialism, such modesty is quite appealing.

Second, fragmentation and disorder is more than a characterization of our scholarly worlds. It attaches to contemporary life and, as every pundit on the global scene reminds us, we live everywhere in unsettled times. The world is being altered — politically, culturally, economically — in a variety of ways. Communication and transportation technologies cut into the social and cultural isolation of societies. Human migrations change the character of villages and cities, regions and nations. Multinational organizations cross borders with impunity seeking new markets and remaking, sometimes obliterating, old ones. Global contrasts are omnipresent as people become increasingly aware of how things are done elsewhere. In changing times — when the Big Mac is in Moscow and sushi is part of the staid New Englander's diet — previously unquestioned cultural understandings and traditions unravel. Stories conveyed by cases are therefore vital; perhaps all we have in an uncharted world.

Third, with cultural practices on the move and unsettled, variability rather than stability is the norm. With variability, older modes of analysis that take-for-granted the unity and value of social constructs such as culture, organization, occupation, role, identity and so forth become problematic and thus challenged. A good example in this regard is Michael

Porter's (1990) influential notions about the competitiveness of nations. Porter's well known view holds that certain national characteristics such as market size, labor characteristics, barriers to entry, state support and so forth determine the economic health and future of organizations that operate within country boundaries. But a good deal of recent work looks beyond "the five forces" to regional and local variation via detailed, highly contextualized case studies. Much of this case work argues that the nation as a unit is far too distant, abstract and general a force to act in the ways Porter claims. There appears to be virtually as much variance within nations as there is between them. Local peculiarities (and advantages) are readily apparent in Saxenian's (1994) account of California's Silicon Valley or Locke's (1995) treatment of the textile regions of northern Italy. Consider, too, the influential role played by the Economic Development Board in Singapore as a unique element in the country's rise to economic power as chronicled in a case study by Schein (1996). These studies (and more) suggest that local, historical and rather unpredictable (if not entirely idiosyncratic) features are far more crucial to the building of concrete and supportive environments for economic growth than previously thought. Aggregate concepts and theories derived from variable analysis simply fail to provide the fine-grained analysis of economic activity and the social context in which it occurs offered by in-depth, narrative case studies (Granovetter, 1985).

Finally, to end my list of reasons why I think case studies have rebounded of late, some old-fashioned pragmatism and a little preaching. There are many good things to say for the practicality of case studies. The ease, comfort, relatively low cost and timeliness in which such studies can be conducted has much to recommend it in these times of rapid change, scarce resources and pinched research budgets. Case studies are typically small, flexible and nimble endeavors. To my mind, they are rather attractive counterparts to the elaborately designed, big budget, over controlled studies whose findings are sometimes obsolete before they reach print. Equally important is that the case study remains something of a solo act and thus the work and results are filtered through one head rather than many and hired hand problems are not a concern. A consistent point of view, a sense of moral and ethical responsibility that comes from personal identification and responsibility, and a set of craft-like norms are perhaps more likely to be in place and respected when a study is conducted by a single scholar.

All this is to say what is in my title: Case studies are important and perhaps more important today than ever before. The goals of this work in my view are to expand our horizons, to reflect seriously and intimately on the events that surround us here, there and everywhere, and to increase the range of human possibilities for both thought and action. By learning how and sometimes why real people, in real places, at real times act as they do, these aims can be advanced. The case, as many good judges have said, is to be continued.

References

Abbott, Andrew (1992). What do cases do? Some notes on activity in sociological analysis. In Charles C. Ragin and Howard S. Becker (Eds.), *What is a case?* pp. 53–82. New York: Cambridge University Press.

Bulmer, Martin (1984). *The Chicago School of Sociology*. Chicago: University of Chicago Press.

Boulding, Kenneth E. (1958). Evidences for an administrative science. A review of *Administrative Science Quarterly*, volumes 1 and 2. *Administrative Science Quarterly*, 3: 1–22.

Clemens, Elisabeth S., Powell, Walter W., McIlwaine, Kris & Okomoto, Dina (1995). Careers in print: Books, journals and scholarly reputations. *American Journal of Sociology*, 101: 433–494.

Feagin, Joe R., Orum, Anthony M. & Sjoberg, Gideon (1991). *A Case for the Case Study*. Chapel Hill: University of North Carolina Press.

Fine, Gary Alan (1995). Introduction. In Gary Alan Fine (Ed.), *A Second Chicago School? The Development of a Postwar American Sociology*, pp. 1–16. Chicago: University of Chicago Press.

Firebaugh, Colin (1997). Editorial statement. *American Sociological Review*, 62: 13–14.

Glaser, Barney & Strauss, Anselm (1967). *The Discovery of Grounded Theory*. Chicago: Aldine.

Goffman, Erving (1981). *Forms of Talk*. Philadelphia: University of Pennsylvania Press.

Granovetter, Mark S. (1985). Economic action and social structure: The problem of embeddedness. *American Journal of Sociology*, 91: 481–510.

Gusfield, Joesph (1990). My life and soft times. In Bennett M. Berger (Ed.), *Authors of Their Own Lives*, pp. 104–129. Berkeley: University of California Press.

Harvey, L. (1987). *Myths of the Chicago School of Sociology*. Aldershop: Avebury.

Kondo, Dorinne (1990). *Crafting Selves*. Chicago: University of Chicago Press.

Kunda, Gideon (1992). *Engineering Culture*. Philadelphia: Temple University Press.

Locke, Richard M. (1995). *Remaking the Italian Economy*. Ithaca, New York: Cornell University Press.

Marcus, George E. (1994). What comes (just) after "post"? The case of ethnography. In Norman Denzin and Yvonne Lincoln (Eds.), *The Handbook of Qualitative Research*, pp. 565–582. Newbury Park, Ca.: Sage.

Platt, Jennifer (1995). Research methods and the second Chicago School. In Gary Alan Fine (Ed.), *The Second Chicago School?*, pp. 82–107. Chicago: University of Chicago Press, .

Porter, Michael (1990). *The Competitive Advantage of Nations*. New York: Free Press.

Pugh, Derek S., Hickson, David J. & Hinings, C. Ransom (1969). An empirical taxonomy of work organizations. *Administrative Science Quarterly*, 14: 115–126.

Ragin, Charles C. & Becker, Howard S. (Eds.) (1992). *What is a Case?* New York: Cambridge University Press.

Saxenian, Annalee (1994). *Regional Advantage: Culture and Competition in Silicon and Route 128 Valley*. Cambridge: Harvard University Press.

Schein, Edgar H. (1996). *Strategic Pragmatism: The Culture of Singapore's Economic Development Board*. Cambridge: MIT Press.

Van Maanen, John (1998). Different strokes: Qualitative research in the Administrative Science Quarterly from 1956 to 1996. In John Van Maanen (Ed.), *Qualitative Studies of Organizations*, pp. 1–33. Newbury Park, Ca.: Sage.

Vaughan, Diane (1996). *The Challenger Launch Decision: Risky Technology, Culture and Deviance at NASA*. Chicago: University of Chicago Press.

The Contexts That Transform Learning

Ai-Yen Chen
National Institute of Education
Nanyang Technological University, Singapore

Joyce James
Regional Language Centre (RELC),
Southeast Asian Ministers of Education Organization
(SEAMEO) Singapore

Synopsis

This chapter focuses on analyzing the *problem of context* in learning situations in higher education from multiple perspectives: personal, social and cultural. The analysis is based on three key questions:

1) What context or conditions facilitate(s) learning and the *artistry of practice* in higher education?
2) Who improves or enhances the conditions of learning and *artistry of practice*?
3) How and why the learning occurs in the context or under those conditions?

The discussions that follow show clearly the complexity and unpredictability of the conditions that facilitate learning. They are not confined to the mental, emotional, social, physical and technological conditions of the learners, professors or practitioners. In understanding the context of learning and in solving problems in work places, the learners should be equipped with vision, sustainable values and capabilities for the profession, the institutions and the larger than life itself.

The Contexts that Transform Learning

Ai-Yen Chen and *Joyce James*

Introduction

In recent years, much interest has been generated by several communities of people studying the problem of *context* in learning and teaching situations. Context is meant by some learners and teachers to be the "setting" or "physical environment" for learning. In reality, contexts have far more dimensions than the mere physical or practical. Besides the physical and practical meaning, context can be viewed and analysed from different perspectives, for example, the personal, social, and cultural, or more specifically the language, value and "shared-ness" among the learners and teachers.

This chapter will focus mainly on the *context of learning* in higher education from the dimensions of the individual learner or teacher, the education institution or learning community, and in terms of language and culture. Since the writers of this Book come from different countries, cultures, and professional practices, their views of cognitive and organisational development, Eastern and Western philosophical ways of thinking and approaches to relationship building, meaning construction, strategies for designing instruction and learning will have important bearing on the case analysis, presentation, and discussion. Three key questions will be raised in our analysis of the context of learning: 1) What *context* or *conditions* facilitate(s) learning and the *artistry of practice in higher education*? 2) Who improves or enhances the conditions of learning and artistry of practice? 3) How and why the learning occurs in the context or under those conditions?

Irrespective of the individual writer's perspective and construction of the learning context, each case contains an account of the learner's needs and the learning environment, be it conventional as in a classroom, or innovative as in cyberspace. Such narratives sometimes include content analysis which also embeds the specification of learning objectives and the learner's level of entry knowledge and skills. Generally the cases contain the professional teacher's reflection on the process of change from one stage of a learner's development to another culminating in an evaluation of the practice.

Context: Its Roles And Meanings In Learning

The word *context* as mentioned earlier means different things to different people. In layman's language the word context can answer the question, "what is going on?" The answer to this is not a simple "this" or "that" but a complex, potentially volatile issue. Taking an extreme viewpoint, every situation is unique to the individual and can never be shared fully by others even within the same institution. However, when one talks about "code", there is the notion of shared context. Hence the difference between the private and the public is the difference between more shared-ness and less shared-ness. The relationship between the "you" and "I" is known as the "tenor". Where the relationship is further apart, the distance tends to be more maximal.

In a teaching-learning situation, the relationship between the "you" and "I" can give rise to different kinds of teacher roles. Teachers who are more autocratic tend to allow students fewer negotiations and choices. On the other hand, teachers who are more democratic allow for more learner negotiations leading ultimately to more learner autonomy in ways of learning. Similarly in a working situation, the relationship between the employer-employee can also give rise to different roles for the professional or the worker. An inquiry into the practice of a professional, be it teaching or engineering, dentistry or business administration, therefore involves more than a "you and I" relationship, or the content or substance of the discipline or profession but also the situation or contexts within which the relation is evolved, and the learning/working process is integrated. The central binding threads are shared-ness in thinking and meaning-making, more specifically reflection or reflective thinking and the language, both verbal and non-verbal language, used by the participants in the process of negotiations, learning, working and decision-making.

Context can also relate to the field of inquiry or the discipline, and the profession under study. In a discipline such as literature which deals with the cognitive as well as the affective and social domains, there is greater flexibility in accepting differences in interpretation than in disciplines like mathematics and the sciences, or in professional studies such as dentistry, engineering, law, and teacher education. Factors that may influence one's viewpoint, learning and thinking can be related to personal and community knowledge of the discipline and profession, beliefs of the individual and community about rights and freedom versus institutional rules and privileges, as well as organisational and individual cultural differences.

At the root of many of the contextual issues, we are likely to find communication failures and cultural differences and misunderstandings that prevent the parties from framing the problem and dealing with it constructively. To prevent some of these failures and misunderstandings and to bridge cultural, institutional, social, and political differences, a discussion on the various dimensions is pertinent in the consideration of what Schon (1990) would describe as the *artistry of reflective practices* when the problems, dilemmas and puzzles of one's practice are perceived in a new light. More importantly, when they are understood, solved and accepted in a different way.

The Cultural and Linguistic Dimensions of Contexts

In the cultural and linguistic dimension, one's viewpoint about context is derived from anthropology and socio-linguistics and is linked to the tradition of Malinowski (1923, 1950), Geetz (1968), Vygotsky (1978, 1981) and Halliday (1974). Malinowski saw context as the situation surrounding the action, that is a situation context. Geetz defined culture as "a historically transmitted pattern of meaning embodied in symbols, a system of inherited conceptions expressed in symbolic form by means of which men communicate, perpetuate and develop their knowledge about and attitudes towards life".

(Geetz, 1968, p. 641).

For Vygotsky, the concept of culture offers a way of linking the history of a social group, the communication activity of its members and the cognitive development of its children. Hence his use of *cultural* development almost interchangeably with *historical* development. For Halliday (1977, 1978) coming from the Firthian tradition, "context of situation" is an abstract notion. The *context of situation* refers to "the whole set of external features considered relevant to the analysis of an utterance such as phonetics, grammar and semantics" (Crystal, 1985, p. 72). Hasan (1996) refers to it as the "motivational interaction" in as much as they bear upon the talk in all its aspects. What makes up the context of situation? The **field**, the **tenor**, and the **mode** constitute the context of situation. As discussed earlier, "field" refers to the field of inquiry or the disciplines involved. "Tenor" refers to the affective domain or the practice of the discipline that is the relationship between the participants involved in the activity of meaning-making. The "mode" of the context refers to the part language is playing in the activity, whether it is in the written or the spoken channel, that is, language could be in the graphic medium or in a phonic medium or vice versa. The differences in the "field", "tenor" and "mode" give rise to different contextual configurations. These in turn constitute differences in learning, thinking and working. Different contextual configurations constitute differences in learning, thinking, feeling and working. A critical point in learning and thinking is that it is a result of an interplay of multiple facets of contexts: for example, political context, pedagogical context, context of specialised content, physical context and others including verbal and non-verbal contexts.

In the cases presented in this volume, the critical contexts for the way learning and thinking take place differ. Each of the case studies presented is a dynamic context embedded in multiple contexts giving rise to unique learning, thinking and working sites and situations.

In the case study entitled the "Talking Addict", an American university teacher narrated his transformation as a self-centred teacher believing that "the more dramatic the presentation, the more brilliant the content, the better the teacher." He was what he believed in his classroom. Silence was hence alien to the talking addict. This resulted in his "unwittingly" creating "a glass wall" between him and his students. What was tragic was the fact that the talking addict was unaware of this invisible barrier. In the course of time, the talking addict underwent a radical transformation and began to understand how his actions and beliefs are inevitably linked with students in an "educational ecological system". The talking addict's recovery occurred after his "reflection-on-action" (Schon, 1983) stimulated by a parent-counselling session not at his teaching site — the university — but at his son's school in Maine. The university teacher's transformation was brought about by another mentor in another social context. The change began with the teacher's recognition of his personal and teaching problem. He realised that he had not been giving his students a chance to negotiate what they wished to learn and discover their strengths and potentials just as his son was pronounced a problematic learner and a potential drop-out because of his *attention deficit disorder* (ADD) condition. From that day onwards, he tried to adopt a more social transaction — interaction mode of teaching. Shuttling between the contexts of a group counselling event to that of a private individual heart-searching event, Schmier, the history professor learned how to improve his teaching by allowing his students to discover, experiment and share their thoughts and experiences rather than getting them to passively learn from his expositions about Nazi Germany and Europe in the Second World War.

The above case showed the development of a university teacher who operates from an individual transmission mode to that of a social transaction mode of learning and teaching. Vygotsky (1933, 1978) in his book "Thought and Language" explicated the idea of *zone of proximal development* (ZPD) of a child quite clearly in his description of how a mother facilitated a child's language and thought development and her role in facilitating a child's larger zone of proximal learning by mental stimulation like questioning. Proximal learning and mental scaffolding are essential features in his sociohistorical theory of learning. In laymen's terms, the university teacher and his students both learned in a new way because of the transformation in the teacher brought about by another social context. The teacher not only changed his content and mode of delivery but also his relationship with his students. His changed behaviour facilitated his students' development. They not only enjoyed what they learned but also were morally committed to actively learn on their own.

The university teacher's confession reflects the values and cultures of schools and the society in the United States — the value placed on degrees and certain kinds of professions and the fairly rigid assessment system of formal schooling. His thoughts and emotions are quite typical of parents with ADD children and his style of teaching reminiscent of most teachers of the arts and humanities. His realization which brought about a change in his pedagogical beliefs and a shift in his own self-esteem and teaching action could only take place because of the heart-searching incident at the school in Maine.

In Kirpal Singh's case study entitled, "Cross-Cultural Readings: The Case of King Lear" there is a versatility in the way some cross-cultural messages must take on a global meaning. The questions that need to be asked are (1) What causes some of the essential differences in student readings? These can be attributed to different cultural, religious backgrounds. (2) What can be differences? What can be universal? If all were differences — we will not be able to have any shared meaning. There cannot be all similarities because there are cultural, social, religious and other differences. The important question to ask is, "are the differences peripheral or crucial to understanding the underlying meaning of the text". At the social and learning contextual levels, another question may be asked: "Will the understanding of the underlying meaning of the text and the multi-cultural, multi-religious differences in interpretation facilitate the multi-cultural appreciation as well as religious tolerance and harmony among the student teachers?" Such questions are important when considering dialogues and negotiations in a professional programme which emphasizes the development of lifelong learning and reflective practice among the teachers.

Kirpal Singh's literature class learned about the multiple perspectives and multiple interpretations in the reading of *King Lear*. The Singapore students' heightened awareness of their religious and cultural differences might have increased their understanding of each other's cultural perspectives. Through class discussion led by the lecturer, the student-teachers might develop their cultural understanding and higher level of literary appreciation but whether they simultaneously attained religious tolerance and cultural assimilation was a different matter. This realization is important in their intellectual growth. They should know that their ability to discuss and negotiate for shared meaning do facilitate their development as lovers of literature but their progress in the artistry of a reflective literature teacher is a life-long process.

From the above, it is clear that the ways of communicating the content and the mode of delivery are further contextual considerations. The "what", "why" and "how" of delivering the content is a contextual issue. Effective teacher and student communication is more than "correct" verbal and non-verbal behaviour. It is associated with the rapport between the two parties which cannot be easily defined by role and functions of a teacher, a learner, or that of the language used. It goes beyond the linguistic context. The main effect is the culture of communication.

Similar research findings on the complexity of interactions between learning, teaching and development have been reported in other parts of the world. There may or may not be any direct connection between school learning and knowledge transmission, self and collaborative reflection preceding the internalization of that knowledge by the learner-professionals. But the professionals' will to reflect on their practices, to recognize or frame the problems of learning and teaching and realize their roles as problem solvers are critical to their professional development and growth.

In the case of the Sydney 5th and 6th grade teacher observed by Watson, his pedagogic knowledge is derived from what Shulman has called "the wisdom of practice" (1987). It includes what has been called the "craft knowledge" of teachers...that capacity to analyse teaching situations and apply appropriate strategies (Batten, Marland and Khamis, 1993; Brown and McIntyre, 1993). This craft knowledge is a result of multiple and repeated dialogue and negotiation between the teacher and his pupils in K-6 Australian classrooms for a prolonged engagement of 11 years. He has learned from his pupils, colleagues in the school and the teacher education institutions and the larger society before reaching the level of "higher teaching competencies".

In Hong Kong, student-teachers of English language were trained by Kwo, their teacher educator-practicum supervisor, to reflect on their classroom practices in order to attain higher teaching competencies. By writing journals, analysing data collected and doing action research into their own teaching experience in almost homogeneous ethnic classrooms with other cultural variations, they developed a greater sensitivity to their own mental and emotional conditions in response to the social and organizational demands and expectations. They were able to relate their personal beliefs to institutional espoused theories and draw some conclusions regarding their personal and professional development.

The tension of cultural and individual differences in social contexts often generate extreme behaviours in organizations. If not understood and moderated in time, these extreme behaviours of avoidance or withdrawal, assertiveness or aggressiveness may be problematic and become barriers to organizational learning in working towards a common vision and some supportive strategies for bringing about change not only at the personal level but also at a higher organizational level for the common good.

Through teaching her students to cooperate in their geography lessons in small groups, Lee and Ng's in-service teacher learned many lessons from her mistakes and failures to bring about collaborative efforts in a competitive school and society. Through self-review and questioning, she subsequently developed her own skills in becoming a more reflective practitioner. The importance of dialogue and negotiation in such cooperative classroom is once again brought home to the researchers.

Through the use of Chinese classical texts from the Book of Warfare and Book of Change, Loi and Teo discovered the use of analogy and problem-based learning in a business law class. The close link between nature, thought and action is established by the ancient writers and can be applied to solving real life problems.

The Social and Organizational Dimensions of Contexts

The culturally based quality of learning is represented by Vygotsky's colleague Leont'ev (1981) but developed and extended to the classroom by Newman, Griffin and Cole (1989), and to the workplace by Brown and Duguid (1991). According to Newman et al. (1989, p. 62), it was proposed by Leont'ev as a socio-cultural alternative to Piaget's biological metaphor of "assimilation". Brown and Duguid (1991) in proposing a unified view of organization learning, working and practice, appropriate the learning of precepts and procedures as a bridge to working and innovation. They advocated the close matching of working, learning and innovation as interrelated and compatible and thus are complementary and not conflicting human activities. They advocated the creation of shared understanding in beliefs and practice by a "thick" detailed description of the way work actually progresses in an organization. This takes place optimally in three specific stages: shared narration as members of the learning community describe to each other in detail the successes and failures of their practices; collaboration as they discuss and cooperate in improving the practice and finally, the social construction of the practice. The social construction of a practice has two parts. First and most evident is the construction of a shared understanding out of "bountiful conflicting and confusing data". This constructed understanding reflects the participants' view of the world. Such an approach is highly situated and highly improvisational (Brown and Duguid, 1991). The second feature of social construction of good practice or an innovation gives the participants *identity and community membership.* (Lave and Wenger, 1993). The development of higher mental skills are mediated by language. The higher processes are acquired through social interaction with others who are more skilful or knowledgeable. Supervision, guidance and discussion allow less experienced people to participate in and complete tasks that would have been impossible alone. Another feature associated with Vygotsky's ZPD is the idea of play in mental development in addition to instructional and social interaction. In integrating these key ideas of developing shared understanding, and membership identity, many university teachers of professionals have developed active learning strategies that employ simulation and role play to increase motivation for learning and maximize cognitive, affective, and social development.

Such ideas about social construction of knowledge were implied in the writings of organizational psychologists such as Argris and Schon (1974) in their book on *Theory in Practice* and Argris (1993) *Knowledge for Action*. In the first book, the authors proposed the influence of one's espoused theories and theories-in-use in any kind of practice. They termed it as "a double-loop learning" in complex situations when members make use of mistakes and difficulties to learn to frame problems, solve problems in contexts and develop more sophisticated espoused theories in attempting to make them congruent with theories-in-use. Both the individual and the other group members' reflection and action are intricately intertwined and reflective practices emerge from the thoughtful and creative artistry of professionals working together (Elliott, 1991:70; Kemmies and McTaggart 1988:14; McKernen, 1991:29; Schon, 1987, 1990), in a tripartite interactive relationship among the learner-apprentice and the coach and the "material" or the "content" of practice. In his latter publication, Argris suggested the use of some tools and procedures that managers and researchers could use to identify a correct defensive positions and political problems in organizations and change adversarial relationships into productive partnerships.

Organisational sociologists such as Schein (1993) and Van Maanen (1983, 1987) analysed the socialisation processes and the attitudes and behaviours of members in organisations based on their personal experiences as members of the Sloan School of Management at the Massachusetts Institute of Technology (MIT). Both Schein and Van Maanen advocate personal involvement in the process of researching into action-on-reflection. Schein believes in "clinical data" as a source of better theory. Van Maanen (1987) uses the term "field" to represent the setting of the organizations and the entire scope of study with the inquirer observing the happenings at first hand. To both of them the importance of personal participation and sensitivity to the situation or in relation to the stages of development of the institutions are prerequisites to understanding and framing the problems to be solved. They do not believe in collecting data to fit a prescribed or established theoretical frame. This sensitivity and the deliberate effort to work towards coupling individual or organizational learning styles with the developmental stages of organizations are emphasized. However, Schein (1993) differentiates dialogue from face-to-face communication of the sort we learn in group dynamics in sensitivity training. The latter emphasises active listening, the former focuses on getting in touch with the underlying assumptions of the parties concerned. Dialogue is focused more on "the thinking process and how our perceptions and cognition are pre-formed by our past experiences... An important goal of dialogue is to enable a group to reach a higher level of consciousness and creativity through the gradual creation of a shared set of meanings and a common thinking process".

Writers such as Schein and Senge who study organizational development and individual learner's abilities to cope with changes and challenges (Holly, 1994; as Lawler, 1992; Mumford, 1994; Schein, 1994; Senge, 1990; Swieringa and Wierdsma, 1992) believe strongly in making businesses and industries learning organizations that can respond quickly to changes and new opportunities. Schein deals with the fundamentals such as the crucial role of leaders and how they could identify, nurture and shape the culture and integrate or mesh the sub-cultures of organizations — in any stage for development — to achieve their goals and fulfil their missions. Senge spells out the core disciplines that build learning organizations which include personal mastery of reality, necessary mental models, shared vision and team learning. To Senge the identification and change of the limiting factor is the first step to resolving conflicts, some structural, some human. This should be done by a team with the same vision of reality, even of "defensive routines" and "structural conflicts" not just by the leader alone. Perhaps what he has in mind is what Schon might have termed "reflection-on-practice" in the process of aiming for artistry or satisfaction and development in a job which is more than being productive.

Most of the case writers of the book do not refer to the above organizational development aspects — contexts that could have influenced their inquiry. They write mainly from personal historical perspectives and how they develop their understanding about their students' learning and the contexts of learning. However, the more interesting cases are those that examine critically the nature of professional judgements which teachers of professionals have to make in educating their students. These judgements may be based on the university teachers' knowledge of their students' backgrounds, learning and thinking styles and personality characteristics, but the most critical may be on their own practices. In operating at such a high level of awareness and realisation, their desire to frame their problems in the context of higher education would perhaps also be sharpened. This resonates with Rowland's view that "the constant of teaching is not the student, or the technique, but the nature of professional judgements we have to make" (1993); and with Ramsden's assertion that improving teaching involves: "a process of conceptual change analogous to the process of student learning" (1993).

Lori Breslow from the Sloan School of Management in the United States and Liao Ziqi of the School of Accountancy and Business in Singapore are both concerned with the ways the multinational students with different learning styles and personalities in their classes interact with each other. Cultural sensitivity and consideration for one another are key ingredients in nurturing a cooperative learning environment. They are also important in developing a shared vision and team work in a learning organization. Insistence on individual rights and differences of perception, justification for gender and racial biases create obstacles to effective communication in learning situations.

In making the learning of Business Law more real to life, two university teachers in business became aware of the power of using "market-place" wisdom from ancient Chinese classical texts such as the *Book of Change – I-Ching* (易经) and the *Art of War* (孙子兵法). Teo and Loi discovered the use of the principles and analogues of nature and war strategies to explicate concepts such as "the Making of a Contract". The idea of associating nature, thought and action expounded by the ancient writers could be applied to present problems that are prevalent in a variety of situations, for example, in personal relationship, business and other kinds of human transactions where contracts might be necessary. The principle of "Sung" (讼) or "conflict" is cited as one that is appropriate for use in such a case. "Sung" highlights the appropriate timing and approach for an action which requires astute judgement in a situation that may lead to conflicts of interest. In such a case it is important to be cautious and carefully balance the virtues of patience and courage, the timing of assertion or submission, and the motion of stand-still and action.

The contexts of learning and thinking have evolved alongside the tools and technologies for learning as they are connected with the development of the organization or the institution. Every time these tools evolve there is a corresponding reason for the use of the tools, and the tools in turn make it possible for new kinds of learning in new and challenging learning contexts. For example, with the development of information technology, there have been corresponding changes in the modes of learning and thinking. Learning takes place not only in traditional classrooms and in the field or laboratories but in electronic learning systems and environments. Each of the learning systems be it in a specific web site or across several sites in the World Wide Web, or in a computer tutorial or simulation system, or over distance learning and teleconferencing link-ups, provide a different learning context for the learners. Learning not only takes place in different contexts, the contexts also serve different or overlapping purposes. Because of the importance of context there cannot be idealised learning and thinking situations and methods. On the contrary, the systems and tools must allow for individual autonomy and preferences in learning, for variation in learning styles, and for lifelong learning. Of important consideration, there should also be different ways of assessing the different desired learning outcomes based on the use of these systems and tools.

Marnie O'Neill, for example, attempted to show how a Western Australian university tried to develop a video disc programme to develop its novice academic staff members. The lecturers were asked to view interactive video excerpts of "expert" classroom teaching and give their critical views and comments after hearing comments by the more skilful teachers and their students. She believes that an increased awareness of the weaknesses and strengths of one's own as well as others' teaching is the beginning of self-correction. In getting university teachers to comment on others' teaching using cooperative learning, O'Neill hopes to share not only the reflections of the experts and their students, but also to provoke reflective behaviour in the users, as well as offering examples of what to reflect upon and ways of thinking about it.

Personal and Psychological Dimensions of Contexts

Closely associated with the studies of organisational psychologists and sociologists are cognitive and learning psychologists who advocate situated learning in context (Bransford et al., 1992; Brown and Champion, 1985; Chaiklin and Lave, 1993; Lave, 1989; Rogoff, 1990; Suchman, 1992); and those who propose communities of practice as sites of innovation (Collins, 1995). A distinctive feature of their practice is in creating authentic tasks using modern technology to enable the students to learn to solve real life problems to prevent the accumulation of inert knowledge that is useless in real life. Their research into "expert" practitioners' thinking and development, in some ways, parallel the work of other educational researchers into teachers' thinking, teachers' behaviours including the development of reflective practices in the past decade (Calderhead, 1991; Calderhead and Gates, 1993; Chen, 1985, 1987, 1993, 1996; Day, Pole and Denicolo, 1990; Rubin, 1989; Fullen, 1994).

In her study of expert or experienced teachers and novice teachers' reflection in Singapore, Chen (1985, 1993) found that a reflective practice in secondary and higher education is at the same time personal and social. There is great similarity between the development of American professors in a Mid Western university as those in Singapore universities and schools (1996). The level of teaching does not contribute significantly to the professional teachers' reflection. The teachers' own thinking style and their response to the culture of the situation played a more important role. Generally speaking, university and school teachers found it difficult to be reflective in a logical, scientific and pragmatic way when confronted with a teaching or learning problem. They tend to be more reactive. However for those teachers whose past negative experiences stimulated their attention on the students; individual needs, appropriate instructional strategies and assessment modes to be used and other contextual factors, social, economic or political, they become more reflective and may subsequently improve their practice.

The case of the American professor of History is a good example of a personal response to a negative stimulus, almost behavioural in nature.

Most of the reflective and effective teachers managed to rise above their dilemmas and to realize that the changeable in a learning environment is usually accomplished not in product-oriented ways, for example, based on examination grades of the students. Often the teachers realize their roles and ability to change a situation or an action in a process-related manner through negotiation with the students such as the case of the literature professor or the law lecturer in Singapore. Sometimes it is the use of the most appropriate technology and involvement of the administration in making a decision that facilitate the establishment of conducive learning environments, the design and development of a curriculum or a set of learning materials that promote better practice as in the case of the Western Australian university.

Most writers on reflective practices agree on the balanced use of thinking and acting. Chen (1993) recommended "*action-on-reflection*" and "*action-in-reflection*" as distinct and important processes in the development of a reflective professional practice. These are the additional two components to Schon's *reflection-on-action* and *reflection-in-action* in his arguments for working towards the artistry of a reflective practice, where there seems to be a greater emphasis on thought rather than on action which is the other equally important side of a reflective practice.

In an attempt to facilitate the spiral of thoughts, self evaluation as well as collaborative inquiry among the university teachers in the Postgraduate Diploma of Teaching in Higher Education (PGDipTHE) programme, Chen (1996) created the *5-R Reflective Thinking Framework* during a series of group discussions. One of the PGDipTHE participants is a dentistry professor in Singapore. Lim introduced the problem-based learning PBL approach into a saturated curriculum to promote critical thinking and problem solving among the dental students. In her orthodontics course, a holistic problem-solving approach was proposed in the management of a patient's problems. The students were grouped. They were asked to collectively manage a patient's gum disease. The case is complex because the patient is a diabetic and a smoker. The students by incorporating clinical skills, communication skills and knowledge of medicine successfully managed the case. Reflecting on her action, Lim felt that the attempt though time-consuming was worthwhile because over 80% of the students gave positive feedback. They felt that they had achieved better understanding of a subject by analyzing a problem critically and solving it collaboratively.

Learning to make good judgements and to select the most appropriate approach for a group of pre-service or in-service professionals is crucial in any professional practice. In his reflection on forty-four years of teaching, Mehlinger is convinced that the most fundamental questions for any teacher to ask are: "Are my students learning what they need to know?" and "Do I know enough about the subject I am teaching that I can fulfil the role of a teacher"? Through the years as he developed in his professional practice as teacher, curriculum material designer and developer and teacher educator-administrator, Mehlinger realized the importance of getting his students to reflect on what they know and use their knowledge in constructive ways. Above all, he has learned that "being a teacher is not possessing a body of knowledge that is passed authoritatively to others; being a teacher is being a learner, and helping others to learn effectively."

Lori Breslow in teaching her MBA business communication for managers becomes more convinced of the truth of Alfred North Whitehead's saying that "the purpose of education is to stimulate and guide their self-development" particularly in the area of interpersonal communication. This requires a different set of skills from the management of people, products, and resources including technology. These interpersonal communication skills include not only listening and speaking skills, but a range of skills related to emotional intelligence. These include how to empathize, how to correct misunderstandings when they occur; how to negotiate, how to motivate and compromise. From a bad class situation of students in conflict, Lori learned some precious lessons that are useful beyond the classroom but have implications for life in general:

❑ Communication is best learned when students are given the opportunity to practice the principles of the discipline.

❑ Teachers must pay attention not only to content, but also to relationships and process.

❑ The proper balance between the role of facilitator and the role of "authority" is hard to achieve.

❑ Instructors are responsible for balancing the interests of sub-groups in their class as well as balancing the needs of individual students against the rights of the class as a whole.

❑ Teaching is a moral art.

Implications of the Study of Contexts for Reflective Practices

Three key questions have been raised in our *analysis of the contexts for reflective practice* as they are reflected in specific as well as in general terms in the cases in this book. These questions are related to the "what" and "why", "who" and "how" to create reflective practices in both the professional schools as well as in the professions. Some contexts have the power of transforming the members of a learning community or the institution of higher education. Other contexts suggest actual or potential conditions that could impede or slow down the development of the *artistry of professional practices*.

To the first question on the conditions that facilitate learning and the *artistry of practice in higher education*, there is no clear cut answer but a combination of factors. Irrespective of the discipline or profession, the artistry of reflective practice hinges on all the members of the learning community, in particular the leaders or the teachers, to sustain the good and create even better learning environments to lift the professions to higher levels. The second question addresses the quality of academic leadership among the higher education teachers. These teacher-researchers are expected to guide their students to generate higher-order problem solving and creative thinking competencies. They are supposed to have the mental ability not only to understand the multi-layered nature of the learning contexts but also to create new opportunities for learning and for the creation of new knowledge and new products. They are sensitive to the deepest human and professional needs and show a passionate commitment to doing the best in the practice yet thinking all the time how best to improve it.

The conditions that facilitate learning are not confined to the mental ability of the leaders and their great communicative competencies and total commitment? Rather, the leaders' vision for the institutions and commitment to the professions so inspire the other members of the learning community that all strive in unity despite diversity of backgrounds and abilities for the highest, perform their best, and break new grounds using the most up-to-date tools and technologies. There is a close match between the personal visions and goals of the members and that of the organization culture, vision and goals. This is seen in the language used in all dialogues and communications within an organization where there is much shared-ness in artifacts, values, assumptions and personal beliefs. It is also because of the excellent example of the leaders whose outstanding mental capacity, emotional intelligence and sensitivity to people and situations and the larger issues in life that inspire a unified reflective spin among the members. The reflective practitioner, thus transform students' learning and community growth by

❏ Improving the understanding and meaning construction in any learning situation;
❏ Increasing sensitivity towards larger issues in life, and
❏ Enhancing the education of reflective practitioners.

Conclusion

The cases presented in this book are reflections of good practices from different perspectives: personal, institutional, and cultural. Each case is an example of the configuration of multiple levels of artifacts, values and assumptions of both the personal and the institution. These elements contribute to the artistry of different professional practices where the practitioners have to adroitly combine thinking, learning, working and innovating in their everyday life. This process is a complex one likened to the kaleidoscopic effect of a landscape. Each case is complete in itself having its own contexts of learning, yet it is part of the bigger tapestry of the spiral of reflective spins.

In analyzing the cases, we have used the *5-R Reflective Thinking Framework* for both analysis and synthesis of the creative and effective actions performed by various experienced teachers in higher education. The process of reflection is often recursive not necessarily progressing from reflection, to recognition, to realization, to response and to resolution. But the efforts are deliberate and sustained. We have advocated for a balance between thought and action from both Eastern and Western perspectives. We have also argued for a more comprehensive, multi-dimensional and flexible approach to educating professionals in learning organizations that may be in different developmental stages. In whatever conditions, the demands of the professions and the time would require different strategies for learning and teaching, and different kinds of decision making, and styles of coping in an era of rapid economic, social, political and organizational change.

References

Argris, C. & Schon, D. A. (1974). *Theory in Practice: Increasing professional effectiveness.* San Francisco: Jossey Bass.

Argris, C. & Schon, D. A. (1978). *Organisational Learning.* Reading, MA: Addison-Wesley.

Brown, J. S. and Duguid, P. (1991). Organisational learning and communities-of-practice: Toward a unified view of working, learning and innovation. *Organisational Sciences*, 2(1), 40–56.

Brown, & McIntyre, D. (1993).

Calderhead, J. & Gates, P. (1993). *Conceptualising Reflection in Teacher Development.* London: Falmer Press.

Chen, Ai-Yen (1985). *The Role of Instructional Consultative for Educational Development in Higher Education.* Unpublished doctoral dissertation, Indiana University, January 1985.

Chen, Ai-Yen (1993). Experienced and student teachers' reflection on classroom practice. *Education Research and Perspectives*, Vol. 20, No. 1, pp. 46–63.

Chen, Ai-Yen (1995). Enhancing reflective practices among teacher professionals in higher education. Paper presented at the Annual Meeting of the American Educational Research Association, San Francisco, U.S.A. April 1995.

Chen, Ai-Yen (1996). Towards Exemplary Teaching Through Collaborative Inquiry. Paper presented at the 16 Annual Conference on Teaching and Learning in Higher Education, Ottawa, Canada, 12–15 June, 1996.

Crystal, D. (1985). *A Dictionary of Linguistics and Phonetics.* 2nd Ed. Oxford: Basil Blackwell.

Elliot, J. (1991). *Action Research for Educational Change.* Milton Keynes: Open University Press.

Fullan, M. (1994). Teacher leadership: A failure to conceptualise. In D. Walling (Ed.), *Teachers as Leaders: Perspectives on the Professional Development of Teachers*, pp. 241–253. Bloomington, IN: Phi Delta Kappan.

Geertz, C. (1968). Religion as cultural system. In D. Cutler (Ed.), *The Religious Situation.* Boston, MA: Beacon Press.

Halliday, M. A. K. (1977). Text as Semantic Choice in Social Contexts. In V. T. A. Dijk and J. S. Petofi (Eds.), *Grammars and Descriptions.* Berlin: W. de Gruyter.

Halliday, M. A. K. (1978). Language as social semiotic. *The Social Interpretation of Language and Meaning.* London: Edward Arnold.

Hasan, R. (1996). Ways of saying: Ways of meaning. In C. Cloran, D. Butt and G. Williams (Eds.), Open *Linguistics Series.* London: Cassell.

Holly, P. (1994). Striving for congruence: The properties of a learning system. In C. Bayne-Jardine and P. Holly (Eds.), *Developing Quality Schools.* London: Farmer Press.

Kemmies, S. & McTaggart, R. (1988). *The Action Research Planner*, 3rd Ed. Victoria: Dearkin University Press.

Leont'ev, A. N. (1981). *Problems of the Development of Mind.* Moscow: Progress Publishers.

Lawler, E. (1992). *The Ultimate Advantage: Creating higher involvement organisation.* San Francisco, CA: Jossey Bass.

McKernen, J. (1991). *Curriculum Action Research.* London: Kogan Page.

Mumford, A. (1994). Learning styles and learning designs. Paper presented at the BEMAS Annual Conference, Manchester, September 1994.

McLean, M. and Blackwell R. (1997). Opportunity knocks: Professionalism and excellence in university teaching. *Teachers and Teaching: Theory and Practice*, 3(1), 85–99.

Mercer, N. (1992). Culture, context and the construction of knowledge in the classroom. In Light P. and Butterworth, G. (Eds.), *Context and Cognition: Ways of Learning and Knowing.* New York: Harvester, Wheatsheaf.

Newman, D., Griffin, P. & Cole, M. (1989). *The Construction Zone.* Cambridge: Cambridge University Press.

O'Sullivan, F. (1997). Learning organisations — reengineering schools for life long learning. *School Leadership and Management*, Vol. 17, No. 2, pp. 217–230.

Ramsden, P. (1993). Theories of learning and teaching and the practice of excellence in higher education, *Higher Education Research and Development*, 12, pp. 87–97.

Rowland, S. (1993). *The Enquiring Tutor.* London: Falmer Press.

Schein, Edgar H. (1993). On dialogue, culture, and organisational learning.

Schon, D. A. (1983). *The Reflective Practitioner.* New York: Basic Books.

Schon, D. A. (1987). *Educating The Reflective Practitioner.* San Francisco: Jossey Bass.

Senge, P. (1990). *The Fifth Discipline: The art and practice of the learning organisation.* London: Doubleday.

Shulman, L. S. (1987). Knowledge and teaching: Foundations of the new reform. *Harvard Educational Review*, Vol. 7, No. 2, pp. 4–14.

Swieringa, J. & Wierdsma, A. (1992). *Becoming a Learning Organisation: Beyond the learning curve.* Workingham: Addison Wesley.

Van Maanen, John (1983). Golden passports: Managerial socialization and graduate education, *The Review of Higher Education*, Vol. 4, pp. 435–455.

Van Maanen, John (1983). *Tales from the Field.* Newbury Park: Sage Publications.

Section
TWO

Reflecting
On
Self and Text

Confession Of A Recovering Classroom Talking Addict

Louis Schmier

Valdosta State University
Valdosta, Georgia
United States of America

Synopsis

The article chronicles the spiritual journey of a university professor of 25 years who moved from being a "talking addict" regarding his students as "just bodies" and himself as merely a transmitter of knowledge, to the realization that the essence of teaching is not methods and grades, but the care of the student, nurturing talent, awakening potential, faith and worth. In so doing he moved out of personal and professional stagnation as he re-examined his own life and values, strengths and weaknesses and rid himself of a "second son" mentality. He moved into a new "vision, a mission, a commitment into the practice of teaching."

Confession of A Recovering Classroom Talking Addict

Louis Schmier

I am a talking addict. It was only until a few years ago, in late October, 1991, to be precise, that I despised silence. In class, I feared it. I was controlled by it. It was my dreaded enemy. I couldn't tolerate it. I worked hard to avoid it — at almost all cost.

Up to that fateful moment in 1991 I gorged my habit with my natural, sweet gifts of both the orator and the thespian, for when I talk, I act out. I don't talk with just my voice. I speak with my eyes, face, arms, and torso — a raised eyebrow here, a tightened lip there, a sweep of the hand, countless muscles operating to make an outward gesture. Delivery is my strength. I am a master at impromptu. I can — vocally — dance on my feet at the drop of a hat. I have a great sense of reading people. I can turn a phrase and play with words. I can talk to a group of people and each individual in the audience at the same time; I can feel those in the audience and tune into each of them, and alter my presentation in midstream if necessary.

For me, it was always a time to talk. "Boring," "dead," "routine," "dull," "monotonous," and "monotone" were not words used to describe my lectures. To the contrary, unofficially, according to the student grapevine, I was constantly voted the professor in whose class you would least likely fall asleep — the most entertaining and the most informative professor. So I guess it was natural that I was able to believe — to delude myself into believing — that the more dramatic the presentation, the more brilliant the content, the better the teacher I was.

Silence made me feel personally self-conscious and awkward. It made be feel professionally inept and derelict. Any vacuum of sound hung like

70

a shroud of some kind of deadly inadequacy. There was no subtlety about it. Silence, for me, was a flashing, bright, eye-catching neon sign advertising "FAILURE," "FAILURE," "FAILURE." I conjured up the demons of inadequacy, insecurity, and fear that tormented my ego and that were always whispering in my ear at the slightest lowering of decibels "Nothing is going on," or, "You're not getting to them," or, "They're not learning enough of the subject," or, "They can't do it," or, "Jump in, they need you," or, "They can't be trusted," or "You're screwing up." or, "What the hell are you here for?" And I was listening to them — enslaving myself to them.

And so I measured my teaching by decibel meters and word counts and gestures. I felt that teaching was more authoritative pronouncement, though I often said otherwise. If the students hesitated for the slightest moment in dealing with a question, or if there was the slightest lull during a discussion, I imposed myself. Just as nature doesn't like a vacuum and rushes in to fill the void, I didn't like the silence, and I rushed in to fill it with sound and authority. I look back now, I see how all but the fewest students were pulling my string. Once they got wise, all they had to do was remain silent and they knew I would immediately get them off the hook by talking.

Silence was the intimidating experience. Inwardly, it threatened to expose to myself my humanity, my frailties, my weakened self-confidence and self-worth, and my sense of failure. Worse, outwardly, silence meant absence. It was synonymous with being ignored, being taken for granted, being unwanted, and being invisible — and I'd had enough of that growing up — contrary to all the reasons I wound up in the classroom.

What was really going on was that I was struggling to hide my sense of failure in the process of which I had desecrated myself. All around me were the subtle signs that I was a failure, for everywhere I turn I continued to be haunted by the image of my youth; of being the ignored, taken-for granted, invisible, diminished unloved second son. I did not see the Ph.D. so much as a membership card in an exclusive intellectual club as a second-class degree for cerebral second sons compared to the more prestigious and lucrative M.D. so wished for me by my parents. The classroom had little glitter of prestige. By all of society's standards, it was a place for life's second sons. There was the pervasive attitude that when a person couldn't do anything else he or she could always teach. In higher academia — whose priorities dwelled on the length of the scholarly resume of awards, grants, consultancies, conference papers, and publications — a teacher was tolerated at best as an academic second son. Moreover, my discipline — History was often academia's second son, at the low end of both the social totem pole and salary scale. The imagery of being the second son came to me every time I heard the demeaning statements about the uselessness of History and people's dislike for what one student described as a "boring memorization of a bunch of stupid dates, places, and names." In a society that demanded practical application History was a discipline that always had to fight for recognition. For me Valdosta State College in South Georgia carried the image of the second son, not the fabled fame, fortune, and prestige that I thought I needed to bring me attention, happiness, peace, well-being, and love.

And so, I tried to become something I was not; I dreamed and fantasized of doing things I could not; and I failed to appreciate fully my own untapped inner strengths: my energy, creativity, imagination, individuality, self-reliance, and sensitivity. My barreled definition of success and my shallow appreciation of myself left me with a sense of humiliation at ending up as a teacher at a small out-of-the-way college in a region of the country and a state known more for *Tobacco Road* and *Gone with the Wind* than its intellectual accomplishments. Later, as a published scholar, national reputation as one of the foremost experts in my field notwithstanding, I found myself once again as the second son in an area of history that more than one fellow historian denigrated as "an insignificant countryside show to the big tent of this sub-field of American history."

I ran after things I thought would bring me inner contentment — things like getting parental approval, degrees, publications, tenure, promotion, reputation, and prestige. I have to admit that all they got me was heightened anxiety, a greater disturbance of my inner sense of peace, a deepening prejudice against myself, greater limits on my sense of self — and a subtle disdain for students who were a constant reminder of my shortcomings, who were a barrier to achieving scholarly recognition, and who were, as a colleague said, a "nuisance necessary to pay the bills."

I didn't see how I had been bringing my Ph.D. and scholarly resume into the classroom with me. I didn't realize that while I had been "professoring" my subject, I had unwittingly erected a glass wall between me and most of the students. The glass wall was invisible to me, even though it acted like an opaque curtain that shut out the sights and sounds of the classroom. I didn't see it or feel it; I didn't know it was there; I didn't know what I was letting it do.

It was a wall unseen, a wall between me and most students that was the foundation of my other reputation: I was avoided like the plague as the "Battling bastard of the History department" — where I had a reputation as one of the most unreasonably demanding and most distant professors, when my class dropout rate and stopped-coming-to-class-at-the-end-of-the-quarter rate hovered around a staggering 30%, when my classes were the last to fill up, and when there was a waiting list of students rushing to drop out of the course during the first days of drop/add. But, for all this exodus, I placed the onus on the student.

I used to regularly "joke" disparagingly about the students by saying that at Valdosta State, we had on campus 1,700 people, of whom 1,200 were "just bodies" and 500 were students. "It's just a joke," I'd always say to myself. "It doesn't mean anything." After all, I always said it with a self-deceiving smile. I never "poormouthed" any student with a disparaging tone or a sneer on my face. I always cheered students on with a "rah, rah, rah, you can do it." Lord, was I good with the academic pom-poms, cartwheels, and back flips.

I didn't want to be bothered with the distracting work, the wasteful energy, the unappreciated and unrecognized labors, and the time-consuming attention. What was the use of making the difficult effort of engaging with bodies I had perceived as unengaging, of trying to reach those I had already subconsciously decided were unreachable? So I didn't really bother trying to discover what I could do to reach out with a helping hand to help them learn how to learn and become their own learners, how to cope, how to hope and dream, and how to believe in themselves. I felt I had done enough just to let them grace my presence and share in my knowledge.

My "recovery" began on that fateful October day in 1991, during a "challenge session" at The Family Learning Center at Hyde School in Bath, Maine, which my younger son, Robby, was then attending. I, at the age of 50 and after 25 years at the head of the classroom, experienced an unexpected and uncontrolled explosive emotional nova of liberating self-reflection, self-examination, and spiritual revelation that ultimately was to shake me out of personal and professional stagnation. It opened personal issues — ones that were long suppressed, denied, or ignored — that had been crucial in shaping who I was and what I did, and that were crucial to face if I was to reshape both myself and what I was doing. It launched me on a never-ending journey of examining my values, reviewing my priorities, ripping away my masks, questioning my identity, examining my purposes, reviewing my life's personal and professional goals, identifying my weaknesses, and discovering my strengths.

The sad thing — the releasing thing — I started discovering on that day was that despite my self-professing good intentions, my ever-present smile, and my cheerleading of the students, that "just bodies" joke *did* reflect my beliefs, beliefs which tended to denigrate rather than elevate, boo rather than applaud, bemoan rather than exalt, ridicule rather than praise, spotlight weakness rather than celebrate strength, and ignore the advice of the 1940s song by accentuating the negative while eliminating the positive.

You know, we teachers know the importance of asking questions. Our mission is to teach students how to ask their own questions. But we so seldom turn important questions on ourselves. Not the questions in search of knowledge, but the questions in search of meaning and purpose about who we are and what we do. Not until that day at Hyde, did I start to have a very uncomfortable feeling. I started realizing that this joke was not talking about the students. It was talking about *me* and of the need to reflect on, examine, and evaluate my personal educational values, attitudes, and priorities. It talked of my prejudices towards myself as a professor and towards the students, my subtle arrogance, my unrecognized aloofness, my separation from the students. This joke did not reflect a professor who has faith in his students and holds them in high esteem. It did not reflect a professor who has visions of success for the students, to whom teaching is not just employment but his life's work, who cares for the students, who affirms the strengths and beings of the students, who gives a high priority to benefitting them, who has a love for the students, who has a faith in them, who treats them with respect and dignity.

The questions that now faced me were: do I continue doing what I loudly do so well, or do I do something different; Do I take the risky and courageous steps to re-invent myself?

This deep, painful, and honest ongoing conversation with myself is still and will always be a part of me. From that moment on, as a colleague wrote about me, there was and is and always will be what a jazz musician might call a personal and professional "back beat" of words that keep challenging me, keep me growing and learning: Who am I? Why am I doing what I am doing? How do I feel about what I and others are doing? Why do I teach? What is meaningful about what I do? What are things I need to do, should do, and can do if I am to have the chance of being a truer person as well as a truer teacher?

I have discovered over these past years, however, that as I walked the hard road and asked myself the hard questions about myself and what I do, and did not rest until I started getting the honest and painful answers, I began entering into another world. I found something no one could give me. I found something I did not think I possessed. I discovered that I am stronger and worthier and more talented inside than I ever thought I was.

As that epiphany brought on a dawn that, in turn, penetrated my own personal and professional darkness, I slowly started leaving my degrees and resume — and my noise — at the door. I slowly discovered that I had little to fear from silence. It took me years to stop loudly looking important and to silently do what was important. It took me years to change my profession from one of professing my subject to one of caring about students and helping them. It took me years to discover that until I stopped being a screaming but passive cheerleader and came down from the summit to become a silent but active and involved climbing coach —

concerned with equipping students for the climb and teaching them the techniques of the climb, and concerned with each person having to make the climb — I wouldn't know the power of a little sincere "I truly care about you," a bit of concerned "I'm on your side," a supporting "I really want to teach you," an encouraging "you really count," a genuine "I'm glad you're here," and an honest, empathic, and real understanding of "I know what it's like to ..." And as I came to know that power, I've been experiencing that almost indescribable, wondrously fulfilling, meaningful and purposeful feeling of making a difference.

To paraphrase a line from Jerry Garcia, what a long, strange trip it's been these last five years. I know that because the students have spoken. Now, the drop rate in my classes is almost 0%! My classes are the first to fill up, and there is a waiting list of students clamoring to get in. I have journeyed to become what almost all students see as the most engaged, caring — although still demanding — real, honest, and humane teacher on campus. In the eyes of the students, I have transformed into the "most loved teacher" on campus.

It is a journey that involves what I suppose you might call a shift of mind and heart, a silencing of my mouth and a shouting of my spirit. I call it "a dawning of my soul" — a spiritual journey overcoming the inertia of dark, deeply embedded perceptions about who I am, who the students are, and the purpose of what I do. It's a journey of overcoming barriers, building bridges, and creating community between me and myself as well as me and others, especially students. Above all, at the core, it is a painful journey of truth, from the darkness of unknowing and unconscious deception to the dawning truth that made me see the reality about myself and everything I do — the ways I was limiting my awareness, deceiving myself, and holding myself back.

It is a journey of truth that has deepened my understanding of how my actions and beliefs are a part of, and are linked with, students in an educational ecological system. It is a journey that has taken me from loudly looking outward for approval to silently looking inward for my own uplifting, aspiring, internal, energizing, directing vision. It is a journey that has taken me from a dreary sense of routine and boredom and failure to excitement and exhilaration and happiness and purpose. It is a journey that has taken me from seeing teaching as a necessary but not-so-serious, income-getting job to seeing teaching as a mission. It is a journey that has taken me from finding fault in, pointing fingers at, and heaping blame on students to pointing fingers at and heaping blame on myself, and to being aware that students are — as are we all — human beings governed by forces that they have not yet learned how to perceive, cope with, and control. It is a journey that has taken me from seeing only myself to a commitment to something larger than myself — to a vision beyond my self-interest that gives me energy, excitement, and enthusiasm that my narrow, self-centered, professional goals cannot.

It is a journey of seeing teaching as a lifelong process — a way of traveling — rather than as a talent I possess and something I do. It is a journey that has led me to see that my mastery of teaching involves not just necessary subject competence and pedagogical skills and techniques, but a spiritual vitality that allows me to approach life with creative force. It is a journey that has taken me from being ignorant of the presence of my spirit to becoming *aware* of it and then on to *believing* in its strength and finally on to *knowing* about its source of power.

It is a journey that has helped me see education anew: it has taken me from seeing education as a transmission and taking in of information — "I covered all of the material required by the course" and "I learned all about that in a course" — to seeing education as a means of constant generation, creation, re-perception, and extension — a means of increasing the ability to create the future.

It is an arduous journey that has helped me put a vision, a mission, a commitment into practice. It is a journey that has taken me from loving my subject to loving each student. It is a journey that has taken me from seeing solely with the mind's eye to seeing with the heart's eye as well. It is a journey that has taken me from seeking rewards to seeing that the journey itself is the reward.

I no longer see myself as an expert in a particular subject or as a transmitter who merely delivers knowledge to some distant, impersonal receiver sitting in a chair. I now think that we educators so often confuse method with spirit, quantity with quality, information with knowledge, performance with learning, and grades with achievement. I now think that we worry so much, too much, about teaching methods, subject content, and assessment. I now believe that we're wrong if we think of education solely in terms of being a transmission and reception of stock information. I now think that we're wrong if we believe that IQs, SAT scores, grades, and degrees have real bearing on a satisfying life. In the long run, the development of an ability, the nurturing of a talent, the discovery of a potential, the uncovering of an inner worth, the planting of a faith in one's self, the awakening of a native creativity, and the stirring of a courage to stand the hurt of failure and try again are more important for the student — and the teacher — than the handing out and acquisition of some facts and axioms, the assigning of some grade, and the getting of a degree.

I now teach by the "seat of my soul." I believe that it is more important to ask if the student learned than to ask if I taught. I believe that no subject matter is more sacred to me than a student's growth. I believe that teaching and learning is an act of human relationship, the cornerstone of which must be an honest bond of trust between teacher and student, and to forge that bond I need to share with the students, not just my subject, but me and the truth of my life. I believe that the student, the whole student, is my prime subject. I believe it is more important to reach for students than reaching the height of professional reputation and looking important.

So I have journeyed in the classroom from an instruction mode to a learning mode; from believing that learning is teacher-centered to seeing that it is student-centered; from believing that education requires only an excited teacher to understanding that it requires both an excited teacher *and* excited students; from believing that talent and ability are the preserve of the select to seeing that all students are talented and have ability; from believing that any Ph.D. can teach to understanding that empowering learning is a challenging and complex craft requiring talents other than those needed for research and publication; from sorting and classifying students into those who are college material and those who can't "cut it" — as if intelligence and ability are scarce commodities — to believing in each student and developing each student's competency and talent; from a competitive, individualized learning environment to a cooperative, collaborative, and supportive learning community; from being concerned with performance to being concerned with character.

I have journeyed from wanting to be judged by how well I perform in teaching terms — how long my resume is, how well I lecture, what material I cover, whether I show interest in my subject and have a command of it, whether I have respect for students, whether I engage students — to wanting to be evaluated on whether the students are learning and on what they are learning. I have come to recognise that the chief agents in the process of learning are the students, and, thus, they must be active discoverers of their own learning.

These last number of years since that miraculous moment at Hyde — when I started becoming conscious of that invisible barrier, bursting through it, breaking it, and shattering it, and I started standing in community with both myself and those around me — have been tough years and painful years. But they have also been wonderful years, releasing years of metamorphosis and discovery. Over these past few years, as I've successfully fought to overcome my inner need to be needed, to be seen, and to be important, I've discovered that the more I speak with my soul, the less I have to speak with my body; the more I express spontaneously, the less I have to "work" to feel; the more I exhort my honest feelings, the less I study and put-on and pose and control; the more my spirit is the stock and tool of my craft, the less I need to be heard. The less I need to be heard and seen, the more I listen to and see, *have* to listen to and see, and *want* to listen to and see each student.

And I've discovered that silence, like sound, can be a vital classroom learning medium. In the class, I've slowly taken the risk of not speaking — in order to shrink my ego, create more space for the students, and involve them in their own learning. Slowly, I've begun to make silence an ally in both my teaching and the students' learning. I consider this breakthrough one of the most important personal and professional moments of my life.

On that day at Hyde, I started hammering away at and tearing down walls, and I started to throw the locks and keys away. It was a time to find the strength and courage to admit that I needed to face up to and start letting go of the old illusions and fears, for overwhelming and new possibilities and potentials. As Pink Floyd's lyrics from *Coming Back to Life* say "I knew the moment had arrived for killing the past and coming back to life." By some quirk of fate, I got the opportunity to find a different place for success and inner peace in my life at the same place.

And, on my headstone, I now hope that someone will chisel simply: "He touched a student and changed the world."

Teacher Knowledge and Classroom Teaching

Alan Watson

School of Teacher Education
The University of New South Wales
Australia

Synopsis

This case was about an outstanding young teacher of upper elementary grades reflecting on a series of teaching episodes under the guidance of a more knowledgeable and experienced teacher educator. Through the use of questioning, based on critical issues, the teacher realized the importance of not just relying on content and procedural knowledge but also on the development of teaching skills, classroom management techniques and values that will help improve pupils' learning.

Teacher Knowledge and Classroom Teaching

Alan Watson

Observation and Interview

This case study comprises a series of teaching episodes and the teacher's reflections on those episodes.

The episodes are based on observations of an outstanding young teacher of a 5/6 grade composite class in a southern suburb of Sydney, Australia. The teacher, who had had 11 years experience and taught all grades K-6, was identified as outstanding by the school Principal and the senior professional officer for the area (the cluster director). He had demonstrated high teaching competence by promoting a positive classroom climate, effective instructional management and good pupil progress as shown in formal and informal assessment. Eight 90 minute teaching sessions were observed by the researcher over a period of three months. Detailed notes were made of the teaching behaviour during the sessions. Comments on the incident are derived from a 30 to 60 minute interview conducted by the researcher with the teacher immediately after each teaching session. The purpose of the interview was to probe the teacher's thinking to ascertain why he behaved as he did. The accuracy of the account was verified by having the teacher read and comment on it soon after it was written. The questions for discussion are meant not only to provoke the reflection of the interviewee, but also for other teachers.

Conceptual Perspective

The observations and interviews were based on the idea that much of the knowledge of practice is tacit (Hirst, 1985) and may not be available to the profession unless it is made explicit. This teacher knowledge derives from what Shulman has called the "wisdom of practice" (1987). It includes what has been called, the "craft knowledge" of teachers — that capacity to analyse teaching situations and apply appropriate strategies — and has begun to receive some attention in the research literature (for example, Batten, Marland and Khamis, 1993; Brown and McIntyre, 1993). However, "one of the more important tasks for the research community is to work with practitioners to develop codified representations of the practical pedagogical knowledge of able teachers" (Shulman, 1987, p. 11). Observation of what respected teachers do and then questioning about why they do it was seen as one way to make the knowledge of practice available to other practitioners. These data are part of a larger study of teachers in composite classes (Phillips, Watson and Wille, 1993).

Presentation

The presentation is broken into incidents which are defined as relatively complete episodes of teaching and learning. They comprise a lesson or a segment of a lesson or even a brief exchange between teacher and student. Each incident is focussed on a question (or questions) or a practical problem which the teaching procedure sought to address. The incident provides an example of how one teacher went about solving that problem. The teacher's comments give his rationale for doing what he did.

There are three limitations to the usefulness of the codified pedagogical knowledge such as that presented in the above study (Phillips, Watson and Wille, 1993) which must be recognised.

First, the observations usually did not allow the researcher to follow a teaching series or issue through to its classroom conclusion. Longitudinal data of a kind not available in this study would be needed to do this.

Second, the codified form of its presentation may not necessarily be a suitable one for passing that knowledge on to teachers. A pedagogically suitable form for its presentation needs to be found.

Third, the practice of an outstanding teacher does not provide a guide in itself for other teachers on how they can become better teachers themselves. By their nature, the teacher's actions and rationale are an incomplete answer to the issue raised. The teaching behaviour is always particular to that teacher, that class and even that specific moment. The subtle differences of teacher style and student needs and personality mean that even the best knowledge must undergo a transformation if it is to be used by another in another situation.

Nevertheless, the teacher's actions provide a valuable starting point for beginning or experienced teachers to discuss the issue and to think of other approaches which are likely to suit their teaching style and situation.

It is desirable that the form in which it is presented should assist in the necessary transformation. This chapter will seek to present knowledge gained by observation and interview in an open-ended form which promotes discussion and thought and so helps the practitioner in the transformation of knowledge.

EPISODE 1: Spelling and Cheating

Issues

1. How can individual spelling lists be taught in the class context?
2. How can cheating be discouraged?

When the reading lesson is over, the teacher lifts his gaze from the small group he has been teaching and says, "Right. Individual list spelling work......Go". There is a flurry of activity as children at the front spring up and move to their seats. All take out their lists and begin in pairs to test one another on their words.

"They have all developed their own list from their previous errors from all subjects and new words I give them chosen from a standardised graded list. They know the routine for learning and testing. This system works because they have practised and learnt the procedures. If a child does not have his own list, the rule is he must be tested on his partner's list'.

The teacher moves about the room asking questions to check vocabulary, hearing children spell words or correcting some who are distracting others, ("Mr Booth, let Mr Stephens do his own work, please!"). He notices Emma surreptitiously looking at her list as she writes the words dictated by her partner. "What are you doing Emma?" the teacher asks. "Cheating," she admits. "Obviously you'll have to put in a special effort on that list, won't you Emma?" he chides. Emma, rather embarrassed, smiles in agreement and stops looking at her list as the pretest continues.

> "She can take it. It's better to do it that way than to make a song and dance about it." She knew she had done wrong. The teacher, by his questioning, brought her to admit it. She had sufficient confidence in him and self assurance to acknowledge her own cheating. Hence strong reproof was not necessary. A low key response is non-threatening to the children. They are developing a sense of responsibility for their own actions and a questioning approach gives them scope to fake responsibility and so fosters independence.

Discussion

1. What other instructional components are likely to be helpful to teach spelling with individualised spelling lists?
2. What are the advantages and disadvantages of an individualised spelling program?
3. What are the limitations of this low-key questioning approach to the discovery of a child cheating?
4. What other strategies can the teacher employ if a child is found cheating?

EPISODE 2: Fractions and Humour

Issues

1. How can concrete materials be used to teach fractions?
2. How can humour be used to enliven classroom proceedings?

When the spelling is finished, each fifth grade child is given a crossword based on mathematical operations to complete and told they can do the maths puzzle in their workbooks if they finish it. The sixth grade children are called to sit on the carpet at the front of the classroom where the teacher has three boxes of Deines multi-based arithmetic blocks ready for their use. Andrew, who is completing a teacher assigned job at the back of the room, is told "We'll start without you. You're good at maths and can catch up. But don't be too long".

On a 10 x 10 grid which each child has been given, they are asked to cover various fractions of the grid using blocks which are 1 x 1(1/100) or 10 x 1 square centimeters (1/10) in size. "Show me ... (cover) 1/10,... 4/10,...1/100,...11/100,... 22/100, the teacher instructs. As they get to the last couple, Andrew joins the group. Most children have completed their arrangement of 22/100 using two 10 x 1 and two 1 x 1 blocks but Andrew worked laboriously to show 22/100 by using only 1 x 1 blocks, placing them on the board one at a time. The teacher says, "You're doing it the hard way, Brainstormer", and the rest of the children laugh. Andrew looks up, completes the last few blocks and smiles a little sheepishly.

"Andrew is well known as the best in the class at maths. His good intellectual capacities have earned him the nickname, "Brainstormer", from his peers. Some cannot take a joke against themselves but Andrew is self-assured and able to fake a joke of this kind without distress." The teacher's use of the peer group nickname reveals a sensitivity to children's attitudes towards a peer and echoes their high regard for Andrew while at the same time pointing out that even the best do not always choose the quickest and most efficient solution. In this way, the others are complimented for their good work.

How does the teacher know that Andrew can fake a joke of this kind?

"I watch how children react to me in class and with their peers. I don't know....perhaps it's a sixth sense? All can accept a joke in some measure but the joke has to be carefully chosen not to exceed an individual's capacity. Some who may be undergoing the stress of parental break-up or who may have a poor sense of self worth would not be a suitable target for such remarks."

As the teacher is working with the sixth graders, the fifth graders are working at their desks, but one fifth grade boy starts to wander about the room. The teacher looks up to him and says "You're fifth. You're half way to sixth (it is about half way through the year). Only sixth may be out of their seats". He accepts the mild reproof and sits down promptly.

"Some can accept a blunt or more direct correction but gentle management is best with that child."

Cameron was the last to complete the next example with Deines blocks. All others were watching him. The teacher said, "Pressure Cameron". Cameron smiled wryly. It helped to relieve the tension as he arranged his last few blocks.

This tactic of putting students' feelings into words was a form of mild teasing and humour. It works with some but not with others. Cameron is the top sportsman in the school and in sport he is used to handling pressure. For example, he represents the school and the district in softball as pitcher and is frequently under extreme pressure to perform well. He will not be distressed by this kind of remark. Though he was slow completing the task, he could do it well. The teacher's remark helped to hold the attention of the other children so that they would be ready for the transition to the next problem as soon as Cameron finished.

Discussion

1. How could the teacher use this equipment to teach other concepts about fractions?
2. What does this incident suggest about the relationship of the teacher to Andrew? ... and to Cameron?
3. What place (if any) should these kinds of jokes have in a teacher's instructional repertoire?

EPISODE 3: What is an Aussie?

Issue

1. How can one teach a complex concept like national identity?

The class, sitting on the carpet at the front of the room, is providing answers to the question, "What makes someone an Australian?" The teacher writes their answers on the board without comment.

"You have respect for your country"

"Someone who likes vegemite"

"Those who feel like they are"

"Someone born here"

"Has citizenship papers"

"Speaks English"

"Has an Aussie accent"

"Someone proud of the national anthem"

"One who calls Australia home"

"Lives here the majority of their life"

"Does things like an Aussie"

"Has tastes like an Aussie"

"Some of these", the teacher says, "are common to a lot of Australians but do they include all Australians? For example, 'someone who likes vegemite'. Hands up those who don't like vegemite'. Four or six hands go up. "What does that do to your theory?" "Or someone who has an Aussie accent. Has our Canadian [a Canadian pupil in the class] a different accent?" He asks him to speak which he does with a strong Australian accent. "He speaks like an Aussie. Is he an Australian?"

The teacher then runs through the list asking children, "Who thinks this is an important part of being an Australian?" The 'voting' is rather inconclusive and there is some confusion especially amongst the fifth graders.

> "They need help to think more about this and I will do it with fifth and sixth separately. The fifth graders are a bit lost. The sixth have more experience and ideas and stifle the fifth. And they need to become more tolerant of differences."

Discussion

1. What have their responses revealed about their thinking?

2. How can the teacher help the children to think more about this concept?
3. What further teaching strategies or lessons could be used?

EPISODE 4: Keeping the Noise Down

Issue

1. How can the teacher allow activity but keep noise within limits?

Although there is frequently a hubbub of work-related noise, especially when one or both grades work in small groups, the classroom is generally managed so that the teacher's voice can be heard easily without him shouting. The class is organised in ability groups for reading and the usual seating arrangement is superseded as the groups come together in different corners of the room. As the teacher works with a small group at the front of the class a boy raises his voice to complain about a girl who has temporarily occupied his seat. "Get out of my seat," he shouts. The teacher raises his head. "Cameron, you know I'm the only one in this room who is allowed to shout". "Yes," he acknowledges. "Don't let me hear you shout." and moves him to work in the front seat (for a short time).

> "They know I don't like noise. He was shouting for effect — to get the attention of the other kids. To see how far he could go. It wasn't a serious offence but I had to nip it in the bud before it got out of hand. The reproof matched the kid".

Discussion

1. How important is it to match the reproof to the child?
2. What other strategies are useful to keep class noise within bounds?

EPISODE 5: Transitions and Incentive Systems

Issues

1. How can the transition between lessons be managed smoothly and quickly?
2. What place can incentive systems have in class teaching?

Students were slow to change lessons. They had to place their books and materials away (under desks or in bags) and come to the front. The class was rather noisy. The teacher stood by the board and said, "I have a duster and chalk in my hands. I hope I can use them to change your status." There was an immediate silence and quick movement to the front.

How did the teacher achieve so great an effect with so little effort?

A group points system with a term prize for the whole group is used to give the teacher a good control mechanism. The children sit in table groups of six facing one another. Suspended from the ceiling above each group is a card with the group's name and its members listed on it. Points are given for good behaviour, for good answers to questions, for volunteering for class tasks and other desirable conduct. Points are never deducted for misbehaviour. At the end of the day the points are added and recorded on the card. At the end of the term the winning group gets some small prize, e.g., a ruler with the school logo on it, for each member and the group shares all the jelly cakes which remain in the jelly snake jar. This 1 kilogram sized jar begins the term full of jelly snakes which are slowly given out as prizes for individual achievements or competitions. It is replenished during the term as it becomes empty. The system has been used and refined over the past ten years. It works! And it works best when the students are allowed to sit with a chosen partner in their chosen group. In this incident the effect of the reward system was heightened because the teacher himself took the chalk and moved to change the position on the board. Usually the child praised is asked to come to the board and make an addition to the points tally.

Discussion

1. Name other efficient methods for the transition between lessons.
2. What features of the system described make it require minimum effort from the teacher?
3. What are the drawbacks or limitations of an incentive system?
4. Why do you think some good teachers swear by them while other good teachers refuse to use them?

EPISODE 6: Anticipation of Problems

Issues

1. How can anticipation of difficulties help class management?

"This next section could get very noisy but I'd rather it didn't". The teacher made his point very distinctly. The class (a fifth/sixth composite) had been working as a whole unit on the Social Studies lesson. "What is an Australian?" They were seated on the carpet at the front of the room. The teacher wanted to break the class into small discussion groups. Perceiving that this discussion could become noisy and that the children could lose their task focus, the teacher gave this warning. He then told them to discuss their ideas in small groups and was able to maintain an orderly class while they did so.

> I know that putting them into small groups to discuss a contentious issue is potentially very disruptive and might lead to unruly and noisy behaviour.

Discussion

Anticipation of a behaviour problem may sometimes even suggest that misbehaviour to a child.
1. What determines the usefulness of this strategy?
2. Can you give other examples where it could be used?

EPISODE 7: Vocabulary and Derivations

Issue

1. How can vocabulary be taught?

The class is broken into ability groups for the reading lesson. One group is practising a play to present to the class, others are answering written questions from a passage, another is seeking information for a social studies project. The teacher, after ensuring that each group has its work assignment and is busy, moves to help a fifth grade group reading a story aloud. He stops the child who is reading and repeats the last words read, "Pray you hearken unto me". There's an unusual word. "Who can tell

me what 'hearken' means?" No child can answer so the teacher gives some
help. "What word can you see in 'hearken'?" "Hear", says one child and
the light has obviously dawned. "So what do you think hearken might
mean?" "It means to hear or to listen to someone".

The children continue reading in turns. As the teacher listens, he
commends the child reading for his good expressive voice. The next child
reads very expressively, obviously stimulated by the teacher's praise of the
last reader. The children come across the word "bidding" and the teacher,
asking them what it means, directs them to the context. Seeing that it is
an auction, they recognise it means offering a price to purchase an object.
The teacher leaves that group to continue its oral reading and moves
around briefly giving help to other groups. After a time the teacher tells
the children to finish their activities and put away their reading assignments
until tomorrow.

> "Although the sixth graders would probably have known the word, 'hearken',
> I was fairly sure the fifth graders would not know it."

> "If they can work out the derivation, it will frequently help them to guess
> what the word means. It will also act as a kind of peg on which they can
> hang the meaning and bring it to memory when they see that word again.
> Study of other languages can be a great help in this process. My study of
> Latin helps me understand many English words. As an extension subject
> many of the class are studying Italian with a special teacher. When we
> came across the word 'sedentary' they were able to link it with 'la sedia',
> the chair in Italian. This helped them to understand the meaning".

Discussion

1. What are the advantages of using this incidental approach to teaching
   vocabulary?
2. What other methods might be used to teach vocabulary?

EPISODE 8: "Snoopy" for Neatness

Issue

1. How can children be encouraged to do neat work?

A well handled wooden statue about 30cm tall sits on the child's desk. It is the bust of a dog, "Snoopy". The boy seems very proud to have it on his desk.

> "Snoopy is an award for neat work. But it is an award of the children not of the teacher." Each Monday the children choose their neatest work from the previous week and display it on their desks. The child who held the award for the last week becomes the judge for the next winner. If a Grade 5 child held it, he or she chooses a Grade 6 child for the next week and vice versa. To ensure there is an award for each grade each week, another carved figure of a dog, "Oscar", is given in the same way but to the other grade. The encouragement of the teacher is sufficient to ensure there is a measure of impartiality in the award procedure."

> "Peer assessment and status from peer recognition of neat work is effective."

Discussion

1. What other means can a teacher use to promote neatness?
2. How important is it, anyway?

EPISODE 9: When the Lesson Falters

Issues

1. How can one use a small group practical exercise to teach volume?
2. What can a teacher do when the lesson doesn't work very well?

In a previous lesson, the class has had instruction and demonstration on measuring volume. They need practical experience so they can gain confidence in doing it themselves. The teacher has prepared a worksheet with several practical exercises for the children to do in groups of three or four using a measuring tape to determine the volume of objects such as their desk, a cupboard and some different sized boxes.

The teacher begins to introduce the lesson as they sit at their desks. "You measure the top, sides and ends of the object". But the class is restless and attention is variable. Quickly sizing up the situation he says, "Bring yourselves to the front". They all move quickly and quietly. With

them all seated on the carpet at his feet, he completes his instructions with
much better attention and then says "Form yourselves into groups. You've
got 15 seconds". They do this quickly and begin to work.

Soon, however, the class becomes rather noisy. There is evidence of
some confusion over what to do and the beginnings of off-task behaviours.
The teacher moves about seeking to help the groups. But the noise gets
too much. He stops working with one group and addresses the whole class,
"Hands on heads, everyone". The children stop their activities and comply.
"Take the desk as a solid rectangular prism", he instructs. "Count the legs
as the edges of a box". The measurement proceeds and the class is less
noisy for a time. But the noise increases again and something seems to be
going wrong with the lesson.

"Finished or not", the teacher says above the noise, "come to the
front". He checks some of the answers, collects the work sheets and
terminates the lesson.

The teacher's awareness of the students' flagging attention leads him
to take corrective action, bringing students to the front to explain the
procedures.

> "It's always easier to speak with the class when they are seated on the
> carpet at the front. They don't have so much to fiddle with as they do at
> their desks. Furthermore, you're closer to them and over them, taller and
> looking down on them. Especially for the restless ones the body language
> has a quietening impact. I learnt to have children sit at the front of the
> classroom when I was teaching an infants class in my first appointment.
> It is common practice at that level. Even though this is a Fifth/Sixth
> Grade/6 class (10–12 year olds), I still find it is a good practice. All
> classes are quieter and it's easier to hold their attention if they are sitting
> on the floor in front of you. As well, the act of moving from desks to the
> front gives a change of posture which is helpful."

As he moved amongst the groups he saw further difficulties developing
and took steps to remedy them. But problems remained. "I don't think I
gave clear enough instructions to start with".

Questions

1. Is it appropriate to have 10 and 12 year olds sit on the floor at the front? If so, in what circumstances?
2. What are the indications that tell a teacher a lesson needs to be brought to an end early?

References

Batten, M., Marland, P. & Khamis, M. (1993). *Knowing how to teach well: Teachers reflect on their classroom practice.* ACER Research monograph No. 44. Hawthorn, Victoria: Australian Council for Educational Research.

Brown, S. & McIntyre, D. (1993). *Making sense of teaching.* Buckingham: Open University Press.

Hirst, P. H. (1985). Educational studies and the PGCE course, *Journal of Educational Studies*, 23(3), 211–221.

Phillips, R. D., Watson, A. J. & Wille, C. Y. (1993). Teacher knowledge and teacher behaviour in composite classes, *St George Papers in Education.* Vol. 1 (1), The University of New South Wales.

Shulman, L. S. (1987). Knowledge and teaching: Foundations of the new reform. *Harvard Educational Review*, 57(1), 1–22.

Embedding Chinese Classical Ideas In A Business Law Course

Soh-Loi Loi and Jack Teo Cheng Chuah

School of Accountancy and Business
Nanyang Technological University
Singapore

Synopsis

Ranked as one of the top ten universities in Asia, lecturers at the Nanyang Technological University use not only theories from contemporary Western educationists but also rely on classics from the East to help them formulate their teaching strategies. In this chapter, Jack Teo and Soh-Loi Loi show how they have managed to merge Chen's Reflective Thinking and Collaborative Inquiry Framework (1995) with two Chinese classical texts, in order to promote an understanding of business contracts amongst undergraduates at the Nanyang Technological University.

Embedding Chinese Classical Ideas In A Business Law Course

Jack Teo Cheng Chuah and *Soh-Loi Loi*

Introduction

The Bachelor of Business (BBus) program at the School of Accountancy and Business (SAB) was launched when the Nanyang Technological University (NTU) became a full fledged university in 1991. NTU's BBus program is unique in Asia as it allows students to select one out of ten specializations in which to major. These specializations are Actuarial Science; Applied Economics; Banking; Financial Analysis; Hospitality and Tourism Management; Human Resource Management; Industrial Management; Insurance; Marketing and Quality Management. Since its inception in 1991, the program has gone from strength to strength and the current enrolment in SAB now stands at approximately 2,000 students.

Specialization in the BBus program starts only from the second year. In the first year, all students read the same eight core modules. These are Financial Accounting; Business Statistics; Business Communications; Organizational Behavior and Management; Principles of Economics; Principles of Law; Marketing and Information Technology. While the course content of the first year BBus program is homogenous, the students are not. First year SAB students have a varied background with the majority entering the university after completing their two year General Certificate of Education (Advanced) Level courses (GCE 'A' Level) at junior colleges. A smaller number are top Diploma holders from the polytechnics with a few mature students making up the balance.

Due to this diversity in the backgrounds of the students, it has been difficult to find any *common ground* on which lectures could be structured.

98

This problem is especially acute when it comes to the teaching of *Principles of Law*, the first year law module which forms part of the core curriculum of all SAB students. The greater part of the *Principles of Law* course deals with contracts and one of the authors, Jack, noticed that a common difficulty recurs year after year. Students continue to have misconceptions about when a contract is formed and whether the contract has to be in writing. It is beyond the scope of this article to plumb the depths of contract law, but basically, a contract is formed when the four necessary legal requirements (or elements) are present. These are: offer (Do you want to enter into a contract?), acceptance (Yes), consideration (the *quid pro quo* between the parties) and an intention between the parties that the contract be legally binding. There is no additional requirement that a contract must be in writing. Many contracts, e.g., the purchase of food/drink at a cafeteria or a bus or taxi ride are not in writing. Contracts are made in writing only where there is a requirement for it to be so (for example, in Singapore, contracts for the sale and purchase of land must be in writing) or in a situation where performance of the contract by one or more of the parties is deferred, for example in the case of a contract where goods are sold on a credit basis or in the case of a contract to build a ship. When performance is deferred, the need for writing arises to avoid the possibility of disagreements between the parties over what was decided in the first place. Despite the simplicity of the legal analysis involved, students continue to have difficulties in recognizing when a contract has been formed in instances where the contract is not in writing.

Reflection

Jack had already taught the *Principles of Law* course for a number of years but none of the approaches which he had tried appeared to bring much success. Jack's process of reflection led him to realize that a piecemeal approach was the cause of the problem. It was no point focussing in the abstract on the presence or absence of the four elements forming a contract. The solution lay in the adoption of a holistic approach. A global approach had to be taken in which the question of whether one should enter into a contract in the first place had to be considered. If we could show students whether they should or should not enter into a contract, they would then be able to see when a contract has been formed and whether that particular contract should be in writing. To paraphrase Hamlet, the solution lay in getting the students to ask themselves, "To contract or not to contract? that is the question." However, Jack was unsure as to what strategies he should use in order to put this plan into action. As a person who has spent his whole academic life grounded in the law, he was unfamiliar with the loftier planes of strategic planning or management.

It was at this point that a chance remark put Jack on the right path. At the time when this problem was on his mind, Jack was a participant in the Postgraduate Diploma of Teaching in Higher Education (PGDipTHE) program which was being conducted at the National Institute of Education (NIE). One evening, the Program Coordinator, Dr Chen Ai-Yen casually mentioned the possibility of applying the principles which have been laid down in centuries old Chinese classics to the classroom context. This remark led Jack to follow up with his colleague, Dr Soh-Loi Loi who was a fellow participant in the PGDipTHE program. Although, a specialist in Actuarial Science, Soh-Loi is well versed in Chinese classical literature and was able to point Jack in the right direction. According to Soh-Loi, the fresh approaches which Jack was looking for could be found in Sun Tzu's *Art of War* (孙子兵法) and the *I Ching* (易经).

Sun Tzu's Art of War (孙子兵法)

The author of the *Art of War*, Sun Tzu was a brilliant military strategist who lived during a very turbulent period in Chinese history called the Spring/Autumn Period (770–476 BC). These three centuries were called the Spring/Autumn Period because China was, at that time, split into many small kingdoms which warred interminably with each other. Many of the weaker kingdoms resembled flowers which bloomed and flourished in the cool of spring only to wither under the heat of autumn when they were conquered by one of their stronger enemies. The state of Chi was one of the stronger kingdoms. This was due, in no small part, to the prowess of

Sun Tzu, the commanding general of the Chi army. To share the knowledge which he had gained from his victories, Sun Tzu wrote a book detailing the strategies which he used. This treatise which he called the *Art of War*, is now considered to be the oldest military manual in the world (there are several English translations of the *Art of War* in print but the one favored by the authors is Samuel Griffith's translation which was published in 1963).

Although Sun Tzu's work concerned itself primarily with the means by which victory could be achieved in warfare, it has become fashionable in recent times to cite Sun Tzu as an authority in a large number of disparate fields, most notably in business and management (McNeilly, 1996). However, other than for a paper delivered by the authors themselves, at the 7th International Conference on Thinking (Loi and Teo, 1997), no researcher has, to date, attempted to apply the strategies of Sun Tzu to education and the classroom. The authors found that many of Sun Tzu's doctrines are of general application and can *mutatis mutandis* be used in the context of modern education and the classroom. To an educator or teacher, education or teaching can be likened to warfare with the objective of securing victory over the enemy which, in this case, is the students' misconception on how or why contracts are formed.

Sun Tzu placed great emphasis on the fact that warfare was of the utmost importance to the State. In the very first verse of chapter 1, Sun Tzu states that:

> "War is a vital matter of State. It is the field on which life or death is determined and the road that leads to survival or ruin. It must be examined with the greatest care."

Prima facie, it may be difficult to see how the authors could relate Sun Tzu's statement to the problem of teaching students whether they should enter into a contract or not. This is made clearer in the next verse when Sun Tzu sets out the factors by which the examination of war is to take place. These five fundamental factors (as they are called) are *dao* (literally, 道 – the way), *tien* (天 – sky), *di* (地 – terrain), *jiang* (将 – command) and *fa* (法 – law). In an assessment of *dao*, several dimensions have to be considered. These include an assessment of objectives, systems, programs, mission, authorities and embodiment of the ideals. *Dao* is listed first because it is crucial to success. *Tien*, climate and *di*, terrain, represent environmental factors like the prevailing political climate, economic conditions, the available human resources, the existing cultural heritage and state of technology. *Jiang*, refers to leadership, whose purpose is to provide vision and strategic intent. Finally, *fa*, emphasizes organizational effectiveness, chain of command and a structure of logistical support; factors which are crucial to the implementation of strategic change and control. In our analysis of business contracts, *dao* would refer specifically to the objectives which we are trying to achieve by entering into the contract. *Tien* and *di* refer to the economic conditions prevailing at the time of the making of the contract. *Jiang* refers to the leader (CEO) of the contracting company who must possess five characteristics: wisdom, integrity, humanity, courage and discipline. The CEO is the one who will make the decision whether to contract or not. Finally, *fa* is akin to the concept of military intelligence. We analyze what knowledge we have of contractual counter-party before we can enter into an agreement with him. These five factors are the distillate of Sun Tzu's wisdom and should be familiar to every businessperson. He who knows them will be victorious; he who knows them not will fail.

By using an analysis of these five factors, Jack has tried to show his students that contracts are not made in the abstract. Instead, these five factors provide the framework by which we can understand what is taken into account by business persons before they enter into a contract. Once the students have understood the *Whats* of making a contract, understanding the *Whys* and *Whens* of contracting becomes a relatively easier task. By using these strategies, Jack was able to make his lessons come alive and arouse his students' curiosity to learn more about the subject. The eagerness in the eyes of the students and the interest shown by them during their lessons bear testimony to the success of this approach.

The doctrines from *The Art of War* are not difficult to understand because they are of general application and are useful in any circumstance. The usefulness of these doctrines lies in their dynamism and essence which one must master. To be more specific, if a teacher understands *The Art of War* fully, he knows exactly when, where and how to vary these underlying strategies to fit individual teaching circumstances and situations. By applying these doctrines, Jack was able to show students the *Whats*, *Whys* and *Whens* of making a contract but not whether they should enter into the contract. The answer to this question was to be found in the realm of the *I Ching*.

The I Ching (易经)

A wise man once said that, "October is a dangerous month to buy stocks. The other dangerous months are May, February, September, July, November, June, April, January, March, December and August." At no time was this saying more true than in October 1997 when the Asian contagion swept the world. Almost 10 years to the day of the October 1987 crash, the currency turmoil which started with the plunge of the Thai Baht and Indonesian Rupiah rippled into Wall Street and caused the biggest one-day crash in the history of the New York Stock Exchange. No one was spared, at the height of the crisis, the runs continued not only on banks in Hong Kong but on cake shops and games arcades as well!

Stories of the economic turmoil, hot from the press, formed the perfect setting for Jack to explore the issue of whether a contract was to be entered into. The question which he posed to the students was this, "Having satisfied yourselves with an examination of the five factors, would you still proceed with the signing of the contract, given the impact of the current economic crisis on you and your counterparty?"

Throughout the course of history, mankind has grappled with the difficulty of answering questions such as this. A sophistical manner of dealing with this problem would be to throw a coin and assign a certain response to the heads or tails; another way would be to consult a soothsayer, one with the mythical ability of being able to predict the future, like the Oracle at Delphi; the classical Chinese approach was to consult the *I Ching*.

In contrast with Sun Tzu's *Art of War*, the origins of the *I Ching* or the *Book of Changes* have been lost in the mists of time. Enough, however, has been written by scholars about the *I Ching* (like the *Art of War*, there are a number of English translations of the *I Ching* but the two favored by the authors are the translations by Damian-Knight (1986) and Wilhelm and Baynes (1967)) for us to know that it was an ancient book of divination; a tool to forecast or predict changes. In contrast to oracles based on divine revelation, the ancient Chinese philosophy of the *I Ching* was based on the experience gained from observing nature over thousands of years — particularly patterns of change and transformation. Over time, the Chinese came to see these patterns of change as resulting from a universal creative energy or spirit. Dynamic and continuous changes were likened to currents or vortices in air or water. Sometimes these patterns of change were depicted as undulating horned dragons, flowing along wave-like lines of change or dragon veins. Metaphorically, these patterns were viewed as a road or passage, suggestive of a path along which one could act or move.

The text of the *I Ching* consists of a series of sixty-four six-line diagrams known as "Hexagrams". Each of these hexagrams can be divided into an upper group of three lines and a lower group of three lines. These trigrams are formed from a combination of solid (—) or broken (--) lines. The solid lines symbolize *yang* 阳, strength and activity while the broken lines represent *yin* 阴, weakness and acquiescence. Each of these lines is capable of change. Thus when a solid line (—) breaks down, it becomes a broken line (--) which is then denoted by (—x—). When a broken line (--) changes into a solid line (—) denoted by (—°—), the hexagram breaks down and a new one is formed. As each hexagram contains six lines each capable of change, there will be three hundred and eighty-four stages of change altogether. Given three hundred and eighty-four different perspectives from which to observe an occurrence, it would only be a matter of time before the most appropriate suggestion is found and the problem solved. The authors realized that the *I Ching* could be applied to their current situation as they were embarking on a process of change. They were trying to change students with a misconception of business contracts into students with an indepth understanding of these contracts. In the broader perspective, the use of the *I Ching* also served as a guide to show students the process by which businesspersons make a decision on whether a contract is to be entered into.

Essentially, a contract is to be entered into when two parties are potentially at conflict. If two parties are *ad idem* and see eye to eye on how to proceed, for example, with a business adventure, there is little need for a contract to be entered into. However, when two parties have different interests and enter into a contract for different reasons, a contract is necessary. For example, in a sales contract, there would be a conflict between the interests if the buyer only wants to buy at the lowest price and the seller only wants to sell at the highest price. In such a situation, the contract becomes the "social glue" by which two potentially conflicting parties come together, it is the tool for avoidance of conflict.

The relevant hexagram in the *I Ching* which deals with conflict is the *sung* (訟) hexagram (䷅). *Sung is* made up of an upper trigram, *ch'ien* (乾 ☰) which denotes the creative forces and heaven while the lower trigram, *k'an* (坎 ☵) denotes the abysmal depths and water. The upper trigram (representing heaven) has an upward movement while the lower trigram (representing water), in accordance with its nature, trends downward. The two halves which have a natural tendency to diverge represent the two parties and their conflicting interests.

The first line (--) from bottom up tells us that while a conflict is in the incipient stage, the best thing to do may be simply to drop the issue. This is especially so when the adversary is stronger. It is not advisable to risk pushing the conflict to make a decision.

The second line (—) means that in a struggle with an opponent of superior strength, retreat is no disgrace. Timely withdrawal prevents unfavourable consequences.

The third line (--) means that if one succeeds in entering into the contract, one can avoid conflict only if one does not perform the contract merely for the sake of prestige. It is enough if the work is done: let the honor go to the other.

The fourth line (—) refers to a person whose attitude at first lacks inner peace but who subsequently changes his mind and finds lasting peace in being at one with eternal law. This brings good fortune.

The fifth line (—) refers to an arbiter in a contract who is powerful and just and strong enough to lend weight to the right side. A dispute can be turned over to him with confidence. If one is in the right, one attains great good fortune.

The last line (—) refers to the situation where one who has carried a conflict to the bitter end has triumphed. Such happiness will not last. He will be attacked again and again and the result is conflict without end.

The starting point of the analysis of this hexagram shows that one party is sincere but is being obstructed by another with diverging interests. So the first party plans to enter into a contract. By doing so, he has halted halfway and this brings good fortune. If he had insisted on proceeding straight through to the end, this would have brought misfortune instead. If business encounters a conflict, the only salvation lies in being so clear-headed and inwardly strong that one is always ready to come to terms by writing a contract to meet the opponent halfway. To carry on this conflict to the bitter end will not serve any purpose even when one is in the right because enmity would have been perpetuated. It is important then to find a legal way, that is an impartial way whose authority is great enough to resolve the conflict amicably or guarantee a just decision.

This hexagram indicates that the causes of conflict are latent in the opposing tendencies of the two trigrams. Once these opposing tendencies appear, conflict is inevitable. To avoid it, everything must be carefully taken into consideration from the very beginning. If rights and duties are exactly defined, or if, in a group, the spiritual trends of the individuals harmonise, the cause of conflict can be removed in advance. With the *I Ching*, Jack had a means by which he could illustrate to the students the decision making process when a contract is to be entered into in order to prevent conflict from arising between two parties with different interests. Like the *Art of War*, the hexagrams in the *I Ching* are of general application and other hexagrams can be used to guide one through other business or educational scenarios.

Resolve

Encouraged by the success of their methods in the teaching of business contracts, the authors resolved not only to continue the use of these methods but also to try to encourage their use in other courses taught by their colleagues. With the emphasis fast shifting towards the need to create the "educated person" by equipping our graduates with "core skills" e.g., communication, accounting skills and a knowledge of economics and law; the authors believe that their teaching philosophies can also be applied to these disciplines and it is only a matter of time before any misconceptions or ignorance existing in the minds of staff or students alike are eradicated.

Conclusion

In this chapter, the authors have tried to show how it is possible to merge Chinese classical thought with western wisdom. *The Art of War* and the *I Ching* are but two of the classics of Chinese literature in which there has been a recent resurgence of interest. The way in which these centuries old principles are able to fit into late 20th century society is symbolic of the balance of "Yin" and "Yang" which is so important to the Chinese. As a symbol of this harmony, the title of the chapter was chosen not only because it was evocative of the merger of ideas from the East and West but also because it was "reflective" of the contents of the chapter. The word "reflections" was meant as a pun to refer both to the authors' ideas which flowed from their source in the classics as well as to the view from the "stream". Images would then form, in the reader's mind, of reflections coming from a metaphorical "stream" in which the authors have channeled their thoughts. Finally, the expression "Eastern straws" is used to denote the ideas propounded. These "straws", by themselves, can only float in the stream but collectively, will bind themselves into the powerful framework of reflection, recognition, realization, response and resolution which forms the central theme of this book.

References

Chen, A. Y. (1995). *Enhancing Teachers of Professionals in Their Reflective Practices.* Paper presented at the annual meeting of the American Educational Research Association, San Francisco.

Damian-Knight, G. (1986). *The* I Ching *on Business and Decision Making.* London: Rider.

Griffith, S. B. (1963). *The Art of War.* Oxford: Clarendon Press.

Loi, S. L. & Teo J. C. C. (1997). *Sun Tzu's The Art of War: Analogous Strategies for the Classroom.* Paper presented at the 7th International Conference on Thinking, Singapore.

McNeilly, M. (1996). *Sun Tzu and the Art of Business.* New York: Oxford University Press.

Wilhelm, R. & Baynes, C. F. (1967). *The* I Ching *or Book of Changes.* New Jersey, USA: Princeton University Press.

Cross-Cultural Readings: The Case of King Lear

Kirpal Singh

National Institute of Education
Nanyang Technological University
Singapore

Synopsis

Shakespeare's King Lear is a play universally regarded as saying something profound about the human condition. Its principal "messages" are supposedly universal as well: thus few scholars, if any, dispute some of the more "obvious" meanings of the play. However, over many years of teaching it in Singapore, I began to observe that the supposed universality of the play most certainly was in need of revision: at least for some aspects of its meaning. In 1993, I made a conscious attempt to try to document some of the more essential differences in the readings offered by my students, who, coming as they did from vastly different cultural/religious backgrounds, naturally offered quite markedly different interpretations of the play. My "case" outlines this project as an instance in "cross-cultural" reading and invites scholars to test this with their own students/readers.

Cross-Cultural Readings: The Case of King Lear

Kirpal Singh

Introduction

One of the paradoxes of the increasing globalisation of the world is that the old uniformities seem to be eroding to make way for pluralistic perspectives. The former certainties of understanding now meet with complex challenges of shifting responses, dependent upon geography and history. Thus, in the world of education, pedagogic thinking has to reckon with more specific, individual based outlooks.

Some scholars have termed this individual approach "reader response" and more generally, the term "cross-cultural" has been used to refer to contexts where there is no longer an assumed homogeneity of background. Studies in this area are only now starting to surface and as of now no agreed theoretical framework seems available. Indeed, a paper such as this one I would like to believe is itself a modest contribution to the ongoing realisation that literature of all subjects contains the enormous complexities we have now come to realise which link individuals across histories and across geographies.

Increasingly there does seem to be a felt need for a formulation of approaches which will help scholars everywhere deal with these new frontiers of interpretation and understanding. Cultural studies go some way towards addressing crucial questions related to this but on account of their emphases on socio-political-economic considerations the literary arena seems to lack a full and even, perhaps, helpful insight into its own peculiar problems. A cross-cultural theory will, I believe, eventually emerge; in the meantime it is hoped that studies such as this present one will carry the discussion forward.

I want to illustrate not only how the case method can be used to demonstrate fundamental positive factors affecting understanding but also how subtle the contemporary educator/teacher needs to be if he/she is not to register bigotry. My example is the study of KING LEAR, that well-worn Shakespearean play which for centuries held a kind of "universal" appeal through shared meaning.

Contexts

My practical source for a reconsideration of KING LEAR — at least some important aspects of it — would be the students at the National Institute of Education, Singapore during the year 1993. The sample is not quite random as my thinking of this multiplicity of viewpoints has been shaping itself since 1980 when I taught at the University of Papua New Guinea where the students had absolutely no difficulties whatsoever identifying with the witches in Macbeth. Thus, the class of 1993 made up of trainee-teachers with an "A" level to their credit, offered me a test-case to use KING LEAR as an instance of cross-cultural readings.

The Problem

Unlike OTHELLO in the Shakespearean oeuvre, a play which from the very start has been problemmatical on account of its hero's ethnic background. KING LEAR had always been regarded as transcending all borders and universally making the same points to all its readers. Regrettably, the more I prodded my students with instruments of self-articulation, the more I began to sense just how complex the problem of LEAR was: given the differences of gender (usually nowadays taken for granted), race, religion and language, students were interested to yield quite different responses.

Key Issues

I discerned five distinct (though obviously linked) areas of valid cross-cultural readings in my tutorials on Lear. For each of these areas the different pupils, coming as they did from a rich tradition of their own cultures, were prepared to respond in ways not too familiar in the West. For my part, interested as I was, in the *plurality* of readings, I kept a low pedagogic profile, not insisting on any "truth" about the play. I found what is known as *subject-position* to be of prime importance in the teaching of this text. After all, if literature is to continue to have significance it must speak to each and every reader. I found that arguments which many of us take as "given" become highly contentious in multicultural contexts, and sound pedagogy calls for an open discussion of these. I found that an entire final position may be arrived at on account of applying one's own cultural knowledge. Thus for most Asians, brought up as we are on the basic belief that our parents are right and must always be treated with respect, Cordelia's protestations are "a bit too much" and she does not, therefore, elicit from us a similar intensity of sympathy. Area (i) the religious is discussed at considerable length below. I have grouped here brief notes for the other 4 areas for colleagues to follow-up and test with their own students:- These were: (i) the religious, (ii) the familial, (iii) the social, (iv) kingship, and (v) sexuality.

(ii) *The familial*: much of KING LEAR hinges on the opening scene and the interaction between the father and his daughter Cordelia. In the vast majority of readings, it is the King who is felt to be wrong and Cordelia almost always given sympathy and the benefit of the doubt. In this ridiculous exchange between father and daughter it is the daughter whose "I love you according to my bond. Nothing more, nothing less" utterance seems to clinch the argument in her favour. This is not clearly the way many of my students read the play. Invariably, given the family cultures current here in Singapore, Cordelia's *haughtiness*, disrespect for her father, and her unwillingness to indulge are the points raised by the students. A radically different reading is offered in which Lear, far from being the wrathful father, is seen as the quite normal attention-seeking daddy! Also, filial piety runs so strong in the culture of our students that any breach of it — especially in public — is absolutely condemned. Thus Cordelia, in the words of one student, is behaving in a manner totally unbecoming of a daughter.

(iii) *The social*: in a world which no longer recognises the mutually binding nature of social obligations — and, differently, a world which puts a very heavy emphasis on such obligations (such as in the Malay culture) — the social issues highlighted by KING LEAR again warrant plenty of discussion along the lines of individual orientations. The "top-down" nature of the play's main lines of action are subject to interesting shifts in perspectives by students coming from markedly different social backgrounds. Clearly, there is no distinct "social" behaviour pattern which is not, somehow, conditioned by a larger religious or cultural norm — and this makes for a range of readings of the social values portrayed in the play.

(iv) *Kingship*: it was fascinating for me to observe how the different ethnic groups in class responded to this theme. The Malay students felt more 'deferential' to kingship as a norm than, say, the Chinese students. However, for most Singapore students, distanced as they are from any real contact with royalty, this theme was most emphasised. Any attempt to engage them on issues of the nature and role of the kinghead was at best a monologue. Thus, while for many commentators from the West, the theme of kingship is of the essence, for us, it is negligible!

(v) *Sexuality*: as a theme within the play, sexuality is most frequently seen to result in perversity. Many of my students took issue with this, seeing not only the warped nature of this theme within the play (as seen by Western readers as well) but extending it to Shakespeare himself — the author is seen to be "warped" too; thus many students felt that Lear's curses on his daughters were too obscene, too unbecoming of any father and thus a case for censorship was developed by at least one Muslim student who felt

intensely angry at the author for such fumigatory utterances/
curses. Many other students felt distressed by the frequent
references within the play to unhealthy sexual behaviour, and did
not take kindly to the "wit" which Shakespeare's poetry relies
upon to make the necessary points concerning sexuality.

The Process

As teacher I played the guide.

Teacher
: Okay, let's begin. Perhaps we can start today's tutorial by looking at the passage in Act 4, Sc i, lines 36:

Gloucester : As flies to wanton boys are we to th' gods: They kill us for their sport.

Now, here is Gloucester, a wounded and suffering man, laying it on the line, as it were, for the gods. What do you think? Is he right? Are we flies to the gods? Do gods kill us for their sport?

(general murmur, eyes darting left and right)

Student A
(female/Malay-Muslim)
: Though we believe in something like fate, we cannot just say we are simply like flies. Anyway, there is only one God and He knows what's best for us.

Student B
(male, Chinese-Buddhist)
: I agree, but Gloucester is making a mountain out of a mole-hill, he is making his own personal problem into a universal truth. That cannot be accepted — did he follow the four-fold truth? You cannot simply say this or that without proper knowledge and

who is he to know the gods? Man cannot know God, he cannot even know himself. So this is an arrogant statement.

Student C
(female, Indian-Hindu)   : Sir, gods can do anything they like. They actually have a lot of fun with human beings, but they seldom just kill for fun. I mean, we are like flies, meaning we are really of no major significance, but gods need human beings to make their sport so they are careful what they do with us.

Teacher   : Good, good, now, you appreciate how just these three responses already suggest just how complicated the apparently simple question I asked actually is. The role of the Divine, the role of Fate in human lives is a very complex problem. We know that several characters in LEAR take issue with the gods, question their motives, etc. Let's turn now to the great Storm Scene and see how Lear himself relates to Nature, the elements — maybe we can begin to piece together something of an argument which may run through the whole play?

Lear   : Blow, winds, and crack your cheeks! Rage! blow!
You cataracts and hurricanes, spout
Till you have drench'd our steeples! Drown the cocks!
You sulph'rous and thought-executing fires,
Vaunt-carriers of oak-cleaving thunderbolts,
Singe my white head! And thou, all-shaking thunder,

Strike flat the thick rotundity o' th' world,
Crack Nature's moulds, all germens spill at
once
That make ingrateful man!

(3, ii, 1–9)

Well, what do we make of this? Is this only
the utterance of a man going mad?

(silence, students seem absorbed, deep in
thought)

Student A
(female/Malay-Muslim)   : He is going mad what, so he just blabbers...
but this is so normal, we all do that some-
times when we are fed-up. And Lear is fed-
up, he's had enough by this time. Of course,
he's being dramatic too, being a King he
feels it more.

Student B
(male, Chinese-Buddhist)   : Again Lear is being self-centred. Here it is
not the wind and the rain that matter, but
he. And he wants to use Nature to hurt
others. Just because he is hurt, he must
hurt others. That's selfish — he has no self-
knowledge. He must learn. He must become
humble. He is too arrogant.

Student D
(female, Chinese-Christian) : You cannot say he's arrogant what, after all
he is a King but reduced to a nobody and
he is out there in the storm when his evil
daughters are warm indoors. Also, this is
pre-Christian right, during the pagan-times?
At that time, the natural elements were used
by men. But even the Bible recognises the

		symbols of storm; but the storm will wash Lear and cleanse him.
Student C (female, Indian-Hindu)	:	We Hindus are very respectful of Nature. Sometimes we can marry with only Nature as our witness, we don't need two human witnesses. Anyway, Nature is made by God so when Lear talks to Nature he is talking to God. It is okay if he is angry — he is being honest and this is good. He will be rewarded, Nature will come to his rescue —
Teacher	:	— I think that's a very remote possibility, don't you think —
Student C (female, Indian-Hindu)	:	— But you see, Sir, Nature will act in its own unique way, when we don't know but it will help Lear because he is an old man and out there alone in the wilderness.

Reflection

The point being made is that no one understanding of these themes any longer apply to a reading of Lear. The above are only five aspects of KING LEAR which immediately recommend a patient, sustained, case reading of the play. Most students reject any 'monolithic' response, and the feeling is that 'subject-positions' and subject-positioning are paramount in literature teaching/learning. Thus the case of KING LEAR is merely one instance of how a popular, universal interpretation which have, naturally, implications for classroom experience. It is vital that in the teaching of literature, attributes which may be assumed as 'given' and 'binding' are radically the frames for dialectic engagements. It would make very minor difference in the teaching of mathematics if students were of a mixed religious background, but in the case of literature, as our discussion of KING LEAR shows, this has a significant, indeed sometimes all-encompassing effect, on the reading of literary texts.

For a sound pedagogy of literature teaching to be obtained it is necessary that many of the points raised through a case study of KING LEAR be incorporated so that sensibilities and sensitivities are not offended. It behoves all of us involved in education that the student's background in terms of religion, culture, ethnicity, etc. be crucially noted to ensure a fair criteria for assessment and discussion are arrived at.

Conclusion

Using the case method in literature teaching is highly desirable because it allows for clear, specific discussion and documentation of the many issues raised and talked about. If our teaching methods — and more importantly teaching habits — are not to be found offensive, it behoves us to become more sensitive to cross-cultural readings. The above example of teaching Lear in Singapore could be used to test other instances in other parts of the world — my own belief is that this is already being done with a high degree of excitement in many parts of the Western world. Such an approach underlines openness, transparency and offers students a good way into the texts.

Traditional ways of discussing Lear have not paid sufficient emphasis on varied and different readings, though feeble attempts in this direction have been made. If KING LEAR can and does mean different things to different people, then there is yet another very rich and rewarding source for scholarship in this field. Students feel freer to answer questions put to them and, on the whole, a fresh perspective is often obtained through such discussions and interactions. The globalisation of our world means, in part at least, giving each individual a valid voice in terms of intellectual understanding. Perhaps in the long term greater harmony may be possible through a result of cross-cultural readings of texts which matter and have mattered to humanity.

Section
THREE

*Learning
in
Community*

Teacher Perspectives: As A Tool for Reflection, Partnerships and Professional Growth

Christine Bennett

School of Education
Indiana University
United States of America

Synopsis

The paper explores ways of assisting teachers to articulate assumptions about teaching from a variety of perspectives, with the view to empowering the teacher.

Working on the underlying assumption that knowledge about one's own beliefs about teaching and learning is critical for teacher effectiveness, the researcher uses a case study approach with pre-service middle and secondary teachers in the Teachers as Decision Maker Programme (TADMP) at Indiana University.

The theoretical perspectives for the study are drawn from pedagogical schemes, professional knowledge, thematic teacher education and teaching perspectives.

Exploring these four components, seven case studies are presented in a non-threatening manner highlighting the strengths and limitations of each. The researcher concludes by stating that the multiple perspectives have assisted students to gain a better understanding of themselves, their peers and mentor teachers.

Teacher Perspectives: As A Tool for Reflection, Partnerships and Professional Growth

Christine I. Bennett

A good teacher knows the subject, is sensitive to students all the time ... he has to be a scholar and a psychologist.

A good teacher is able to impart knowledge to students in a way that the knowledge will stay with them.

Sensitivity to students' needs is important to me. A good teacher is one who watches you in class and can pick up on your facial expressions to see how you react to something.

These quotes offer a glimpse into the strong and differing perspectives held by the pre-service middle and secondary school teachers I have worked with since 1988 in the Teachers as Decision Maker Programme (TADMP) at Indiana University. Even the simple question "What are the characteristics of an excellent teacher?" evokes extremely diverse answers from students who enter the programme. Like many other teacher education researchers, I have discovered that initial teacher perspectives change very little during student teaching or the first few years in the classroom, despite challenges and contradictions faced in school contexts (Bennett and Powell, 1990; Bennett and Spalding, 1991, 1992a, 1992b). As a result I have begun to explore ways of helping teachers make explicit their assumptions about teaching, to identify multiple perspectives from which teaching may be viewed, to consider how their teaching might be enhanced by incorporating additional perspectives, and to realise that there are many ways of being a good teacher.

Knowledge about one's own beliefs about teaching and learning is a critical component of becoming an effective teacher. It is well known that among beginning teachers, self knowledge is essential to self-confidence as a teacher, which in turn leads to higher self expectations and greater success in the classroom (e.g., Kagan, 1992). Yet even experienced teachers (including teacher educators) are often unaware of their own beliefs and unaware that there are viable alternatives to the beliefs they hold. When teachers have not reflected upon how their own beliefs, values, and attitudes influence their teaching, they may react to difficult situations by blaming themselves, their students, the school, or society when their beliefs do not help them solve problems or indeed even cause problems (Bennett and Spalding, 1992b).

In this paper I will review the theoretical framework that underlies TADMP inquiry and the development of a conceptual framework of seven teacher perspectives. I will also explain how these seven perspectives have helped TADMP pre-service teachers gain a better understanding of themselves, their peers, their mentor teachers, and other teachers they come in contact with as they enter the teaching profession.

Theoretical Framework

The TADMP has drawn heavily upon the recent contributions of numerous teacher education researchers, particularly those who have focused on teacher thought processes, perspectives, and socialization. The theoretical framework that guides TADMP research, as well as the nature of the programme itself, contains four components: pedagogical schemata, professional knowledge, thematic teacher education, and teaching perspectives (Bennett and Powell, 1990; Bennett, 1991).

Pedagogical Schemata

"Pedagogical schemata" refers to mental constructs that contain knowledge about teaching. These schemata are "the complex cognitive structures that include both theoretical and practical knowledge and an understanding of the interrelatedness of these knowledge sources for informing judgment and action" (Barnes, 1987, p. 17). This knowledge may or may not be accurate and appropriate, and may be based on misconceptions about teaching. This is especially true among pre-service teachers who are likely to "have an unrealistic optimism and a self-serving bias...believing that the attributes most important for successful teaching are the ones they perceive as their own" (Pajares, 1992, p. 323).

As a framework for cognition, schemata have been used to examine knowledge that underlies teachers' actions (Carter and Doyle, 1987), to compare knowledge structures of pre-service and experienced teachers (Livingston and Borko, 1989; Peterson and Comeaux, 1987) and to analyze the type of knowledge experienced teachers accrue during interactive classroom teaching (Nespor, 1984; Lienhardt and Greeno, 1987). In addition, Barnes (1987) has used a schema to study the type of pedagogical knowledge pre-service teachers acquire in teacher education programmes.

The importance of examining schemata that contain pedagogical knowledge in pre-service teachers has been made clear by various teacher educators. Carter and Doyle (1987) hold that pre-service teachers' pedagogical schemata reveal the knowledge they use during interactive classroom teaching. Beyerbach (1988) examined pedagogical schemata to discover the type of knowledge pre-service teachers acquire as they interact with their teacher education programmes. Furthermore, Beyerbach concluded that when pre-service teachers examine their own knowledge schemata with such methods as concept mapping, they can become more aware of the development of their own pedagogical knowledge. Calderhead (1987) supports the view that research on knowledge contained in pre-service teachers' pedagogical schemata provides insight into the processes of professional development during teacher education.

According to Berliner (1987), an examination of pedagogical schemata can reveal the knowledge teachers use to set their instructional pace, determine students' intellectual level, establish a work orientation, affect the classroom value system and influence classroom organization and management. Berliner further states that individuals who possess rich, relatively complete schemata about certain phenomena need very little personal experience to learn easily, quickly, and retain well information pertaining to those phenomena (p. 61).

The TADMP is based on the assumption that teachers with more fully developed schemata have a better understanding of the classroom and are therefore more effective. This assumption is supported by the work of Peterson and Comeaux (1987) who discovered that well developed schemata containing both practical and theoretical pedagogical knowledge enabled teachers to go beyond the obvious literal features and have a better understanding of the classroom. Similar findings have been reported elsewhere (Calderhead, 1981; Livingston and Borko, 1989). Furthermore, teachers with less developed pedagogical schemata appear to be limited in their effectiveness (Livingston and Borko, 1989; Roehler, Duffy, Conley, Herrman, Johnson and Michelsen, 1987). Thus, it seems highly desirable that teacher education programmes foster the growth of relatively complete pedagogical knowledge schemata in pre-service teachers. If developed early in a teacher education programme, such "rich, relatively complete schemata" might enable pre-service teachers to assimilate more quickly the techniques and skills they need to be effective in the classroom (Joyce, 1980).

Professional Knowledge

Schema theory, in particular the notion of a cognitive schema (Anderson, 1977, 1984; Howard, 1987; Neisser, 1976; Rumelhart, 1980), has become an important vehicle to examine teachers' knowledge. What remains unclear, however, is what constitutes powerful and appropriate schemata. The type of knowledge that actually comprises well developed professional knowledge schemata in pre-service as well as beginning and more experienced teachers has been the focus of ongoing discussions among teacher educators (Barnes, 1987; Livingston and Borko, 1989; Peterson and Comeaux, 1987; Shulman, 1986, 1987; Smith, 1980; Wilson, Shulman and Richert, 1987; Tamir, 1988).

The conception of teacher knowledge that underlies the TADMP is based primarily on the work of Shulman and Sykes (1986), Shulman (1987, 1988) and Tamir (1988). A modified version of Tamir's framework for teachers' knowledge (1988) was used to develop the TADMP's academic programme and to study changes in the professional knowledge schemata of TADMP students as they moved through the programme (Bennett and

Powell, 1990). The concept map in Figure 1 contains six areas of inquiry and three areas of practice that provide an overview of the professional knowledge base emphasized in the TADMP.

Figure 1
Teaching Perspectives as a Color Wheel

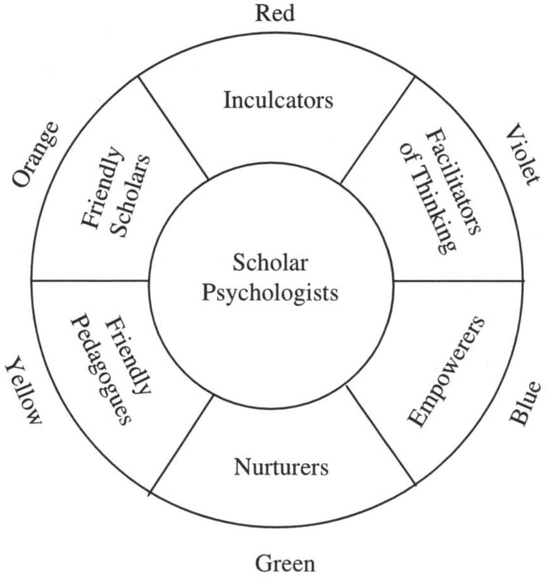

Thematic Teacher Education Programmes

Thematic teacher education programmes have emerged as a means of helping pre-service teachers build elaborate and well-organized schemata that guide teacher action (Barnes, 1987; Borko, 1987). They represent the application of cognitive psychology to teacher education which, as Barnes points out, may be as appropriate as applications of cognitive psychology to classroom teaching.

Just as naive conceptions and misunderstandings imbedded in existing schemata inhibit pupil learning of natural phenomena, such as photosynthesis and light, naive conceptions of teaching also impede attempts to build appropriate schemata for teaching. The preconceptions and images of teaching that prospective teachers bring to their formal study of teaching frequently remain unexamined in traditional teacher education programmes and persist in spite of exposure to contradictory models. Altering the structure of the programme, could significantly increase the power of formal teacher preparation to overcome students' naive conceptions about teaching and create alternative views of effective teaching practice (Barnes, 1987, pp. 13–14).

The literature identifies three necessary components of thematic programmes. First, thematic programmes should be characterized by a unifying theme or metaphor that accurately reflects the central intent and character of the programme (Short, 1987, p. 6). In addition to the decision maker theme that has been used in a number of settings, other examples include the Teacher as Broker of Scholarly Knowledge and the Teacher as Reflective Practitioner.

Second, thematic programmes require a structure or conceptual framework that helps "students develop schemata for teaching that are complete, well-organized, and stable" (Barnes, 1987). This conceptual framework reflects the programme's assumptions, goals, purposes and philosophy and serves as a means to organize the knowledge and experiences provided to participants.

And finally, thematic programmes should foster the development of a mutually supportive cohort, a community of learners. Programme participants are encouraged to develop a sense of group ownership, belongingness, and concern for the well being of all members.

An underlying assumption held by advocates of thematic programmes is that a more sophisticated pedagogical schema will enable pre-service teachers to make decisions like those made by more experienced teachers. Barnes found that professional decision making in pre-service teachers can be effected by thematic programmes. She collected data from pre-service teachers' about their beliefs toward teaching and about their perception of themselves as teachers and decision makers. She found that participants in the thematic programme did not significantly differ from their traditional counterparts in their educational beliefs. However, she did find that thematic participants do differ in their perception of professional decision making. Thematic participants indicated they would rely more often on theoretical knowledge and research data when making interactive decisions. Moreover, a significantly higher number of thematic pre-service teachers held higher expectations regarding social behavior of students and were more willing to work with less motivated students.

The TADMP is a thematic teacher education programme aimed at developing reflective teachers who can make wise decisions in middle and secondary school classrooms. The underlying assumption is that teachers who make well informed, appropriate decisions in the classroom are more likely to foster their students' learning, growth, and development than teachers who do not. Students move through the 12–14 month programme as a cohort, experiencing a common core of coursework and field experience that are guided by the decision maker theme.

Teacher Perspectives

As a complement to the cognitive focus of professional knowledge schemata, a perspective refers to the personal attitudes, values, and beliefs (Rokeach, 1968) that help teachers interpret and justify their classroom decisions and actions (Posner, 1985). A perspective provides the lens through which teaching is viewed and affects the way teaching is perceived and interpreted. Goodman writes, "Teacher perspectives take into account how situations within schools and classrooms are experienced; how these situations are interpreted given different teachers' backgrounds, assumptions, beliefs, and previous experiences; and how their interpretations are manifested in actions" (1985, p. 2).

Zeichner and Tabachnick (1985) used teacher perspectives to study the socialization of pre-service teachers into the profession, and to describe the continuities and discontinuities between the socializing conditions of student teaching and the first year of teaching. Based upon a two-year study that explored the extent to which beginning teachers modified their teaching perspectives during their first year of teaching, they refuted the "commonly

accepted scenario of a loss of idealism during the first year of teaching"
(1985, p. 19).

Zeichner and Tabachnick's use of social strategies as a conceptual
framework for exploring the socialization of beginning teachers provided
initial guidelines for studying teacher perspectives during the first two
years of the TADMP. Developed originally by Lacey (1977), the framework
contains three distinct strategies:

(1) internalized adjustment, where "individuals comply with the authority
     figure's definition of a situation and believe these constraints to be
     for the best;"

(2) strategic compliance, where "individuals comply with the constraints
     posed by a situation, but retain private reservations about doing so;"
     and

(3) strategic redefinition where "successful attempts to change are made
     by individuals who do not possess the formal power to do so"
     (Zeichner and Tabachnick, 1985, pp. 9–10).

Initially, the idea of "strategic compliance" framed TADMP teacher
perspective inquiry in terms of "resisters" and "non-resisters" and proactive
and reactive teachers (Bennett and Powell, 1990). Follow up research that
explored linkages between teacher beliefs and classroom behavior greatly
expanded this teacher perspective framework and identified seven primary
perspectives: Scholar Psychologist, Friendly Scholar, Inculcator, Facilitator
of Thinking, Empowerer, Nurturer, and Friendly Pedagogue (Bennett and
Spalding, 1991, 1992). The latest phase of research has explored the utility
of this teacher perspective framework as a tool for reflection, partnerships
and professional growth.

Development of the Teacher Perspective Framework:
First Phase of Methodology and Findings

In this section I will review the methodology and findings of TADMP
teacher perspective research between 1988 and 1992 which led to the
development of seven teacher perspectives conceptualized as a color wheel

(Bennett and Spalding, 1991, 1992a, 1992b). The next section reports inquiry into the color wheel of teacher perspectives as a tool for reflection that has continued since 1992.

Participants

The first phase of research involved 68 TADMP pre-service teachers who have entered the programme since its inception in 1988. The teachers represent a highly select group in terms of academic preparation and/or work experience, interpersonal communication skills, and commitment to teaching. They range in age from 23–51 and come from many careers, including law, banking, business, homemaking, engineering, nursing, theater, social work, and college teaching. Their areas of teacher certification are as follows: 20 in social studies, 18 in science, 18 in English, 6 in math, and 6 in foreign languages. 31 males and 37 females comprise the group.

Data Collection

Four techniques were used to study the students' teaching perspectives during the programme and during their first years of teaching: (1) autobiographical interviews, (2) concept mapping, (3) stimulated recall interviews, and (4) classroom observations with follow-up interviews. Brief descriptions of each technique follow. (For detailed descriptions, see Bennett and Spalding, 1991; Bennett and Powell, 1990; Bennett, 1991).

Autobiographical Interviews

Each year, upon entering the programme, the students were interviewed in depth by a programme assistant. All interviews were audiotaped and subsequently transcribed. The questions were grouped according to personal background data; early socialization, including school experiences; teaching perspectives, including motivations, values and conceptions of teaching; conceptions of knowledge in the selected content area; and the role of schooling in society.

Concept Mapping

Using free association concept mapping procedures (Beyerbach, 1987), students were asked to construct concept maps around the central organizing concept of "teaching." Maps were created at four strategic points throughout the programme: upon entry, end of summer coursework, end of fall field experience, end of student teaching. After completing their first and last concept maps, the students were asked to explain their maps and interpret their development over time. These interviews were audiotaped and transcribed.

Stimulated Recall Interviews

Four lessons (at beginning of summer coursework, during fall field experience, beginning and end of student teaching) taught by each student were videotaped and analysed in a follow-up interview that was taped and transcribed. Stimulated recall interviews were conducted immediately following each lesson. The interviews contained three distinct components:

1) questions about planning;
2) stimulated recall through viewing the videotape and focusing on three critical incidents/points of saliency in the lesson; and
3) reflective analysis of the lesson (Borko, Livingston, McCaleb and Mauro, 1988; Norton, 1987).

Classroom Observations and Follow-up Interviews

During their first, second, and third years of teaching, six teachers from each cohort were videotaped for at least one full class period. A two person research team conducted the observations and follow-up interviews. The teachers were asked to describe their classroom and feelings about teaching, and to answer questions related to teaching perspectives (e.g., values and conceptions of teaching and learning, conceptions of knowledge in their content area, and the role of schooling in society). All follow-up interviews were audiotaped, transcribed and analysed.

Data Analysis

Each participant was assigned a coded I.D. number to indicate the cohort, individual, subject area, and gender. Original units of analysis were taken from the autobiographical interview transcripts and categories were developed using Lincoln and Guba's index card system (Merriam, 1988). This card sorting yielded the seven teacher perspectives described in the findings.

Table 1
Teacher Perspectives of TADMP Teachers

Teacher Perspective	Description
Scholar Psychologists	Emphasize academic knowledge and understanding nature of the learner; emphasize relevance in the subject area and helping students become intelligent decision makers in the future.
Friendly Scholars	Emphasize academic knowledge and teacher personality characteristics; stress immediate relevance in the subject matters; subject areas help students solve personal problems and understand current issues and events.
Inculcators	Emphasize academic knowledge; transmission of fundamental knowledge and values; teacher as inspirational role model; subject matter as cultural literacy.
Facilitators of Thinking	Emphasize thinking, decision making and learning processes; subject area important in helping students think critically and become lifelong learners.
Empowerers	Emphasize values, critical thinking, decision making, self-actualization, and social action; subject matter important in effecting change on a societal or global scale.
Nurturers	Emphasize teacher-student interaction, empathy and caring relationships; subject area less important than development of the learner.
Friendly Pedagogues	Emphasize instructional strategies, well-planned lessons and student feedback; subject area important as a tool for understanding.

Table 2
Seven Teacher Perspectives: Description of Classroom Actions of TADMP Teachers

Actions Pre-spective	Classroom Leadership Style	Student Roles/ Behaviors	Content Emphasized	Preferred Instructional Strategies	Responses School Contexts
Scholar Psychologists	Control through connections and questioning	Cooperative participants	Textbook as a resource/ springboard	A wide range	Adaptability
Friendly Scholars	Control through charisma and connections	Passive recipients and admiring fan club	Text plus supplementary materials	Lecture, questioning, demonstrations	Adaptability
Inculcators	Control through authority	Passive recipient or potential disrupter	Textbook as centerpiece	Lecture, teacher explanation	Frustrated by constraints unless supported by school culture
Facilitators of Thinking	Student self-control through responsibility	Active Participants and decision-makers	Primary source materials	Higher level questions, student projects	Adaptable, but frustrated if expected to "cover the text"
Empowerers	Student self-control and teacher charisma	Passive recipients to Active Participants	Multiple resources	Discussion, groupwork, student projects	Frustrated by constraints unless supported by school culture
Nurturers	Student self-control through teacher contact	From caring cooperation to testing the boundaries	Textbook plus hands-on materials	Teacher explanation and student seatwork	Willingness to adapt
Friendly Pedagogues	Control through performance and continuous activity	From appreciative to captive audience	From a rich array of resources to textbook medium	Discussion, Groupwork, individual study projects	Happy in resource-rich non-restrictive environments

In order to enhance reliability, my co-researcher and I sorted the cards independently, discussed and resolved discrepancies, then wrote the perspective descriptions. A colleague not involved in the research was given these descriptions and independently categorized a selected sample of the index cards. Inter-rater reliability was 0.78. Qualitative analysis of concept maps was conducted for the purpose of triangulation. Field notes, videotapes, and transcriptions of other interviews were also studied for this purpose. We asked colleagues who are teacher educators to comment on our emerging findings and conducted member checks with the teachers observed after they had completed the programme, most of whom have concurred with our analysis. The perspective descriptions we developed from this analysis are found in Table 1.

The videotapes of classroom teaching and transcriptions of the audiotaped follow-up interviews were analysed to explore the classroom validity of the teacher perspective framework (Bennett and Spalding, 1992). First we attempted to see if teaching behaviors in five areas differed according to teacher perspective without knowing the perspective that had been identified for the teacher. In later visits we looked for confirming and informing evidence of the primary teaching perspective. Classroom interactions were analysed in terms of five concepts: the teacher's classroom leadership style, typical student roles and behaviors, the nature of course content emphasized, the most prevalent instructional strategies, and the teacher's general response to the school context. From this analysis we further developed the teacher perspective descriptions to include the classroom actions shown in Table 2.

Seven Teaching Perspectives as a Color Wheel

As we sought a way to represent the seven perspectives visually, we wanted to avoid linear designs that might suggest a hierarchy or compartmentalization of the perspectives. Thus, we chose the color wheel as both a model and a metaphor for our general stance toward the perspectives.

Figure 2

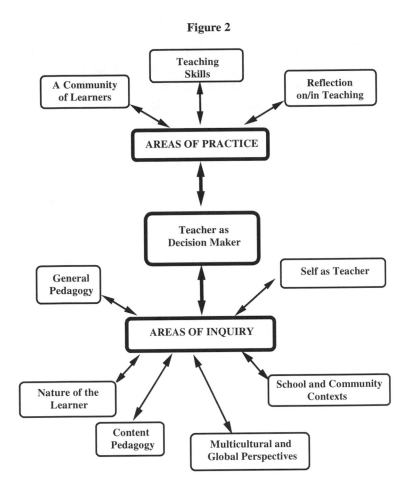

We found that perspectives, like colors, appear most often in "shades." Just as there are few "pure" colors, there are few "pure" perspectives. The color wheel is also intended to suggest a degree of flexibility among the categories. For example, an individual's fundamental perspective may be that of Empowerer, but she may at times act as a Nurturer or an Inculcator. A brief description of each perspective follows, together with elaboration of the color wheel metaphor.

Primary colors

Inculcators (RED) described the transmission of academic content knowledge as central to teaching. Several aspired to transmit "fundamental values" as well. They rarely referred to subject matter relevance, the nature of the learner, or teacher personality characteristics, such as enthusiasm or creativity. They often expressed a desire to "inspire" or be role models. Recurring themes were "control" and "discipline."

Empowerers (BLUE) described teaching in terms of social action or change. They saw academic knowledge as less important than, for example, learners becoming "self-actualized," or "gaining a sense of power and independence and control." Frequently committed to social causes themselves, they hoped to influence students to use political power, understand cultural pluralism, or accept multiple perspectives.

Friendly Pedagogues (YELLOW) defined teaching in terms of lesson preparation and teacher personality characteristics (e.g., "organization" or "enthusiasm"). An eclectic group in terms of educational goals and values, most expressed an aversion to "lecture" or to "being boring," and a preference for questioning and discussions. They stressed the importance of well-planned lessons and student feedback.

Secondary Colors

Facilitators of Thinking (VIOLET) identified thinking and lifelong learning as the principal goals of teaching. Although often scholarly themselves (and therefore similar to Inculcators), they de-emphasized the importance of content. Their emphasis on "critical thinking," "problem-solving," and "learning how to learn" brought them close to the Empowerer perspective, but their recurring focus was cognitive rather than social.

Nurturers (GREEN) perceived teaching primarily in terms of interactions with students. They defined good teachers as "open and responsive," "flexible," and "attainable." Because they emphasized the development of the learner and expressed concerns about children as "our future," they resembled Empowerers. Because they de-emphasized academic knowledge, they resembled Friendly Pedagogues.

Friendly Scholars (ORANGE) shared with Inculcators an emphasis on the transmission of academic knowledge, but, like Friendly Pedagogues, they stressed teacher personality characteristics such as enthusiasm, humor, friendliness. Their transmissive view of learning was balanced by a desire to make knowledge relevant and learning fun.

Scholar Psychologists lie at the center of the wheel, representing the murky blend of colors that results from mixing red, violet, blue, green, yellow, and orange. This was the largest and least clearly defined group, who often displayed characteristics of other perspectives. Like Inculcators, they emphasized academic knowledge. Like Friendly Scholars, they wanted to make knowledge relevant. To do this, they often planned elaborate lessons, like Friendly Pedagogues. Like Nurturers, they wanted to be "sensitive" and "available" to students. They were distinguished, however, by several characteristics. They tended to point out relevance in terms of students' future rather than present lives. They used psychological language in describing students, e.g., "understanding the nature of adolescent development." They saw themselves as counselors to students, willing to listen to their problems but not to become personally involved in them.

The Teacher Perspective Framework as a Tool for Reflection: Three Illustrations

The second phase of this research involved a series of interventions with 16 members of the TADMP's Fifth Cohort and 19 members of the Sixth Cohort. As director and an instructor in the TADMP my approach ranged from consultative to collaborative self-study (Schön, 1991). I designed a series of interventions that were intended to help students clarify their beliefs and assumptions about teaching and reflect upon their teacher perspectives during their 12 months in the TADMP. These interventions are outlined in Table 3.

When students entered the TADMP in June they were interviewed about their beliefs about teaching and aspects of their educational history, taught an unstructured lesson in the microteaching lab, and completed a concept map according to the procedures used with the first four cohorts.

Table 3
Interventions to Initiate or Maintain Teacher Reflection

Early June ....   Autobiographical interview
                             Concept mapping
                             Microteaching reflections

Late July ....   Introduction to color wheel
                             Concept mapping
                             Microteaching reflections

Late August ....   Color wheel with mentor teachers

Late November ....   Color wheel reflections on Ten Day Teach
                             Concept mapping
                             Reflective interview

Late January ....   Color wheel and student teaching anticipations

Late March ....   Color wheel reflections on student teaching
                             Reflective interviews

Late May ....   Color wheel reflections on student teaching
                             Concept mapping
                             Concept map interview
                             Teacher perspective focus groups

I analysed these data sources and identified the teacher perspective that seemed most appropriate for each student. The task was easy in most cases but I felt reassured when, although I had not revealed my choice to them, most students later selected the same perspective for themselves as I had.

The next intervention was an introduction to the *Color Wheel* as a framework for understanding teacher perspectives. During a 2–3 hour seminar I first explained the *Color Wheel* using colored overheads, Tables 1 and 2, and numerous examples of teacher beliefs and classroom practice. Next the students worked in small groups to identify the teacher perspectives in 7 case studies of teachers from previous TADMP perspective inquiry (Bennett and Spalding, 1992). Finally they identified their own primary perspective using the guidelines found in Appendix A. About 6 weeks later the seminar was repeated with their mentor teachers during an orientation retreat. The *Color Wheel* was again used as a catalyst for reflection in mid-autumn after the Ten Day Teach and at several points during the spring semester of student teaching.

The three illustrations that follow show how the *Color Wheel* can enhance self examination and growth during the beginning phases of becoming a teacher. In the third example, possibilities for strengthening partnerships between student and mentor teachers are also brought out.

The Case of Ronald

The son of a nursing home worker and factory worker, Ronald grew up in a close-knit family that emphasized education and hard work. After obtaining a degree in industrial engineering from a Big Ten university, Ronald took a job as a teacher at a Christian school "because they needed somebody who was proficient in math." Although he enjoyed teaching Ronald left the classroom after one semester to work with a major company, realizing that it was a high risk as well as a high paying one... When the economy slumped Ronald lost his job along with "many other supervisors, engineers, and plant workers." An intelligent, dynamic African-American male with exceptional interpersonal skills, Ronald received numerous job offers in his field and he pursued business and engineering for several years. However, after learning about the TADMP he decided to follow his deepest personal convictions and made a career change into teaching.

Ronald's autobiographical interview and initial concept map of teaching strongly indicated the Friendly Scholar perspective. According to Ronald, "A good teacher cares about his or her students. Good teachers have a strong knowledge of what they are teaching, and the ability to get this information across. A good teacher is organized and sets a good example." Indeed, he was the personification of the Friendly Scholar in the lessons he developed and taught in the education lab, using synectics, humor and personal charisma to teach math concepts.

When Ronald was introduced to the *Color Wheel of Seven Teacher Perspectives* he saw himself "most like the Empowerer, with Nurturer second and Friendly Scholar third." He wrote that he was an Empowerer because "I have a definite desire to build self esteem in students. I have a definite agenda of global values that I want to get across, possibly interwoven with math problems. Second, I see myself as a Nurturer because I plan to have caring, warm relationships with my students. Thirdly, I see myself as a Friendly Scholar because in teaching math the students must learn the content (for college entrance and the next course requirements) and I love to make learning fun and help students see the relevance. It is the Friendly Scholar that will be seen most in my actual teaching." Ronald wrote that the Inculcator seems LEAST like him because, "Emphasizing knowledge without showing the relevance would be hard for me. Not seeing how something applied to my life was one of my biggest challenges for learning."

During the retreat with mentor teachers, Ronald again identified the Friendly Scholar as most like him. He wrote, "I feel that academic knowledge is crucial in teaching and want students to feel learning is fun and applicable in the real world." As previously, he saw the Inculcator as least like himself, and wrote, "I had teachers like this and felt they were boring. Learning being fun when possible is important!"

Ronald's fall practicum took place in two advanced high school math classes where academic achievement was emphasized. At the conclusion of his Ten Day Teach, Ronald again identified primarily with the Friendly Scholar perspective. He explained, "Emphasis on academic knowledge and teacher personality characteristics were big in my teaching experience. I wanted the students to like what they learned from me. One of the most thrilling aspects of teaching during the 10 days was that of connecting the material to the real world. This also seemed to grab the students."

Thinking back to his predictions about how an understanding of his teacher perspective might affect his school practicum experience he wrote, "I really felt at first my teacher also was a Friendly Scholar, and so did she. This was not totally the case. She was very friendly and good but the core subject matter was too important to be interrupted by many connections to the real world or anything else." He went on to say that his Friendly Scholar perspective "hindered my enjoyment of the teaching experience since I was placed or pushed more into an inculcator mode, control through authority, etc. Humor and innovation weren't smiled upon. This was a hard pill to swallow."

Asked if knowledge of his perspective helped him identify areas he needs to work on Ronald replied, "Yes. I need to be a Facilitator of Thinking as well. And with Friendly Scholars there is always a potential problem with discipline because students might try to take advantage of their friendly relationship with me."

With classroom teaching experience Ronald's affirmation of his Friendly Scholar perspective became stronger but it did not stifle his growth. Placed in a context that was more conducive to an Inculcator perspective Ronald understood the source of his disease. He accommodated to the demands of his high school experience but his basic perspective did not change. An understanding of his Friendly Scholar perspective helped him identify the source of his frustration without losing respect for his mentor teacher or developing doubts about his own teaching abilities. He was much happier in his middle school placement during student teaching where he could teach as a Friendly Scholar, with shades of the Nurturer and Empowerer. After Ronald's first six week in the classroom his mentor teacher wrote:

> Ronald has a very creative side as well as being very knowledgeable in the research on how students learn. He seeks to develop activities that engage his students in the learning process. Students who are musically inclined, which many students demonstrate in their ability to memorize songs, have enjoyed learning two "originals" by Ronald. To help two students learn properties, Ronald taught them songs and motions that would help them learn two mathematical properties. The motions actually gave meaning to otherwise very abstract ideas. Ronald sets the expectations for his classes with style, making students qualify as supervisors in a candy factory, engineer designers, or captains of a space craft bound for new worlds beyond our own that may take them into another dimension.

Students are required to work together and demonstrate quality in their work if they are to be rewarded or recognized by the end of the class period. Several students have been positively influenced by Ronald's high expectations and have made remarkable improvements. Ronald was so impressed with one student's new attitude toward learning he took the time to call the parents to share the "good news."

The Case of Audra

Growing up near a major industrial city in Pennsylvania, Audra is the granddaughter of Italian and Romanian immigrants. Like Ronald, she comes from a close-knit family that emphasized education and hard work. Her mother was a housewife and her father an electronics technician.

After graduating from a large midwestern university with highest honors in bio-chemistry, Audra took a job with a large pharmaceutical company where she worked for three years as a chemist. When the company moved her into an instructional role Audra discovered that she enjoyed teaching more than working in the laboratory and decided to make a career change into the teaching profession. Her classroom teaching in the TADMP schools is exemplary in the eyes of her mentor teachers and she has found her niche with middle schoolers.

When Audra was introduced to the *Color Wheel* she readily identified with the Scholar Psychologist as the teacher perspective most like her. "Content is really important!" she wrote. "Also the nature of the learner is important to being able to convey relevance. In my interview I remember discussing different types of learners and the importance of being able to teach so that different learners could understand." This dual emphasis on content and learners was also clearly evident in her initial concept maps about teaching.

Audra selected the Inculcator as the perspective that was LEAST like her. She explained, "Although I definitely feel that I emphasize academic knowledge and values I don't want to control through authority. I want control by interesting lessons. I don't want passive recipients but more active participants."

Thinking ahead about how understanding herself as a Scholar Psychologist might affect her school practicum experience Audra said, "It might help me be more in tune with other teachers' perspectives (especially my mentor teachers) and therefore know why they might present material in a different way than I would. Also it may help me to focus on the benefits of perspectives or things that I might want to do differently."

At the completion of her Ten Day Teach in two advanced high school biology classes Audra said, "I still feel that I am primarily a Scholar Psychologist but I am also much more of a Nurturer than I thought." Explaining her Scholar Psychologist perspective she wrote, "I tried to use examples in my circulatory and respiratory system units that related to the students. Also I would spend a lot of time revising or changing lessons to relate to different learners. I spent a lot of time after school thinking about how to reach different students."

Audra felt that her Scholar Psychologist perspective influenced her classroom decision making during the Ten Day Teach. "I gave my students many second chances. I wanted them to be successful. I remember talking to students after class to see why they weren't taking notes or participating. Also I had my students evaluate me at the middle and at the end of my Ten Day Teach and I revised my lesson plans to try to incorporate their suggestions. First I told them about constructive feedback and then I let them evaluate me. They had a lot of helpful suggestions."

In rethinking her predictions about how an understanding of her Scholar Psychologist perspective might affect her school practicum experience Audra said, "Surprisingly, content was less important than getting students interested and involved in learning. I was much more concerned that the students understood risk factors of heart disease and respiratory disease which would affect them in life than knowing the names of the four chambers."

Like Ronald, Audra identified the Facilitator of Thinking as a perspective she would like to incorporate into her teaching. "I would like to work on facilitation of thinking," she wrote. "I feel that is extremely important and it would help keep students interactive."

It is clear that Audra views her classroom teaching through the Scholar Psychologist lens and she is confident and insightful in her self reflections. At the same time Audra is aware of alternative perspectives and uses the *Color Wheel* as a critical tool for effective classroom decision making. After her first week of teaching she sought "constructive criticism" from her students to help her improve her lessons.

The Case of Maria and Diane: Compatible Perspectives Between Student and Mentor Teachers

The daughter of a primary school speech pathologist and a university professor, Maria grew up in a midwestern university town. Reflecting back on her school experience she felt it was mainly positive, but uninspirational. Until college she was "almost always the only student of color" and was exposed to a traditional mainstream curriculum that did not include the history and culture of "the three different nationalities" in her background. However, her family intervened and was influential in helping Maria develop a strong sense of ethnic identity and self esteem. She explained, "I always had my parents who were teachers and who were very inspirational. I was taught at school and then I would come home and be taught a second time because my culture wasn't taught in school and because I come from a multicultural background....It was very important because my parents and grandparents wanted me to know their cultures in addition to the other cultures which represent America. This was an important issue to my family when I was growing up."

Maria entered the TADMP after completing her BA degree with a major in English and a minor in Afro-American studies at a Big Ten university. The teaching profession attracted her because it is "The best way I could find to deal with the critical issues our nation is facing...More than ever children and young people are definitely a major factor in solving our nation's problems. My contribution, the only place I could really see that fit comfortably, and what felt right, was teaching."

The perspective revealed through Maria's initial interview and concept map was classic Empowerer. In her mind the most important goal of teaching was the "empowerment" of students. In teaching, she said, "one of the most important things is to do your job, to teach your subject area, but to make sure when you are gone that the students really have knowledge and skills for themselves. No dependencies. Teaching means being sure that they can think for themselves and are encouraged in their own learning process." Her first concept map of teaching emphasized "Learning to grow, to stretch limits, and appreciate differences among the whole; global awareness and understanding, and craftwork — a word used in terms of the Native American idea of finding one's calling."

Not surprisingly, Maria chose the Empowerer as one of the two perspectives that seemed MOST like her. She explained, "I believe that I would fall into an area that is the combination of an Empowerer and a Nurturer. The reason I feel this is because I feel compassion for students, but more than anything I feel that students should be empowered and in control of their own sphere of learning." She decided that the Inculcator was least like her, "Although I would stress that I can see facets of all of these within my own personal teaching style. I feel there is too much isolation and structure (in Inculcators) which adds up to me to a sense of rigidness and 'control.' I feel controlling behavior is unhealthy and sometimes abusive towards students — it leaves them out of their own sense of learning."

As Maria thought about how an understanding of her teacher perspective might affect her school practicum experience she wrote, "I feel that a weakness of an Empowerer/Nurturer would be a complete lack of structure and resistance to school/curriculum requirements. The benefits, however, would be promoting a love for learning, facilitating empowerment, and enjoying my own working experiences." After her Ten Day Teach in a middle school where she taught an original unit on multicultural short stories she wrote, "I think that having too strong an identification with your perspective is not a good idea. It could limit you." Later she explained that, although her fall practicum experience had been successful and enjoyable, she worried about her ability to plan and organize for student teaching. She viewed Empowerers as being creative but lacking structure and organization, at times.

Maria's mentor teacher for student teaching, Diane, also included the Empowerer as one of her primary teacher perspectives. She wrote, "I would say Scholar Psychologist in most classes, but Empowerer in my poetry class." With over 20 years of experience, Diane explained how her perspective has affected her classroom decision making. Speaking as a Scholar Psychologist, she said, "I try to connect with each student each day, but tend to maintain some distance. I design lessons that demand student participation and that are based on content." Thinking about her poetry class she believes that "success becomes empowerment." Her students see themselves as poets, give poetry readings and plan to continue writing poetry.

Asked how an understanding of teacher perspectives might affect her work with Maria during student teaching she wrote, "Seeing how styles vary will help me see that the same goals can be achieved in different ways. I can see how different styles can affect students and their feeling about the class." Maria and Diane agreed that neither one of them accepted a single teacher perspective category, that "[Which perspective dominates] depends on what we are teaching. The subject and students make a difference." They also agreed that they both emphasized empowerment and that they both tended to be nurturing in varying degrees. They felt that they would probably want similar results and would both be flexible enough to shift perspectives, but they worried that they might *assume* they shared opinions and would need to communicate to avoid misunderstandings and erroneous assumptions.

Empowerers and Nurturers have been rare in the TADMP, and along with Inculcators, have had the most difficulties during student teaching and the first years of teaching. In past years TADMP Empowerers like Maria who hold strong views on social, cultural, and political issues and who wish to foster awareness and activism among their students have often become frustrated or alienated in school contexts that did not enable them to translate their beliefs into practice. Thus a mentor/student teacher partnership between two Empowerers was especially interesting.

Maria began her student teaching with a unit she created for Diane's fifth and sixth period English classes, "Exploring The Diversity Around us and Within Multiculturalism and the Language Arts." Prior to my first visit to her classroom Maria told me that Diane was "a huge help" and she was finally "learning how to be organized and to structure her lesson plans." Furthermore, she had incorporated Diane's plans for the community's "diversity essay contest" sponsored by *the Commission for Human Rights and Multicultural Understanding*. The unit also reflected the multicultural perspectives emphasized in the TADMP as well as Maria's own creativity and beliefs about teaching. She was comfortable and effective as she engaged her students in serious discussions about prejudice and racism, and she was deeply interested in her students' work. She used cooperative teams to implement her writers' workshop and implemented theories stressed in the TADMP such as multiple intelligences (Gardner, 1994) and strategic teaching (Jones 1988). Maria's biggest frustration was with some of the students who did not put forth their best effort, but overall her unit was highly successful and several of her students were selected to compete in the local essay contest.

At the end of her Ten Day Teach, Maria wrote, "I wasn't sure how on target I was about my perspective. What happened was that my teaching experience confirmed and reaffirmed what kind of perspective I fit into." Maria became aware of her strengths and weaknesses as an Empowerer/ Nurturer and took steps to correct her weak areas prior to her student teaching. She worked hard to develop more structure for her students and to better organize her teaching plans. Both of Maria's mentor teachers, an Empowerer/Scholar Psychologist and a Friendly Pedagogue, affirmed her Empowerer perspective by allowing her to develop lessons that were consistent with her beliefs about teaching. They also helped her improve in areas of weakness, in large part because Maria recognized her weaknesses in the Empowerer/Nurturer case studies and sought their help. This request for help is a necessary ingredient for successful mentor-mentee relationships and has contributed to her rapid growth as a teacher.

Discussion

Ronald, Audra and Maria exemplify the Friendly Scholar, Scholar Psychologist and Empowerer perspectives held by many of their peers.

Among the 35 teachers in the Fifth and Sixth cohorts, there were 6 Friendly Scholars, 7 Scholar Psychologists, 4 Empowerers, and 2 Empowerer/Nurturers. Reflecting a pattern that is evident across the six TADMP cohorts since 1988, Empowerers and Nurturers tend to be women, Friendly Scholars tend to be men, and Scholar Psychologists (like the remaining four perspectives) are not associated with gender differences. Six of the eight African-American male TADMP teachers identify with the Scholar Psychologist perspective, while the African-American women identify primarily with the Scholar Psychologist or Empowerer/Nurturer perspective.

Like other Friendly Scholars, Ronald stresses academic knowledge, connects it to the personal lives of his students, and makes learning "fun" through humor, enthusiasm, and creative demonstrations.

Audra also stresses academic knowledge and makes connections with her students' lives. However, like other Scholar Psychologists, her emphasis is on learning that is important for their future (more than personal) lives and she incorporates her knowledge about learning theory and adolescent development into her instructional planning.

Like other Empowerers, Maria has developed a deep commitment to social justice and believes that school can and must make a difference in solving social issues. While her lessons are based on scholarly knowledge, she emphasizes the personal development of her students' creative expression and social values. Unlike most TADMP Empowerers, Maria's desire to create and implement a multicultural curriculum has been supported by her mentor teacher.

Audra, Ronald, and Maria also exemplify aspects of the career change teachers who are attracted to programmes such as the TADMP. Most have resigned from higher paying jobs and enter the teaching profession with strong personal commitments.

This strong commitment does not make them more amenable to reflection, however. A major component of the TADMP has been the encouragement of self reflection on teaching practice through auto-biographical interviews and essays, reflective journals, concept mapping, stimulated recall interviews, discussion of "critical incidents" generated during student teaching, and "action research." Our students have greeted these strategies with varying degrees of enthusiasm. Some regard reflective journals as busy work while others become deeply involved, some look forward to stimulated recall interviews while others find them overly restrictive, most detest concept mapping yet are thrilled at the changes they see in themselves over time, and most are unable to carry out action research projects during student teaching. None of this is surprising, given the intensive nature of a 12-month programme like the TADMP.

After the *Color Wheel of Teacher Perspectives* was developed in 1991 and we began to use it during follow up interviews to our classroom visits of TADMP graduates, the teachers often told us that they wished they had learned about their perspective early on in the programme. This reaction encouraged me to use the *Color Wheel* as a tool to initiate and nurture on teaching, there-by strengthening their professional preparation and classroom practice.

The development of wise decision making capabilities is at the heart of becoming an effective teacher. In the words of Brubacher, Case, and Reagan (1994, p. 18), "Good teaching requires reflective, rational, and conscious decision making." Teachers must be able to justify their decisions and actions and in doing so they cannot rely on "instinct alone or on prepackaged sets of techniques." Instead, a teacher "must think about what is taking place, what the options are...in a critical, analytic way....The teacher must engage in **Reflection** about his or her practice, just as the physician must reflect about the symptoms and other evidence presented by a patient."

Building on the work of John Dewey (1933, 1938) and Donald Schön (1988), teacher educators are increasingly interested in approaches based on "reflection" and "reflection on, in, and for practice" (e.g., Tremmel, 1993; Johnston, 1992; Lampert, 1985; Duckworth, 1986; Clandinin and Connelly, 1990). A growing number of researchers argue that we can strengthen the impact of teacher education programmes by focusing on prospective teachers' initial beliefs about teaching, teaching metaphors, and background knowledge about teaching (e.g., Bullough, 1991, 1992, 1995; Britzman, 1986; Shuell, 1992). Other researchers conclude that sustained reflection on teaching can help beginning teachers develop the rich pedagogical schemata that distinguish effective experienced teachers from novices (Berlinger, 1988). Although pedagogical schemata "are constructed naturally over time,...their development can be encouraged and supported by reflective practice....While good teaching does indeed depend on a strong experiential base, reflective practice can help speed up the development of such an experiential base in new teachers" (Brubacher, Case and Reagan, 1994, pp. 22–23). Given that development of pedagogical schemata and professional knowledge are essential components of the TADMP's theoretical framework, the idea that reflective practice can enhance the development of pedagogical schemata is intriguing. With the development of the *Color Wheel of Seven Teacher Perspectives*, reflection on and for teaching practice has become an integral part of the programme.

In "Zen and the Art of Reflective Practice in Teacher Education," Tremmel (1993) writes that many reflective teaching and teacher education programmes are limited by "technical and analytical views of reflective practice" (p. 434). He argues that these programmes would be enriched "through the incorporation of non-Western notions of reflection, particularly the Zen Buddhist tradition of 'mindfulness'" (p. 434). Drawing upon Donald Schön's concepts of "knowing-in-action," and "reflection-in-action" Tremmel is gently critical of the linear step-by-step approaches to reflective process based on technical rationality.

Over the past two years I have learned that the *Color Wheel* can be a means to initiate self-reflection and to develop what Tremmel calls "the art of 'paying attention' as a way of nurturing reflective practice" (p. 434). It helps teachers make explicit their assumptions about teaching and describes multiple perspectives from which teaching may be viewed. It encourages teachers to identify a primary perspective with which they feel most comfortable and to consider how their teaching might be enhanced by incorporating additional perspectives. By portraying the strengths and potential weaknesses of perspectives derived from the actual classroom instruction of beginning teachers very much like themselves, the *Color Wheel* gently suggests ways they may want to modify their perspectives in various school contexts, should they encounter problems. Having been taught to use the *Color Wheel* early in the TADMP they used it as a critical tool for reflection on practice during the Ten Day Teach and reflection for and in practice during student teaching.

The *Color Wheel of Seven Teacher Perspectives* provides the major framework I now use to initiate and sustain my students' reflections on their teaching. During classroom observations, for example, I try to view curriculum planning and interactive teaching from their primary perspective, rather than from my own, to help them tune into their strengths and build from there. Indeed, my OWN teaching seems to be improving as I develop greater insights into the strengths and potential limitations of MY primary teacher perspective.

Questions about the influence of primary perspective matches/ mismatches between student and mentor teachers were also explored in this research. Both mentor and student teachers were receptive to the *Color Wheel* and felt that it helped them understand their similarities and differences. During the Ten Day Teach and student teaching, an awareness of the perspective held by each partner proved to be more important than a match or mismatch. The advantages of a perspective match were evident with Maria and Diane. However, another situation where the student and mentor teacher selected the same primary perspective became so difficult that the student teacher was placed with a new mentor teacher. While an understanding of perspectives was helpful, particularly for the student teachers whose mentors differed in perspective, it could not make up for personality conflicts or lack of mentoring skill.

In conclusion, the *Color Wheel* provides a complex yet comprehensible way to reflect upon and discuss the multiple perspectives teachers hold. The seven teacher perspectives are presented in a non-judgmental way through seven teacher case studies that highlight the strengths and possible limitations of each. Consideration of these seven perspectives has helped my students gain a better understanding of themselves, their peers, their mentor teachers, and other teachers they meet as they enter the profession. The *Color Wheel* encourages a proactive approach to problem solving by framing problems in terms of potential mismatches between the teacher's perspective and conditions she or he encounters in school.

References

Barnes, H. L. (1987). The conceptual basis for thematic teacher education programmes. *Journal of Teacher Education*, 38(4), 13–18.

Bennett, C. & Powell, R. (1990). The development of professional knowledge schemata and teaching perspectives among career-change pre-service teachers: A study of resisters and non-resisters. Paper presented at the Annual Meeting of the American Educational Research Association, Boston, Mass.

Bennett, C. & Spalding, E. (1991). *Teaching perspectives held by pre-service and novice teachers in an alternative teacher education programme.* Paper presented at the Annual Meeting of the American Educational Research Association, Chicago, IL. (ERIC Document Reproduction Service No ED 335336).

Bennett, C. & Spalding, E. (1992). Multiple approaches for multiple perspectives. *Theory and Research in Social Education*, 20(3), 263–292.

Bennett, C. (1991). The teacher as decision maker programme: An alternative for career-change pre-service teachers. *Journal of Teacher Education.* 42(2), 119–130.

Berliner, D. C. (1987). Ways of thinking about students and classrooms by more and less experienced teachers. In J. Calderhead (Ed.), *Exploring Teachers' Thinking*, pp. 60–83. London: Cassell Educational Limited.

Beyerbach, B. A. (1987). *Developing a technical vocabulary on teacher planning: Pre-service teachers' concept maps.* Paper presented at the meeting of the American Educational Research Association, Washington, DC.

Beyerbach, B. A. (1988). Developing a technical vocabulary on teacher planning: Pre-service teachers' concept maps. *Teaching and Teacher Education*, 4(49), 339–357.

Borko, H., Livingston, C., McCaleb, J. & Mauro, L. (1988). Student teachers' planning and post-lesson reflection: Patterns and implications in teacher preparation. In James Calderhead (Ed.), *Teachers' Professional Learning*, pp. 65–83. Philadelphia: The Falmer Press.

Borko, H., Livingston, C., McCaleb, J. & Mauro, L. (1987). Student teachers' thinking and problem solving. Paper presented at the meeting of American Educational Research Association, New Orleans, LA.

Britzman, D. (1986). Cultural myths in the making of a teacher: Biography and social structure in teacher education. *Harvard Educational Review*, 56(4), 442–456.

Bullough, Robert V., Jr. (1991). Exploring personal teaching metaphors in pre-service teacher education. *Journal of Teacher Education*, 42(1), 43–45.

Bullough, Robert V., Jr. (1992). Beginning teacher curriculum decision making, personal teaching metaphors, and teacher education. *Teaching and Teacher Education*, 8(3), 239–252.

Calderhead, J. (Ed.) (1987). *Exploring Teachers' Thinking*. London: Cassell Educational Limited.

Carter, K. & Doyle, W. (1987). Teachers' knowledge structures and comprehension processes. In J. Calderhead (Ed.), *Exploring Teachers' Thinking*, pp. 147–160. London: Cassell Educational Limited.

Clandinin, D. J. & Connelly, F. M. (1991). Narrative and story in practice and research. In D. A. Schön (Ed.), *The Reflective Turn: Case Studies In and On Educational Practice*. New York: Teachers College Press.

Clandinin, D. J., Davies, A., Hogan, P. & Kennard, B. (1993). Learning to Teach, Teaching to Learn: Stories of Collaboration in Teacher Education. New York: Teachers College Press.

Duckworth, Eleanor. (1986). Teaching as research. *Harvard Educational Review*, 56(4), 481–495.

Goodman, J. (1985). Field-based experience: A study of social control and student teachers' response to institutional constraints. *Journal of Education for Teaching*, 11(1), 26–49.

Grossman, P. L. (1992). Why models matter: An alternative view on professional growth in teaching. *Review of Educational Research*, 62(2), 171–179.

Johnston, S. (1992). Images: A way of understanding the practical knowledge of student teachers. *Teaching and Teacher Education*, 8(2), 123–136.

Kagan, D. (1992). Professional growth among pre-service and beginning teachers. *Review of Educational Research*, 62(2), 129–169.

Kennedy, M. (1991). *Research Genres in Teacher Education*, (Issue paper 91-1). Michigan State University, East Lansing: The National Center for Research on Teacher Learning.

Lampert, M. (1985). How do teachers manage to teach? Perspectives on problems in practice. *Harvard Educational Review*, 55(2), 179–194.

Leinhardt, G. & Greeno, J. G. (1986). The cognitive skill of teaching. *Journal of Educational Psychology*, 78(2), 75–95.

Livingston, C. & Borko, H. (1989). Expert-novice differences in teaching: A cognitive analysis and implications for teacher education. *Journal of Teacher Education*, 40(4), 36–42.

Merriam, S. B. (1988). *Case Study Research in Education: A Qualitative Approach*. San Francisco: Jossey Bass Inc.

Nespor, J. (1984). *Issues in the Study of Teachers' Goals and Intentions in the Classroom*. University of Texas: Research and Development Center for Teacher Education.

Norton, R. (1987). Divining and defining a problem space: An investigation of pre-service teachers' interactive thinking. Paper presented at the American Educational Research Association Meeting. Washington, DC.

Pajares, M. F. (1992). Teachers' beliefs and educational research: Cleaning up a messy construct. *Review of Educational Research*, 62(3), 307–332.

Posner, G. J. (1985). *Field Experience: A Guide to Reflective Teaching*. New York: Longman.

Reynolds, A. (1992). What is competent beginning teaching? A review of the literature. *Review of Educational Research*, 62(1), 1–35.

Roehler, L. R., Duffy, G. G., Conley, M., Herrman, B. A., Johnson, J. & Michelsen, S. (1987, April). Exploring pre-service teachers' knowledge schemata. Paper presented at the meeting of the American Educational Research Association, Washington, DC.

Rokeach, M. (1969). *Beliefs, Attitudes and Values*. San Francisco: Jossey Bass.

Schön, D. A. (Ed.) (1991). *The Reflective Turn: Case Studies In and On Educational Practice*, New York: Teachers College Press.

Short, E. C. (1987). Curriculum design making in teacher education: Policies, programme development, and design. *Journal of Teacher Education*, 38(4), 2–12.

Shuell, T. J. (1992). The two cultures of teaching and teacher preparation. *Teaching and Teacher Education*, 8(1), 83–90.

Shulman, L. S. (1986). Those who understand: Knowledge growth in teaching. *Educational Researcher*, 5(2), 4–14.

Shulman, L. S. (1987). Knowledge and teaching: Foundations of the new reform. *Harvard Educational Review*, 57(1), 1–22.

Shulman, L. S. & Sykes, G. (1986). *A National Board For Teaching? In Search of a Bold Standard. A Report for the Task Force on Teaching as a Profession*. New York: Carnegie Corporation.

Smith, B. O. (1980). *A Design for a School of Pedagogy*. Washington, DC: US Government Printing Office.

Tamir, P. (1988). Subject matter and related pedagogical knowledge in teacher education. *Teaching and Teacher Education*, 4(2), 99–110.

Tremmel, R. (1993). Zen and the art of reflective practice in teacher education. *Harvard Educational Review*, 63(4), 434–458.

Wilson, S. M., Shulman, L. S. & Richert, A. E. (1987). 150 different ways of knowing: Representations of knowledge in teaching. In J. Calderhead (Ed.), *Exploring Teachers' Thinking*. London: Cassell Educational Limited.

Zeichner, K. M. & Tabachnick, B. R. (1985). The development of teacher perspectives: Social strategies and institutional control in socialization of beginning teachers. *Journal of Education for Teaching*, 11(1), 1–25.

Reflective Classroom Practice: Case Studies of Hong Kong Student Teachers

Ora W. Y. Kwo

Department of Curriculum Studies
School of Education
The University of Hong Kong
Hong Kong

Synopsis

This paper addresses the nature of reflective classroom practice in a setting where action research has been undertaken by both the student teachers and the teaching practice supervisor. It is based on a cross-case study of the processes through which student teachers learn to teach. Specifically, the analysis focuses on how student teachers reflect on their experiences in learning to teach. The data are based on student teachers' reported thoughts about their learning over a period of one year. The results contribute to the understanding of reflective classroom practice by highlighting first, student teachers' perceptions about learning to teach and second, their reviews on classroom practice. The discussion also adds to the literature on teacher development taken from the novice-expert research tradition. Accordingly, implications for curriculum development in teacher education are drawn.

Reflective Classroom Practice: Case Studies of Hong Kong Student Teachers

Ora W. Y. Kwo

Critical Issues in Learning to Teach
Meaning of Teaching Experience

A prominent theme in research on teacher development concerns expert and novice teaching. The terms "experienced", "effective" and "expert" have been used widely, in parallel to "probationer", "beginner" and "novice" in many studies. Emerging from the findings are the schema differences between expert and novice teachers: their prior knowledge (Calderhead, 1983; Housner and Griffey, 1985), their awareness of classroom events (Housner and Griffey, 1985; Carter et al., 1987; Peterson and Comeaux, 1987), their prediction of learning misconceptions (Borko and Livingston, 1989), and their concepts of routines (Doyle, 1979; Parker and Gehrke, 1986; Berliner, 1993). While it is reasonable to see teachers' schemata as developing with experience, experience should not be equated with expertise. Amongst the important questions is how novices develop their schemata during initial teacher education.

Within most teacher education programmes, teaching practice is an important component (Stones, 1987). In the teaching practice component of most courses, student teachers spend several weeks in schools where they are guided by tutors from the training institutions and commonly by on-site cooperating teachers. The guidance mostly consists of occasional observations by tutors or cooperative teachers, and their post-lesson comments. Much of the student teachers' time on extended practice is spent without guidance. Calderhead (1987) found that as most students were driven by concerns with assessment, they rarely experimented for effective instruction. They were also resistant to much of the specific feedback from college tutors. Calderhead showed that it was only towards the end of the field experience, when most student teachers knew that they could maintain control, did they become more willing to experiment. However, experimental lessons were rarely supervized.

The limited effects of the conventional practicum call for reconceptualization and reforms. Schon's (1983, 1987, 1991) perspectives on the nature of professional knowledge raises many questions about the meaning of classroom practice in teacher education. As emphasized by Calderhead (1991), learning to teach is different from other forms of learning in academic life: changing teachers' knowledge does not necessarily result in changes in their practice. Student teachers need to be assisted to reflect on their new roles as teachers. Research on reflective teaching should explore how student teachers develop new frames on which new understandings can be built. Furthermore, recent reform efforts are highlighted by partnership and school-based models (see e.g., Booth et al., 1990; McIntyre et al., 1993). To enhance the knowledge base for supervision, the meaning of practicum should be investigated from student teachers' perspectives.

Parallel to this concern, it is important to consider the mixed backgrounds of student teachers on entry to teacher education programmes. Research should generate new insights by exploring whether and to what extent former teaching experiences facilitate their acquisition of the meaning of practice.

The Nature of Reflections in the Practicum

Extended from Stones' (1987) concern for the lack of guidance in the conventional practicum are criticisms on the quality of guidance during the practicum. Alongside the recent trend in practicum which emphasizes theory-practice integration through reflections, many studies document the restricting impacts of supervisory guidance on learning to teach (e.g., Korthagen, 1988; Livingston, 1990; Ben-Peretz and Rumen, 1991). Despite the important arguments for reflections in learning to teach, student teachers do not appear to be readily engaged in significant reflections. Emphasis on reflective teaching by itself is no simple solution to problems in learning to teach. Innovations from an established institutionalized structure naturally create tensions which render the goals difficult to attain. For instance, as pointed by Livingston (1990), student teachers need integrated support from cooperating teachers and supervisors to engage in reflective practice. Student teaching as currently structured provides little time or encouragement for reflection. Alternatively, student teachers' stage of development should be considered. Berliner (1988) argued that novice teachers may have too little experience to reflect on until extensive classroom experience has been acquired. McNally et al. (1994, p. 229) further queried whether it is actually in service that teachers may have a greater need for the input from higher education in promoting reflection, and in re-visiting early experiential learning. In a recent study, the author has noted that, at least in her sample, student teachers develop over time by engaging in more active reasoning and evaluation (Kwo, 1994a). However, despite the increased awareness of problems, generally no major decisions were reached to tackle the problems and alter directions of the lessons. Without suggesting that self-reflection is inappropriate for novice teachers, it is important to be cautious about the ambitious expectations of initial teacher education. There is a need to reach realistic expectations of student teachers from an understanding of the complicated demands on them.

Learning to teach requires the ability to face multi-faceted demands other than those in the cognitive domain. For readiness in learning to teach, student teachers have to move beyond initial concerns, such as socialization into traditional roles (Calderhead and Robson, 1991; McCullough and Mintz, 1992). Teachers should be helped to formulate their individual selves and personal agendas. There are affective domains concerning their coping with their own emotions, such as described in studies of Szpiczka (1990), Woods (1991), Cole and Knowles (1993). There are also social dimensions concerning their communication with cooperating teachers (see Clift et al., 1994) and interpersonal relationships with their pupils (see Kagan and Tippin, 1991). Regarding these competing demands on the student teachers, teacher educators should be sensitive to the developmental stage of student teachers. As critically reporting the alarming effects of an innovative programme which incorporate the latest ideas about reflective pedagogy, Eisenhart, Behm and Romagnano (1991) concluded that students might have been forced to need certain strategies the relevance of which they could not see. Therefore, teacher education should be more sensitive to the needs of novices in order to help them leave the programme with more confidence in the skills they have acquired and a clearer view of the identities they are striving for. The research literature has converged in a general concern to pursue an understanding of how student teachers learn to teach.

The Frame of the Study

The study reported here arises from a concern to narrow the gap between those who primarily do research and those who primarily deliver teacher education. Teacher education is viewed by the author as both a situation for studying learning patterns of student teachers and a factor influencing those learning patterns. It is important to acknowledge the potential for constructive innovations through teacher educators' own integration of research and practice. The context of this study is a teacher education programme which basically follows the academic tradition, with theoretical foundations of professional education, some academic preparation in the subjects that the students are to teach, and the student practicum. The researcher was the supervisor of the student teachers under investigation. Acquiring the spirit of the reflective practitioner in pursuing personal knowledge for her professional role, she attempted to integrate her action research with reforms in curriculum design (Kwo, 1994).

By considering the critical issues in learning to teach, this study focuses on the understanding of student teachers' reflective classroom practices. It aims to investigate the patterns of learning to teach by adopting a "second-order" research perspective (Marton, 1981). Specifically, it addresses the question concerning how student teachers reflect on their experiences in learning to teach. By comparing the reviews of three student teachers with former teaching experience and three student teachers with absolutely no teaching experience at all, the study is able to explore the significance of former teaching experience on readiness for reflections. The analysis focuses on the student teachers' perceptions about learning to teach and their reviews on classroom practice.

Design and Methodology
Setting and Sample

It is often assumed that student teachers in pre-service teacher education programmes have little or no teaching experience. However, this assumption is not always valid. In Hong Kong, graduates are permitted to teach without professional qualification in teaching. However, the initial start and ceiling points of their salary are lower than those of professionally qualified teachers, and many such graduates choose to gain training after entering the profession. This can be done either part-time or full-time. The dichotomy between in-service and pre-service training is therefore blurred; while many participants in the full-time programmes have no teaching experience, others have substantial experience.

The researcher collected a full set of data from 15 student teachers, all of whom are majoring in English language teaching, in the one-year full-time Postgraduate Certificate of Education Programme at the University of Hong Kong. As shown in Table 1, the majority of students were female, and two-thirds of them were native speakers of Chinese. Despite these dominant features, however, the group was heterogeneous in terms of geographic origin, age and teaching experience.

In order to explore the significance of former teaching experience on their reflections, six students were selected for data-analysis. These were the three with most and the three with least teaching experience. The students in the first group are called Susan, Juliet and Heidi, while those in the second group are called Sophie, Joy and Rita (Table 1).

Table 1
Personal data of student teachers

Student Teacher	Gender	Native Language	Origin	Age	Year of T. Exp
1	F	English	England	28	3+PT
2 Sophie	F	Chinese	Hong Kong	22	0
3	F	Chinese	Hong Kong	34	1
4	F	English	Pakistan	42	2+PT
5 Susan	F	Tagalog	Philippines	26	4
6	M	English	Scotland	24	2+PT
7	F	Japanese	Japan	37	PT
8	M	Chinese	Hong Kong	22	PT
9	F	Chinese	Hong Kong	40	PT
10	M	Chinese	Hong Kong	27	2
11 Juliet	F	Chinese	Hong Kong	42	5
12 Joy	F	Chinese	Taiwan	25	0
13	F	Chinese	Hong Kong	41	2
14 Heidi	F	Chinese	Vietnam	30	5
15 Rita	F	Chinese	Hong Kong	22	PT

Structure of the Curriculum

The year's course was divided into three terms. The pattern in each term was as follows:

Term One

Term One was scheduled to provide three weeks of School Experience between two periods of course work on campus. The topics presented prior to the School Experience gave student teachers some basic background for practical teaching. Pedagogical knowledge in the teaching of language skills was introduced with attention to planning, teaching and evaluation.

Through the School Experience, the student teachers were acquainted with a classroom reality in which they could expand learner knowledge and apply the pedagogical knowledge and skills which they had been initially exposed in the course. In this way, they were prepared to pursue knowledge about teaching from practical experience.

After the School Experience, the students' pedagogical knowledge in the teaching of language skills was reviewed in relation to their content knowledge in various aspects of applied linguistics. Building into the skills in planning, teaching and evaluation were perspectives beyond lessons: curriculum design was considered with emphasis placed on the critical use of textbooks and material development.

Term Two

Course work in Term Two focused mainly on the preparation for a seven-week period of Main Teaching Practice. The student teachers were prepared with skills in observation, analysis, and evaluation of video-recorded lessons. These skills were essential prerequisites for peer coaching during the Main Teaching Practice, which demanded capability in problem-solving and communication. The course work before the Main Teaching Practice concluded with an examination in which individuals had to independently analyze a video-recorded lesson after viewing it together in class.

During the Main Teaching Practice, alongside the further acquisition of learner knowledge and application of pedagogical knowledge and skills, each student teacher was engaged in the expansion of his or her teaching repertoires and meta-cognition through conducting a classroom action-research project as the final assignment. The supervisory school visits provided support on both action research and classroom teaching.

Term Three

Term Three covered areas in relation to the student teachers' general progress. Forums encouraged reflection on the Main Teaching Practice. The schedule also included student teachers' presentations of classroom action research, as well as on teachers' global responsibilities and professional development.

Data Sets

Data were collected throughout the year, both during course work on university campus as well as when the student teachers were working in schools for teaching practice. Three major sets of data were generated from the student teachers: their written reviews of their learning experiences during the course; their action research assignments; and videotapes of lessons recorded at the beginning as well as at the end of teaching practice. From the three sets of data, patterns in learning to teach could be studied to illustrate three factors: (i) student teachers' reflections on learning experiences, (ii) their development of personal knowledge about teaching and (iii) their actual development in classroom practice.

The study will eventually aim to reach a triangulation of three sources of data. However, this paper focuses on student teachers' reflections on learning experiences by analyzing the first data-set. In particular, the analyses focus on their perceptions about learning to teach and their reviews on classroom practice.

Student teachers' written reviews of their learning experiences were collected at six points during the course: on entry, before and after two blocks of reaching practice, and at the end of the course. The specific questions to which they responded are listed as follows:

1. On entry to the course:
   What do you see as essential qualities of a teacher which you are striving to develop?
2. Before the School Experience:
   From the course, what do you see as new learning experience to you?
   What are your major concerns/worries about the forthcoming teaching practice?
3. After the School Experience:
   What insights about teaching have you gained from the teaching practice, and in what ways have you developed as a teacher?
   What are the major problems you have encountered, and what are the strategies you have adopted to cope with these problems?

4. Before the Main Teaching Practice:
   (same questions as "Before the School Experience")
5. After the Main Teaching Practice:
   (same questions as "After the School Experience")
6. At the end of the course:
   From your perspective, how far have you developed yourself over
   the course in the essential qualities of a teacher which you have
   been striving to develop? If necessary, elaborate or modify your
   views about the essential qualities of a teacher.

Data Analysis

The data were analyzed in an interactive process of data reduction and
verification (Miles and Huberman, 1984, pp. 21–23). Following that, the
phenomenographic method (Marton and Saljo, 1984) was used. The
analysis emphasized an objective review of the data without any imposition
of theories. The theoretical perspectives were considered only after an
intrinsic understanding of the original data was established. Case descriptions
were examined repeatedly until some apparent categories emerged from the
data. These categories were set up tentatively as hypotheses to check all
the scripts again and again. The categories were revised, when they were
found to be unaccountable for some data. The whole process of data
analysis was iterative and interpretative. Finally, general patterns were
drawn about time changes and variations between the experienced and the
inexperienced student teachers. Although there were some overlapping of
common categories shared by the two groups of student teachers, collectively
the data displayed some specific trends in the changes that took place in
learning to teach. The report of findings which follows begins with a
summary of the data, and then turns to discussion, which is illustrated with
some quotations from student teachers' reported thoughts.

Table 2
Experienced student-teachers' perceptions about learning to teach

SUSAN	HEIDI	JULIET
On Entry: Perception of Essential Teacher Qualities		
* Able to develop student-centred teaching * Character molder	* Help academic and spiritual development * Humble, honest, consistent	* Keen to learn * Positive towards students * Honest, enthusiastic, dedicated
Before School Experience: Perceived New Learning		
* Keen to try out some strategies and check its effectiveness	* Realized my problem in the past: too much teacher talk * Fascinated by the student centred method	* Aware of previous mistakes: too much teacher talk, spent too much time marking, demanded total silence from pupils
After School Experience: Insights and Development		
* Learned to manage mixed ability students * Learned to motivate students by positive feedback * Saw the need to develop a flexible teacher personality	* Realized there is a long way to go to get rid of the old habit of talking too much * Tried out various strategies related to student-centred teaching	* Realized some principles of teaching generalizable for different student levels * Tried out various strategies related to student-centred teaching
Before Main Teaching Practice: Perceived New Learning		
* Realized the shortcomings in previous teaching and wanted to make up for them * Hoped to make a quality leap in teaching methods	* Concentrated on reducing teacher talk * Continued using various strategies related to student-centred teaching	* More confident * Keen to replace rooted thinking from the past with current thinking * Saw the connections between different courses * Improved learning ability
After Main Teaching Practice: Insights and Development		
* Enjoyed developing strategies in teaching * Able to introduce preliminary activities to motivate students successfully * Used a lot of evaluation techniques to measure learning	* Able to plan for teaching * Able to foster a secure climate for learning * Realized that learners are what the teacher expects them to be	* Increased feelings of inadequacy * Able to apply into practice what has been learned from the course without disciplinary problems * Convinced of value of student-centred teaching
At the end: Evaluation of Self-Development		
* Confirmed the belief in student-centred teaching * Prepared to be a student-centred teacher	* Learned to be a facilitator * Confirmed the belief that students could learn even without non-stop teacher talk * Confirmed the belief that students could learn in many ways and modes	* Painful process in getting rid of the old ideas on traditional style of teaching * Expanded my teaching strategies and knowledge of subject matter * Grown into a better person

Table 3
Inexperienced student-teachers' perceptions about learning to teach

SOPHIE	JOY	RITA
On Entry: Perception of Essential Teacher Qualities		
* Not a commander but friendly and helpful * Knowledgeable * Teach systematically and efficiently * Fair grading system	* Patient and loving to students * Fluent spoken English * Good communication skills * Good explanation ability	* Enthusiastic in teaching * Care for students without prejudice * Prepare before lessons * Able to learn continually
Before School Experience: Perceived New Learning		
* Realized that the four skills could be taught in terms of a series of stages * Realized that English can be taught in a lively way, by using different teaching aids	* Realized teaching is a job of a lot of preparation and making assumptions about the learning process	* Changed my conceptions about teaching: not that easy * Realized the use of various techniques was essential for effective teaching * Teaching does not mean testing
After School Experience: Insights and Development		
* Treated students as friends, sisters; helped them but not punished them * Realized that students wanted more participation	* Important to be patient * Able to set up a reasonably good relationship with students	* Strengthened the belief that teachers play a vital role in students' growth * Realized that good relationship with students is important * Be flexible in teaching
Before Main Teaching Practice: Perceived New Learning		
* Learned to produce materials * Acquired techniques in observation * Learned to integrate the four language skills	* Teachers should help each other to improve teaching * More confident to give help to the partners * Not satisfied with the school reality: teachers unwilling to observe each other teach	* Realized the importance of integrated learning * Teachers must work very hard to make a lesson interesting
After Main Teaching Practice: Insights and Development		
* Important to be strict with students * Important to be patient * Should teach students how to behave	* Tried to make every lesson student-centred * Had some good interaction with learners * Observed and learned from peer teachers	* Had good rapport with students * Tried many activities * Got more organized * Learned to adjust teacher talk to students' levels * Learned from peers
At the end: Evaluation of Self-Development		
* Realized that diligence is an essential quality of a teacher * Learned to be patient * Avoid prejudice * Friendly with students	* Critical of myself * Uprooted my previous understanding about teaching * Found many interesting methods to motivate students * Learned to innovate ideas and modify them for teaching different groups of students	* Renewed enthusiasm in teaching * Able to set up good rapport with students

Findings

Perceptions about Learning to Teach

Student teachers' perceptions about learning to teach are summarized in Tables 2 and 3 respectively.

Changing Conceptions of Teaching

With some overlap between experienced and inexperienced student teachers, it is possible to trace similarities and differences in their conceptions of the essential qualities of a teacher. There seems to be a continuum from what a student might look for to a broader awareness of a teacher's professional competence and commitments to a societal role. Initially, it is natural that student teachers with no teaching experience tend to view teacher qualities from the learners' angle, as they themselves have come from many years of classroom experience as students. For instance, they used words like "fair", "friendly", "care without prejudices". In contrast, student teachers with teaching experience apparently began the course with a more sophisticated view about essential teacher qualities which lay beyond classroom instruction abilities, to the extent they were concerned with their personal qualities, and the facilitation of pupils' character development.

A major change which occurred over time concerned an awareness of the meaning of teaching in relation to learning. Teaching has been traditionally regarded as a transmission of knowledge, which may be what most student teachers experienced in their classrooms in the past as learners. According to this concept, fluent teacher talk and good communication skills were important qualities, and this understanding was especially apparent in initial reports by inexperienced student teachers. The course highlighted an alternative concept of teaching which emphasized the facilitation of learning, and most participants were challenged to reconsider the former concept of teaching. Susan was an exceptional case because of her previous educational and teaching experience, (she had been exposed to ideas about student-centred teaching in a short course prior to the P.C.Ed.

programme). She set off with a specific regard for student-centred teaching and concluded the course with confirmation of the value of this regard.

In cases of experienced student teachers like Heidi and Juliet, after only four weeks of course work they reported that they now realized that the problems they experienced in their earlier teaching were caused because the teaching had been teacher-centred. Subsequently, they repeated their concerns about having to eradicate their old thinking and habits to make way for teaching methods aimed at the facilitation of learning. Their established concept of teaching was dismantled, while they were open to reconstruction of a new one. Along a similar move towards more student-centred teaching, the concept of teaching amongst inexperienced teachers like Sophie, Joy and Rita apparently became more complicated over time. They realized that teaching is demanding, if it is to facilitate learning rather than testing learners' abilities. They also reported an expansion of their teaching repertoire by the consideration of a range of methods.

Some illustrations may help to show the change in conception of these teachers. Before the School Experience, Sophie remarked that she "never thought that English composition [could] be taught in class". While her previous English teachers might never have explicitly taught her how to approach the composing of English writing, it is possible that as a student she had never been aware of English composition procedures. Either possibility could change her concept of teaching from a simple to a more complicated one. Similarly, Rita's previous image of an English teacher was simply of one who was always busy with marking. Her report was most illustrative:

> "Drawing my former experience as a student, I suppose teaching English was not to be that difficult except the workload of marking. Teachers only need to go through the textbooks... the course makes me realize that the job of teaching English is not that easy."

Joy also reported seeing teaching as "a job of a lot of preparation and making assumptions about learning". Like the experienced teachers, the inexperienced student teachers also displayed conceptual changes. Their original concept of teaching might have been influenced by their observation of their former teachers. As critically reviewed by Joy,

"I have uprooted my understanding of teaching, which was planted in me long time ago as I was a secondary school student... many of the ways my teachers used to teach me were rubbish... I am glad to have begun to find many interesting methods to motivate and help students to learn."

With a different focus, Rita also mentioned her acquisition of a teaching schema:

"My enthusiasm before joining the course was strong, but it has become more concrete now, as supported by a teaching schema in my mind."

On entry to the course, except Susan all the experienced student teachers saw teaching as transmitting knowledge, whereas the inexperienced student teachers held a rather simplistic view about teaching. At the end of the course, having gone through their personal processes of learning to teach, both groups seemed to have adopted a more student-centred concept of teaching. In general they also reported an awareness of using different methods to facilitate learning.

Learning Processes in the Passage of the Course

Over the year differences between the experienced and inexperienced student teachers in their reviews of learning were apparent. The experienced student teachers were able to identify their problems, and hence the focus of learning, more specifically. With some developed schemata about teaching, they selected what they needed, and in different ways reached a higher level of concept and practice about flow to facilitate learning. In pursuing student-centred teaching, Susan reported her newly-acquired understanding of the teaching process:

"I realized the futility of preparing too many tasks if they do not help learners to understand what is supposed to be learned. Instead, I saw how important it is to be equipped with a direct but well-structured lesson plan designed to meet the cognitive styles and needs of the learners."

Heidi and Juliet were critical of their previous teaching styles, and hence, open to new alternatives. Having identified her problems in teacher talk, Heidi concluded that:

"Students can learn without my non-stop teacher talk — individually, in pairs as well as in groups. They need not be spoon-fed all the time... An effective teacher need not be a walking encyclopedia, but should be one who can facilitate and motivate the learners to learn by themselves."

Along a similar vein in challenging the self in pursuing changes, Juliet's reflections were most vivid:

"After five years of teaching, I have genuinely built up myself with a certain amount of confidence as well as a certain amount of prejudice. It took me almost a year to humble myself, to renew my mind and to refill my teaching life with some fresh ingredients."

Seeing alternatives through their reflective practice, both Heidi and Juliet made fundamental changes in their conception of teaching. While that might have been a slow and painful process, it was most encouraging to see the possibility that the established schemata of experienced teachers *can* be changed.

For the inexperienced student teachers, the initial teaching practice made them realize the complicated demands that exist in teaching, not something they could have understood when they were students. In contrast to experienced teachers, Sophie, Joy and Rita shared a more conspicuous concern for survival while undergoing teaching practice. Instead of applying the ideas they had encountered in the course, they tended to focus more on relationships with students. Compared to the experienced teachers, their practice of student-centred teaching was rather limited and *ad hoc*. Their shared concern for good rapport with their pupils was less specific with regard to pedagogical considerations. For instance, after the School Experience, Sophie described her insights in seeing the importance of student participation and friendly relationships with students, and then summarized what she had learned before the Main Teaching Practice in an itemized list (*see Table 5*). However, there was no elaboration on the meaning of the items. It is likely that her attention was scattered on the mechanics of teaching procedures, as taken from the notes of the course. Unlike her experienced counterparts she was not yet ready to be engaged in extensive reflection to sort out learning priorities.

It seems that given the two blocks of teaching practice which had exposed the inexperienced student teachers to the complicated reality of the classroom, the components for learning were too plentiful for them to select their priorities consciously. With Sophie's emphasis on diligence, Joy's espousing of new methods and criticism of the self, and Rita's renewed enthusiasm for teaching, they had all made some progress. Yet they all seemed to realize that there was a long way for them to go before they would achieve their goals of learning.

Reviews of Classroom Practice

The student teachers' reviews of classroom practice are summarized in Tables 4 and 5. Given the shared direction in conceptual change towards student-centred teaching (as analyzed previously), the study also traces how the student teachers viewed their own practice. The analysis turns to the changes in their focus of attention, identification of problems and strategies. Judging from individual cases, it was difficult to identify common patterns. However, patterns are revealed in comprehensive and repeated reviews of the data.

Focus of Attention

Emerging from the data on concerns and worries about teaching practice is a developmental trend over the course of learning to teach. This trend can be used to map the possible stages of learning. The inexperienced ones may cover the first part of the journey, whereas the experienced ones may cover the latter part.

1. Classroom management

Setting up the basic routines in teaching seemed to worry the new teachers most. The main concerns of Sophie, Joy and Rita before the School Experience were not pedagogically-related so much as how to deal with recalcitrant students, how to cope with students who might deliberately

Table 4
Reviews of classroom practice by experienced teachers

SUSAN	HEIDI	JULIET
Concerns before School Experience		
* Afraid there is not a wide range of audio-visual resources	* Whether I meet students' expectations * Discipline problems * Establish good relations with colleagues * Afraid to work with a difficult teacher-tutor	* No knowledge of students' background and school rules * Does the teacher-tutor have the same philosophy of teaching as mine? * How much can I apply what I have learned to real situations?
Problems and Strategies in School Experience		
* Assessment of teaching practice	* Afraid to teach a large class * Afraid that students are not so cooperative that 1 can't apply theory learned to practice	* Do not have the same worries as those before School Experience * How to make the Main Teaching Practice meaningful to me and students * Wish MTP can reinforce my commitment to teaching career
Concerns before Main Teaching Practice		
* Traffic noise outside classroom -- Used a microphone -- Repeated the important answers -- Used more eye-contact -- Used more individual, pair, group work to reduce teacher talk	* Teacher-tutor not friendly -- Listened to her negative comments without defence * Class teacher: negative about the students -- Ignored negative opinions -- Took a positive attitude -- Set to motivate students	* Took too much time to plan -- Focused on 2-3 objectives * Not enough time to cover what was planned -- Minimized teacher-talk -- Avoided repeating students' answers * Lower achievers were passive -- Talked to them during the lunch time * Not know how to assess their understanding of my teaching -- Got feedback from their facial expressions -- Made instructions clear and simple
Problems and Strategies in Main Teaching Practice		
* Coped with differences between Form Three and Form Six students -- Adjust teaching methods to students' differences in personality	* The teacher-tutor was too busy * Benefitted from the peer-coaching	* Students good at mathematics not motivated to learn English * Students had their own culture: make jokes all the time * Some students never handed in their homework -- Talked to them after class -- Established good relationship with them

Table 5
Reviews of classroom practice by inexperienced teachers

SOPHIE	JOY	RITA
Concerns before School Experience		
* How to break silence * How to deal with naughty students * How to build up friendly relations with students and teachers	* How to keep smiling even if students don't respond * How to assess students' understanding * How to cope with students' different levels and students who might challenge me on purpose	* Nervous when facing unfamiliar faces * My oral English may not be fluent
Problems and Strategies in School Experience		
* School was far away * Students' English was poor * School environment was noisy * How to arouse students' interest in learning English * How to deal with students who finish work faster and keep on talking * How to apply good teaching ideas to the students with low standard	* Too much work * How to treat adolescents properly without hurting them * How to learn more from peer partners without taking too much of their time	* Not enough time to prepare the lessons * Appreciate peer-coaching and how to get more help from the partner
Concerns before Main Teaching Practice		
* One girl hurt herself and two girls felt sick but refused to go to the sick room -- Stayed calm and tried to behave like a sister * Students spoke too softly to be heard -- Encouraged them to speak louder * Very upset about students' mistakes in their exercises: wondering if I am a good teacher	* Hard to meet the teacher - tutor's demand: teach in her ways -- Insisted on practising what I have learned from the course * Hard to finish a lesson as planned * Hard to assess students' understanding * Hard to explain everything in perfect English -- More preparation * Felt uncertain if I should show anger about students' lateness * How to organise the blackboard * Hard to tackle different levels	* Put too much into one lesson and the plan left unfinished * How to deal with passive and inattentive students * Students spoke too softly to be heard -- Repeated or rephrased their answers -- More pair or group work * Not experienced and inadequate knowledge -- Anticipate to learn more from the course
Problems and Strategies in Main Teaching Practice		
* Students' English was poor -- Gave them simple questions to answer * Traffic noise outside classroom -- Used a microphone -- Gave them written work * Boys and girls unwilling to work together -- Set games for them which required competition * Two boys daydreaming -- Got them to answer my questions	* How to develop dynamic interaction with students -- Memorized their names -- Treated different classes differently -- Established direct and active communication * Hard to give precise instruction -- Used cue cards with questions -- Refrained from speaking too fast and thought before responding to questions raised on the spot * Not enough time for marking -- Used weekends -- Introduced peer-checking	* Hard to recognise the students of three classes within seven weeks -- Got the seating plans of each class * Sometimes unable to spot the mistakes in students' oral English -- Improved my English: both listening and speaking * Time constraints: too much work pressure

challenge the new teacher, and even simply how to face unfamiliar faces. Interestingly, the experienced group did not focus so much on classroom management, though Heidi did express concerns regarding discipline.

2. *Self-image and relationship with colleagues*

Again, the concern for self-image and social relationships was related not so much to subject matter or pedagogy as to another aspect in basic survival. Worries about self-image were explicitly mentioned by Sophie:

> "I may be too young to be a teacher. I laugh easily, and behave like a girl. I am nervous about speaking in front of a class."

Similarly, Joy was concerned about her image, and wondered how she could keep smiling even at a lack of student response. On the other hand, experienced student teachers did not mention their self-image. Instead, both Heidi and Rita expressed their concerns regarding relationships with their colleagues, especially their teacher-tutors. Susan showed no concern regarding this aspect.

3. *Pedagogy*

The focus on pedagogy shows a concern for the applicability of teaching methods, use of materials and audio-visual resources. To experienced student teachers, this is a central concern. Even before the School Experience, Susan expressed her worry about the possible lack of audio-visual resources. By the time of the Main Teaching Practice, her concern had extended to assessment. The concern about "applying theory to practice" was mentioned by both Heidi and Juliet. Juliet's concern was particularly ambitious: she wanted to make her Main Teaching Practice so meaningful that it would reinforce her commitment to the teaching career. In contrast, the inexperienced student teachers' expressions of this concern were rather vague. As reviewed by Sophie after the School Experience,

> "What we have learnt is useful, but it may not be applicable to students of lower ability, they hate speaking in English. If we don't correct them, they will never know that they are wrong."

While her view may be considered simplistic, by then her focus had apparently gone beyond basic survival and had moved to the complexities in applying teaching methods.

4. *Learners and learning*

The concerns for learners and learning are also shared by both groups, although their responses to this concern were quite different. An instance can be drawn from their thoughts about learners' low standard. By the Main Teaching Practice, Sophie was concerned about learning, but felt rather helpless about the learners described by her teacher-tutor:

> "She told me that I have to teach a remedial class, and the students are very passive and most of them fail in a test... I fear that I would be disappointed, I recall how upset I was in the School Experience, when my students made lots of mistakes in their exercises."

It seemed that her limited practice did not lead her to a state of confidence in coping with this concern. In contrast, the response by an experienced student teacher, Heidi, to the similar encounter was very different. As reported by Heidi:

> "Without defence, I listened to my teacher-tutor's negative comments about the class. But then I ignored these comments, and took a positive attitude to motivate the students."

In her later experience, she concluded that "learners are what the teacher expects them to be", and she was pleased that the class considered to be the second worst actually improved a lot in response to her effort.

The Self in Relation to Problems

Focusing on the data on student teachers' identification of problems and coping strategies, it is possible to trace a pattern of their learning process: from passively tolerating environmental constraints to actively initiating changes. Again with some overlap, this trend revealed differences between the two groups. The inexperienced student teachers tended to identify problems as arising from the environment rather than from their personal abilities. Furthermore, the inexperienced student teachers reacted rather passively to environmental constraints, expressing very little of the power from within themselves. In contrast, the experienced ones were more ready to be critical of themselves and were able to identify personal weaknesses. They were also able to search within themselves for resources to initiate changes in the environment. The learning process seems to be characterized by a change in self in relation to problems. Apparently, personal maturity plays a part, as the process of learning to teach requires the student teacher to move from a learner role to a teacher role. During the School Experience, Sophie seemed to be daunted by numerous environmental problems concerning which she had little mention of coping strategies. Her overall query of whether she was "a good teacher" probably added to her sense of inadequacy. By the Main Teaching Practice, she was still bothered by non-pedagogical issues — such as the distance to the school, and the students' low standard of English. Nevertheless, she began to identify some pedagogical problems, and mentioned what she could do about them. This shift in the perception of the self in relation to problems showed her significant progress in learning to teach. Both Joy and Rita also shared this pattern in the move towards the search of strategies from within the self. In particular, Joy seemed to have made considerable progress. During the School Experience, she identified many problems, but had few coping strategies. In contrast, her Main Teaching Practice was completed with a rich exploration of strategies which focused on improvement of her interaction with students. Amongst the experienced student teachers' more active response to problems, Susan came up with multiple alternatives to deal with the noise outside the classroom, and Juliet reached for some depth in her rapport with students by trying to understand and accept their culture. The data demonstrated that by the end of the two blocks of teaching practice, the student teachers had acquired some clear changes in the ways they identified and responded to problems. While the progress was considerable for many, the teaching practice can only provide a start for them to see the growing strength in themselves in dealing with problems. There is a longer way, beyond the course, for further maturing, both personally and as a teacher.

Flexibility and Adaptability

Another feature of their learning emerging from the data on student teachers' identification of problems and coping strategies: a progress towards greater flexibility and adaptability. *Flexibility* refers to their responses to problems, whereas *adaptability* refers to their interaction with students. Some overall differences between the two groups can be identified: the experienced student teachers tended to be more flexible and more adaptable than the inexperienced student teachers. From different starting points, however, they showed a common direction in their progress.

In tackling the noise problem outside the classroom, Susan's considerations were multi-faceted, ranging from using more eye-contact to balancing teacher-talk with other learning activities. While using the microphone, she was also trying to deal with its constraint to her mobility within the classroom by reducing the reliance on teacher-talk and involving students in independent work in pairs or groups. Her flexibility was shown in the ways she searched for different strategies, while being aware of the conflicting nature of the chosen strategies, e.g. although a microphone could be used to tackle the noise problem, it presented another problem by restricting her interaction with students. Facing a similar problem, Sophie had a less elaborated response: apart from the use of a microphone, she resolved the noise problem only by giving students written work. In comparing flexibility, another example can be located in their relationships with teacher-tutors. During the School Experience, Joy handled her disagreement with her teacher-tutor through direct confrontation, which led to an unhappy relationship between them. Compared to Heidi's quiet work on alternatives (as discussed previously), Joy was not tactful, and lacked flexibility in reaching a compromise. This incident illustrated a new teacher's dilemma in dealing with competing demands. Often, when there is a lack of flexibility, a painful option has to be made in coping with both demands. Over the pedagogical strategies, Joy, however, made considerable progress in becoming more flexible. In order to improve her teacher-talk, she came up with different strategies, ranging from the use of cue cards, to a conscious effort to refrain from speaking too fast, allowing herself time to organise her response to impromptu questions.

Adaptability was more apparent in experienced student teachers who were rather observant of the differences between students. Susan gave a detailed description of her students:

> "I found Form Three students quite playful and talkative, while the Form Six students were very serious and quiet. They wanted to learn more about life. I included more games and discussions about teenagers in my Form Three class, but focused more on serious topics (e.g. friendship, communism etc.) in my Form Six class. I also had to change my personality, when going into a different class. I was very serious to my Form Six class, but more ready to crack jokes with my Form Three class."

In her development of a warm rapport with students, Juliet faced an unexpected dilemma in finding that the students were too casual with her and she felt threatened. However, she decided that she had to "develop a stronger sense of humour and become more adaptable to their culture in order to minimize the generation gap". That provided another illustration of the adaptability of an experienced student teacher. Although in less depth, inexperienced student teachers also considered students' characteristics in the Main Teaching Practice. Rita was conscious of the importance of recognizing students personally, even though she had to take up three classes, and thus had little contact time with each class. Joy mentioned "designing tasks to channel the students' energy and modifying activities according to the levels of students". At different points in their process of learning to teach, both groups of student teachers seemed to demonstrate more adaptability over time.

Former Teaching Experience and Readiness for Reflections

The findings of this study add to the literature on student teachers' professional learning. The meaning of learning from course work and practicum was drawn from student teachers' perspectives. In particular, by analyzing the differences between experienced and inexperienced student teachers, the paper highlights the significance of former teaching experience for various aspects of student teachers' reflective classroom practice.

Although the student teachers with no former teaching experience did not enter the learning process with such developed teaching schemata as their experienced counterparts, they did have some entry perspectives about teaching which were challenged during the course. Equally, rather than merely expanding the existing schemata, the experienced student teachers had to get rid of some old ideas in order to make space for changes. The course on which this study was based was designed to address the critical issues about training effects. Through engagement in various forms of reflection, such as classroom action research and regular reviews of their learning experiences, student teachers were required to play an active and constructive role in their own learning. Consequently they all underwent critical reconsideration of their former conceptions of teaching, as inherited unconsciously during years of socializing experiences in classrooms as learners. To a certain extent, in having re-lived the socialized experiences as teachers, those with teaching experience, prior to initial training had to carry more weight when going through the critical reviews. On the other hand, once they realized their weaknesses, they tended to approach their learning processes with better focus, whereas the inexperienced student teachers faced initial difficulties in prioritizing their learning focus.

While former teaching experiences certainly played a part in reflective classroom practice, findings of this study do not agree with Berliner's (1988) assertion that novice teachers may have too little experience to reflect on until extensive classroom experience has been acquired. Despite the limitation of time, the inexperienced student teachers were able to get into elaborate reflections of their practice. They tended to come up with more problems than coping strategies. From a comparison of the detailed accounts of concerns, perceptions of problems and new insights of the two groups of student teachers, some essential features of various patterns of reflections were captured. The question is not so much whether student teachers are ready to reflect, but rather the support or guidance needed in their course of learning to teach. A further question concerns the extent to which they can be expected to benefit from their reflections. The necessary support went beyond what the supervisor's classroom visits could offer. As mentioned in the reviews, peer coaching was a valuable source of support. Concerning the question of whether the student teachers might have benefitted from reflections, it is necessary to consider the data from the video-lessons. Meanwhile, it is worth acknowledging the power of video-recording as a powerful source of stimulus in assisting recall of what had actually taken place in class. By reviewing the video-recorded lessons, the student teachers were sensitized to critical details which they would not otherwise have noticed. It was probable that the multiple resources in the course had facilitated the student teachers to be engaged in reflections. Former teaching experience is therefore not necessarily a prerequisite for readiness to reflect.

Implications for Curriculum Development in Teacher Education

As the major objectives of the course included facilitating student teachers to explore and experiment with a broad range of approaches in teaching, and to pursue a wide repertoire of problem-solving strategies (Kwo, 1994b), the findings indicate the ways student teachers responded to their course experiences. The extent to which the objectives were achieved were partly revealed in student teachers' own words, their own assessment of their learning experiences, and how they concluded their own understanding of the nature of teaching. If teacher education has to target at the nature of student teachers' conceptions and competence levels at their entry to the course, it is important to refrain from unrealistic assumptions. This study describes some differences between groups of experienced and inexperienced student teachers. The schemata differences and the range of teaching competence amongst student teachers were apparent. Rather than taking the differences as constraints, the course accommodated the differences by nurturing individual developments through promoting reflective teaching. Individuals started from where they were and progressed over the year in a similar direction towards student-centred teaching, and reached different points of their development at the end of the course. Progress in this shared direction was essentially based on a culture of inquiry ingrained in the practice of reflective teaching. Throughout the analyses, the supervisor-researcher was constantly reminded from the data the importance in acknowledging and accepting the individuality of student teachers in order to facilitate them in their "pursuit of personal excellence" (as explicitly stated in the objectives). Parallel to the student teachers' progress from a transmission mode to a student-centred mode of teaching, the study also enabled the supervisor-researcher to undergo a reinforcement of training practice in the spirit of the course objectives. Learning together with student teachers was vitally crucial in empowering the supervisor-researcher to help sustain the harmonious culture of inquiry amidst the tension each individual had in facing the problems.

The open curriculum of the course provided the framework to build a context of reflective teaching. Rather than being merely a matter of rational planning, the curriculum requires contributions from the participating student teachers as well as the supervisor. This study shows positive signs about the collegiality amongst student teachers, and the benefits in learning they gained from one another. The personality differences amongst the student teachers may be exciting for peer coaching, but they may also cause difficulties when clashes occur — which may be a subject for future research. Parallel to the school context, teaching at the university requires the supervisor to be actively involved in reflections on teaching-learning processes in ways that the student teachers experienced. The self-education of the supervisor-researcher was an implied but essential part of the curriculum for building up the desirable context in training for reflective teaching. Indeed there is an intimate connection between teaching and learning. Learning to teach and teaching to learn are simultaneous activities to both student teachers as well as reflective practitioners who seek to improve themselves. Conditions for reflective teaching include the entire environment and the persons associated with it.

References

Ben-Peretz, M. & Rumney, S. (1991). Professional thinking in guided practice. *Teaching and Teacher Education*, 7(516), 517–530.

Berliner, D. C. (1988). Implications of studies on expertise in pedagogy for teacher education and evaluation. In *New Directions for Teacher*

Assessment. (Proceedings of the 1988 ETS Invitational Conference, 39–68). Princeton, NJ: Educational Testing Service.

Berliner, D. C. (1993). Some characteristics of experts in the pedagogical domain. In F. K. Oser, A. Dick and J-L. Patry (Eds.), *Effective and Responsible Teaching: The New Synthesis.* San Francisco, CA: Jossey Bass.

Booth, M., Furlong, J. & Wilkin, M. (Eds.) (1990). *Partnership in Initial Teacher Training.* London: Cassell Educational Limited.

Borko, Fl. & Livingston, C. (1989). Cognition and improvisation: Differences in mathematics instruction by expert and novice teachers. *American Educational Research Journal,* 25(4), 473–498.

Calderhead, J. (1983). Research into teachers' and student teachers' cognitions: Exploring the nature of classroom practice. Paper presented at the annual meeting of the American Educational Research Association, Montreal, Canada.

Calderhead, J. (1987). The quality of reflection in student teachers' professional learning. *European Journal of Teacher Education,* 10(3), 269–78.

Calderhead, J. (1991). The nature and growth of knowledge in student teaching. *Teaching and Teacher Education,* 7(516), 531–535.

Calderhead, J. & Robson, M. (1991), Images of teaching: Student teachers' early conceptions of classroom practice. *Teaching and Teacher Education,* 7(1), 1–8.

Carter, K., Sabers, D., Cushing, K., Pinnegar, S. & Berliner, D. C. (1987). Processing and using information about students: A study of expert, novice, and postulant teachers. *Teaching and Teacher Education,* 3(2), 147–157.

Clift, R. T., Meng, L. & Eggerding, S. (1994). Mixed messages in learning to teach English. *Teaching and Teacher Education,* 10(3), 265–279.

Cole, A. L. & Knowles, J. G. (1993). Shattered images: Understanding expectations and realities of field experiences. *Teaching and Teacher Education,* 9(5/6), 457–471.

Doyle, W. (1979). Making managerial decisions in classrooms. In D. L. Duke (Ed.), *Classroom Management* (Yearbook of the National Society for the Study of Education), Chicago: University of Chicago Press.

Eisenhart, M., Behm, L. & Romagnano, L. (1991). Learning to teach: Developing expertise or rite of passage? *Journal of Education for Teaching*, 17, 51–71.

Housner, L. D. & Griffey, D. C. (1985). Teacher cognition: Differences in planning and interactive decision making between experienced and inexperienced teachers. *Research Quarterly for Exercise and Sport*, 56(1), 45–53.

Kagan, D. M. & Tippins, D. J. (1991). How teachers' classroom cases express their pedagogical beliefs. *Journal of Teacher Education*, 42(4), 281–291.

Korthagen, F. A. J. (1988). The influence of learning orientations on the development of reflective teaching. In J. Calderhead (Ed.), *Teachers' Professional Learning*. London: The Falmer Press.

Kwo, O. W. Y. (1994a). Learning to teach: Some theoretical propositions. In I. Carigren, G. Handat and S. Vaage (Eds.), *Teachers' Minds and Actions: Research on Teachers' Thinking and Practice*. London: The Falmer Press.

Kwo, O. W. Y. (1994b). Towards reflective teaching: Curriculum development and action research. In D. Li, D. Mahoney and J. Richards (Eds.), *Exploring Second Language Teacher Education*. Hong Kong: City Polytechnic of Hong Kong.

Livingston, C. C. (1990). *Student teacher thinking and the student teaching curriculum*. Unpublished doctoral dissertation, University of Maryland College Park.

Marton, F. (1981). Phenomenography: Describing conceptions of the world around us. *Instructional Science*, 10, 177–200.

Marton, F. & Saljo, R. (1984). Approaches to learning. In F. Marton, D. Hounsell and N. J. Entwistle (Eds.), *The Experience of Learning*. Edinburgh: Scottish Academic Press.

McCullough, L. L. & Mintz, S. L. (1992). Concerns of pre-service students in the USA about the practice of teaching. *Journal of Education for Teaching*, 18(1), 59–67.

McIntyre, D., Hagger, H. & Wilkin, M. (Eds.) (1993). *Mentoring: Perspectives on School-Based Teacher Education*. London: Kogan Page/Kegan Paul.

McNally, J., Cope, P., Inglis, B. & Stronach, I. (1994). Current realities in the student teaching experience: A preliminary inquiry. *Teaching and Teacher Education*, 10(2), 219–230.

Miles, M. B. & Huberman, A. M. (1984*). Qualitative Data Analysis: A Sourcebook of New Methods*. Newbury Park: Sage Publications.

Parker, W. C. & Gehrke, N. J. (1986). Learning activities and teachers' decision making: Some grounded hypotheses. *American Educational Research Journal* 23(2), 227–242.

Peterson, P. L. & Comeaux, M. A. (1987). Teachers' schemata for classroom events: The mental scaffolding of teachers' thinking during classroom instruction. *Teaching and Teacher Education*, 3(4), 319–331.

Schon, D. A. (1983). *The Reflective Practitioner*. London: Temple Smith.

Schon, D. A. (1987). *Educating the Reflective Practitioner*. San Francisco: Jossey Bass Publishers.

Schon, D. A. (Ed.) (1991). *The Reflective Turn*. New York: Teachers College Press.

Stones, E. (1987). Student (practice) teaching. In M. J. Dunkin (Ed.), *The International Encyclopedia of Teaching and Teacher Education*. Oxford: Pergamon.

Szpiczka, N. A. (1990). *Preservice teachers' perspectives on student reaching*. Unpublished doctoral dissertation, Syracuse University.

Woods, Helen E. (1991). *The student teaching experience: A qualitative examination*. Unpublished doctoral dissertation, Oregoii State University.

A Teacher's Use of The Reflective Process In Implementing Cooperative Learning

Christine Kim-Eng Lee and Maureen Ng

National Institute of Education
Nanyang Technological University
Singapore

Synopsis

This is a single-teacher case study. The subject is a secondary school geography teacher who is also a department head at her school. The purpose of the study has been to systematically record, analyse and understand the processes involved as the teacher undertook an instructional innovation within the natural dynamics of the classroom and school. Data collection was primarily through reflective journals and interviews. The case study represents one real-life story of a teacher's struggles in implementing co-operative learning in her classrooms. Insights have been gained of the perceptual changes that have occurred in the teacher herself, the varying outcomes with different pupils and the personal dilemma of accommodating new roles within the context of the school situation.

A Teacher's Use of the Reflective Process In Implementing Cooperative Learning

Christine Kim-Eng Lee and *Maureen Ng*

Introduction

"The debate over cooperative learning has been in swing for a decade now. Yet the positions have not hardened, the discussions are not passed and the interest not diluted" (Venette, 1994).

There are a variety of cooperative learning methods described in the educational literature, each with its own underlying philosophy and the form which it takes in practice. Although there are often important differences in the theoretical perspectives behind the various cooperative learning methods, these methods are not mutually exclusive. There are areas of commonality. All the cooperative learning methods share the common feature of the instructional use of heterogeneous small groups where students work together to "maximise their own and each other's learning" (Johnson, Johnson, and Holubec, 1990). Within cooperative learning groups, students are given two responsibilities: to learn the assigned material and to make sure that all other members of their group do likewise. In cooperative learning situations, students perceive that they can reach their learning goals only if the other students in their learning also achieve the goals.

Formal cooperative learning groups may be used for the learning of specific content in the classroom. The teacher introduces the lesson, assigns students to heterogeneous groups of two to five members, gives students the materials they need to complete the assignment, and assigns roles to individual students. The teacher then explains the task, teaches any concepts or procedures the students need to know to complete the assignment, and structures the cooperation among the students. Students work on the assignment until all group members successfully understand the material and complete the group's task. While the students work together, the teacher moves from group to group systematically monitoring their interaction. The teacher intervenes when the students do not understand the academic task or when problems arise from working together. After the groups complete the assignment, the teacher evaluates the academic success of each student and has the groups discuss how well they functioned as a team. In working cooperatively, students realise they have a stake in each other's success; they become mutually responsible for each other's learning (Johnson & Johnson in Stahl, 1992).

The cooperative learning approach is complex. It is not just another teaching technique for the classroom, easy to learn and assimilate, and to implement without significant challenges to other ways of teaching and operating a classroom. Sapon-Shevin and Schniedewind (1992) suggest that

> "cooperative learning is more than a teaching strategy, more than an instructional technique. It is an entirely different way of viewing the educational process of schools, reshaping them into communities of caring in which individual students take responsibility for the learning of their classmates and respect and encourage each other's diversity" (p. 16).

What does this conception of cooperative learning mean to teachers? Firstly, it is clear that implementing cooperative learning should not be a cookbook approach with teachers eager for ready-prepared lessons and programmes. Rather, teachers should be encouraged to plan their own cooperative lessons and adapt the strategies within the cultural milieu of their own classrooms. It requires teachers to think critically about all aspects of their classroom and their teaching. In particular, teachers need to understand how their roles change when they delegate authority to groups of students. The teacher's role shifts from being a director of learning to a facilitator in which students are encouraged to help each other learn. Secondly, teachers need a clear conceptual understanding of the essential components of cooperative learning, concrete examples of lessons and strategies, and repeated implementation in classrooms over

extended periods of time. Such a conceptual application requires teachers
to understand precisely what they are doing in order to communicate to
others the nature of cooperative learning and to explain how it needs to
be adapted within their specific circumstances. A carefully crafted use of
cooperative learning in the classroom requires reflective deliberations on
the part of the teacher.

The use of cooperative learning in schools has been viewed with mixed
feelings. On the one hand, the approach has the proven capacity to improve
academic performance and attitudes of children toward school, learning
and their classmates (Johnson, Johnson and Maruyama, 1983; Slavin,
1980, 1989). On the other hand, it is neither a panacea nor a quick cure
for the problems of instruction in schools. Kohn (1992) suggests that

> "despite an enormous research literature supporting the value of having
> students work in pairs or small groups to help each other learn — and
> more interestingly, despite the growing awareness of cooperative learning
> on the part of educators — anecdotal evidence suggests that it might
> eventually meet the same fate as many other worthy educational innovations
> (p. 38).

Rich (1990) observes that cooperative learning may remain an instructional strategy seldom used in a systematic manner over the course of a
school year or more. Probably the most important problem in implementation efforts is the user's construction of meaning (Fullan, 1991). In fact,
the "neglect of the phenomenology of change", i.e., how people actually
experience change as distinct from how it might have been intended — is
said to be "at the heart of the lack of success of most social reforms". Yet
in many implementation efforts, the important question "What does this
mean for teachers and students?" as they experience the change is not asked.
This suggests the need to examine more systematically the implementation
process of cooperative learning in classrooms and to consider more carefully
how teachers and students actually experience the changes. Helping teachers
to reflect on their experiences of cooperative learning will facilitate a deeper
understanding of how teachers cope with personal dilemmas in their efforts
to use cooperative learning within the constraints of the classroom and the

school. The insights from teachers' reflections will help in the development of more useful forms of teacher support. As Cohen (1990) has suggested, unless teachers receive useful continuing support, we may see those who try to implement cooperative learning "burn out on the new techniques".

Purpose and Method

The case study reported in this chapter represents one real-life story of a teacher's struggles in implementing cooperative learning within the natural dynamics of her classrooms and school. It is an attempt to gain insights into how the teacher copes with the tensions between the teaching method on one hand and the learning needs of her pupils, the demands of the school syllabus, and the organisational structure of the school on the other. Research data was gathered primarily through reflective journals written by the teacher as well as from open-ended interviews. In the course of journal writing, the teacher was guided by the following key rubics:

  a) Reflect on your philosophy of teaching; your goals for your students and your own personal goals.
  b) Reflect on the cooperative learning approach — the objectives and strategies you used; the adaptations you made and reasons for the changes.
  c) Reflect on your students — describe and account for their reactions to cooperative learning.
  d) Reflect on colleagial support — in what ways was peer support forthcoming or otherwise.
  e) Reflect on the school culture and organisational factors influencing your use of cooperative learning.

Data collection has lasted 18 months and produced rich data relating to this teacher's experiences. In analysing her journals, we have found Schon's framework on reflective practitioners useful. According to Schon (1987), practitioners when faced with situational problems would generally not be able to apply clear-cut "technical means" in their problem-solving. Rarely would the practitioner have the time to begin with a defined framework and then proceed to apply some problem-solving procedure to achieve a particular objective. It is much more likely that he will resort to his "intuitive understanding" of the situation coupled with some improvisation. This process has been called "reflection-in-action" — where the practitioner responds spontaneously to "puzzles and surprises" or situational events over which he has limited control. A different reflective process in which the professional may engage is known as "reflection-on-action". The latter takes place only after the event and entails more ordered, deliberate and systematic application of logic to the problem.

The Teacher and the Process
Teacher Motivations

Ms L, still in her early 30s, teaches Geography in a secondary school. Bright, assertive and effective, she has already been made a head of department though she has been teaching for just five years. In mid-1993, she enrolled in a training programme at the National Institute of Education for professional upgrading. It was during this time that she was introduced to cooperative learning. Her understanding of cooperative learning still fledgling, she had written:

> .... so much more can be achieved through cooperation... Cooperative learning is providing me with an alternative way to teaching — mastering & understanding of information becomes an effort of the group. There is a developed sense of accountability towards one another as they (the students) move together towards the same goal. The reward system .... recognises their efforts and increases their sense of achievement.

Her attraction to cooperative learning was sparked by her affinity to a more personal method of teaching and learning. In her years of teaching, she noted that some of her students seemed to lose self-confidence while others seemed to develop more "selfish and individualistic" attitudes. These, she believed, were a result of the highly competitive school system. She hoped that cooperative learning would counteract the trend and help the students understand the importance and value of teamwork and sharing.

First Encounters with Cooperative Learning (Semester 1, 1994)

Ms L started out by conducting a school-based workshop in which she shared what she had learned about cooperative learning with her school teachers. The cooperative strategy she selected was *Jigsaw*:

> I found a combination of *Jigsaw I* and *II* very appropriate for the teaching of Geography, History and Social Studies as the teaching of these subjects require the imparting of huge amounts of information, facts and understanding of concepts.

> This method is excellent for building a sense of positive interdependence as the students need to work together in order to get information and are individually accountable as each student needs to learn all the information in order to impart the information... The structure forces the students to be active learners... The student not only becomes individually accountable for his or her own learning but learns through being interdependent on others. Learning is no longer a lonely road to excellence and achievement.

Following the workshop, some teachers in her department implemented the *Jigsaw* method in their classes. The lessons were observed by Ms L, who later recorded this in her journal:

> My teachers found *Jigsaw* effective as the students were forced to take an active role in learning. There is definitely an increase in student interaction and discussion. They asked more questions and learned actively. This cuts down on spoon-feeding. Students had no opportunity to dream and they had to grapple with the information and learn to work with one another.

> The majority of the students however prefer a teacher-centred lesson, with the exception of the boys from Sec 1A and Sec 3D. This is rather revealing of our students nowadays and reflective of our education system. In the strive towards attaining excellent results, the teacher ends up preparing all the notes for the students. This has resulted in students becoming passive learners waiting for the teacher to provide them with the information. The students do not think for themselves and also do not trust themselves to learn on their own.

While recognising some student resistance, Ms L's enthusiasm remained strong:

> ... as teachers we must continue to modify and slowly change those perceptions. Motivated teachers who continue to focus on student learning will ultimately succeed. The road ahead is long and it is going to take time. However it will be time well invested as ultimately, the best teacher is the one whom the students do not need when they leave school.

The Teacher uses Cooperative Learning (Semester 2, 1994)

On completing her course, she returned to teach and proceeded to implement *Jigsaw* with her two Geography classes — Secondary 4A and Secondary 2J (years 10 and 8 respectively). As she used the approach with the two classes, the relevance of the practices to students of different abilities and motivations became more clear to her:

> Sec 4A is the best class in the *Express** level... I wanted to carry out a revision lesson on "Rubber" with this class. I told the pupils to get into their groups and arrange their tables in clusters. I numbered them and gave them the expert topics. This was more like a revision lesson for them. I gave them 10 minutes to master the information, another 15–20 minutes to share the information and then half an hour to tackle a structured question worth 25 marks.

> The class took it seriously and during the expert topic discussions, they were eagerly clarifying. I felt that the groups were too big. I divided the pupils of one expert topic into 2 so that there would only be 4 in each expert group.

---

*"Express" and "Normal" refer to educational tracks in the Singapore secondary school. Higher ability students generally take the Express course which leads to the GCE O-levels in 4 years. Lower ability students take the Normal course which is a 4-year course leading to the CSE N-levels.

Peter's group was very enthusiastically sharing information — there was of course also an exchange of jokes and wise cracks... I am a bit concerned about Wendy's group. I saw her trying to lead the group and share the information — generally very quiet even when they are sharing. There doesn't seem to be any form of discussion or clarification... Rachel's group doesn't seem to be working well either. Rachel and Janet seem rather dominant and more enthusiastic. Chiang Bee, Jonathan and John are not as interested. I had to prod the group along, especially Jonathan who was trying to copy Janet's notes... Hazel's group seems to be the most balanced — clarifying and sharing with one another what they have found out.

As she continued to use Jigsaw with Sec 4A, she recorded these thoughts:

I am becoming more conscious of cooperative learning techniques now and I think so's the class. They are automatically in their groups now... I see leaders emerging, students who take the initiative to organise themselves and other members of the group to contribute their ideas... As I walked around the class, I noticed that some groups worked faster than others. I then moved them into the next stage of discussion...

As they were discussing, Peter's group raised their hands to clarify their interpretation of the question. Later I found that other groups had the same problem. I told them to decide by themselves which they think is the best approach and we would discuss it later.

I realised that the answers were of much better quality and they were very conscious of the techniques of approaching the questions. Through this process, we commented on the answers and clarified the points. We didn't have enough time so we had to continue in the next lesson.

Although a lot of time was taken up just to discuss one question, through their presentations we could discuss the most appropriate approach to the answer and identify the pitfalls. At certain points of the lesson, the discussion became rather heated. However they were able to come to appropriate conclusions. For the next lesson, I decided to try something different — I gave them the questions to prepare for the next lesson.

Adapting the *Jigsaw* Model

Ms L had more difficulties using the *Jigsaw* with Sec 2J, the weakest class among the three *"Normal"* classes in the school. The strategy had to be adapted to suit the students who, she felt, lacked the skills and motivation assumed by the model. She decided to cut out the expert group discussion and put in an "individual study" phase before the test:

> The (Sec 2J) boys are rather unmotivated. I planned to use *Jigsaw* without using the expert groups for the topic "Decision-making in a farming area".
>
> The students were divided into groups, given the questions and pages that they were supposed to refer to in the text. They were asked to find the information to these questions and write their answers in the exercise books and then exchange their answers.
>
> The students took quite some time to settle down, get themselves organised and gather the information. It became more difficult when they had to share their answers because they just allowed one another to copy from their books... The lesson was quite disastrous.

Ms L noted that she should have realised that such problems could occur, as the weaker students would not have the skills of note-taking and peer teaching. Further adjustments were made in the following lesson:

> I tried using the same approach on a different topic on "Industrial location in Singapore". This time, I typed a worksheet with questions and space for them to fill up their answers. I allowed them to divide the questions among themselves and search for the answers.
>
> During the period of sharing, they still allowed one another to copy from their worksheet. One particular group was disbanded and I allowed 3 individuals to work on their own as they did not trust one another.
>
> I've discovered that with weaker pupils, such strategies are not so appropriate till the teacher encourages them to establish rapport with one another as well as teach them the techniques of note-taking, sharing information, etc. The pupils (especially the boys) do not actively play a part and very often the girls prefer to work on their own as they do not trust the boys to do the work.

> Three periods a week actually limits the time that can be used for *Jigsaw*. I would need to try other cooperative learning techniques which are simpler. Motivating the pupils to study is more immediate.
>
> I found that I needed to guide and motivate these pupils. Teaching them the information-processing and study skills was very much more important before carrying out the *Jigsaw*.

Ms L at this stage concluded that weaker pupils did not have the prerequisite social and information-processing skills to use *Jigsaw* effectively. She has encountered some unmotivated students, whose lack of enthusiasm during smallgroup work had resulted in a less than satisfactory lesson. The success of cooperative learning, she discovered, required the establishment of mutual trust among the group members as well as the development of self-directed learning skills and attitudes. The heterogeneous smallgroup arrangement brought with it tensions between the girls and boys, and one group was consequently disbanded. As Ms L's focus among the slower learners shifted toward "motivating" them and teaching them information-processing and study skills, she still believed that with older and more able students, *Jigsaw* was applicable in its entirety:

> I found it easier and more fruitful with this class (Sec 4A) as they had already acquired the information-processing and study skills and this strategy enabled them to voice their thoughts, opinions and encouraged them to speak and argue. I did not need to provide detailed worksheets for this class. I encouraged the class to keep a notebook. This strategy has made them more willing to share. Even the quieter ones are sharing their thoughts.

Continuing to use Cooperative Learning (Semester 1, 1995)

Now in a new academic year, Ms L has five new classes — a Sec 2 (Normal Technical) social studies class and four Sec 4 (Express) classes. Her journal entry, made just one week after the start of the school term showed a shift toward simpler cooperative techniques — *Think-Pair-Share* and the *Sequential Roundtable*:

I carried out a simple *think-pair-share* approach.... on the topic of marine processes.... I posed them a question... describing the erosional features that I discovered at St John's island. This was rather strange as Singapore is supposed to be part of a constructive wave environment. This led to quite a bit of discussion among the pairs. I then asked the different pairs to share their answers.

Among all the classes, Sec 4D seems to be the most enthusiastic... 4E seems the most distant..... 4G did not have a problem either.... 4A — the best class is rather quiet and expressionless. They don't seem to want to volunteer their answers.....

Through the *think-pair-share* strategy, we managed to come to certain conclusions. However, the level of enjoyment and satisfaction differed from class to class. I need to establish a rapport especially with 4A and 4E as their learning styles definitely differ from mine. The two classes prefer a chalk and talk method. They are not comfortable with sharing answers, what more [even less] to ask questions.

The *sequential roundtable* — I tried that. I notice that pupils are very concerned about what is not written in their notes. They feel rather insecure that it [the information] is going on this common piece of paper. So what I have done is mainly use rough paper. They write their points down, after that I will gather the points from the different groups and write them on the board. After the class has decided on the acceptable answer, they then copy it into their exercise books. So in the end everybody still gets their notes and we don't have notes hanging on pieces of paper. I find that this has worked.

Combining the use of Cooperative Learning with Information Technology

Ms L decided to begin a new project integrating cooperative learning and information technology (using CD ROMs). She wanted to get her Sec 4 students to collaborate in a group investigation project on the "Oil industry in India". They were to undertake group research using library resources and computer software. To encourage cooperation, specific roles were assigned — computer expert, time keeper, resource manager and encourager:

...there was definitely insufficient time for the pupils. I shifted the deadline of the project to after the school holidays — to give them more time.

I decided to find out how much they had done by meeting them again in the reference room. They sat in their groups and each group had a drawing paper and a marker pen. I taught them how to draw a mind map — how they went about gathering information on the project. I asked them to focus on how they divided their roles, how they went through the books, which books they went through, how they searched through the CDs, what were the problems faced and the benefits received.

Most of them preferred to use the CDs (rather than the library books) because it was easier to search for information and it was interesting. They thought it was fun as they saw [this as something implying] that they did not have any lessons. They divided themselves according to the subtopics.

I am looking forward to marking their projects, to go through their post-test and another structured question on oil. It will be interesting to see how the pupils fared when they had not been taught any form of content at all. The pre-test results showed a lack of knowledge. Most of the students failed the test except for a handful in 4A and 4D.

When Ms L marked the students' projects, she was pleased with the quality of the work of some of the groups but there were also other groups which did not do well:

I was amazed at the amount of information they found out. Certain groups summarised and synthesised the information and had diagrams within the text. These groups did well.

The groups that did not do well because they had problems working with each other.

Upon reflection, Ms L decided that the next time round, she will need to give the students time to discuss their group project with one another in class. This would give her the opportunity to observe how well her students cooperated in their groups and to intervene and facilitate the spirit of interdependence within the groups where necessary.

Discussion

Reflecting on teaching can be an arduous task and involves looking at the teacher's beliefs about education, the learning process and the academic subjects. Doing so requires the ability to:

(a) identify and analyse problems and situations in terms of significant educational, social and ethical issues,

(b) use a rational problem-solving approach in educational situations,

(c) make intuitive, creative interpretations and judgements, and

(d) take action based on a personal decision and monitor the effects of that action (Ross, 1987).

For Ms L, we believe that the reflective process has helped her to articulate her ideological beliefs about teaching and learning and to consider the efficacy of specific practices when using cooperative learning. She began with a firm belief that cooperative learning would help pupils learn better and also develop desirable personal and social skills. She believed that the teacher should not just teach but "empower students to assume control over their own learning" (Sapon-Shevin, 1992). She also felt that learning in groups would be less daunting for the weaker pupils. Moreover, Geography presented opportunities to use the *Jigsaw* strategy as the subject is content-based and entails discussion. The students would be engaged in "clarifying geographical concepts with one another and explaining them to their teammates". The "ideological congruence" (Rich, 1990) between cooperative learning and her personal beliefs about education led her to adopt and persist with the approach for over a year following the training she received, in spite of constraints of curriculum time and classroom space.

But, there were traces of discomfort with the approach — a fear of "losing control" in the class on the part of the teacher and the resistance to greater classroom participation on the part of the students. Cooperative learning involves the creation of a supportive environment and classroom practices that help the students to learn through sharing. It brings with it "uncertainty" in place of "predictable progressions through a prepared lesson plan" (Kohn, 1992). Myers (1992) in his personal journey with cooperative learning however, attests that a "little discomfort in one spot can encourage movement".

As Ms L continued with the approach, she shifted to describing how some students were uncomfortable with *Jigsaw*. Whereas cooperative classrooms should be "communities of caring" in which students see themselves as having specific responsibilities to one another, she noted that there was apathy toward discussion among some of the boys and some girls preferred to work on their own because they "did not trust the boys". In addition, a large majority of the students preferred a teacher-centred approach and did not trust themselves to learn on their own.

At the same time, Ms L was concerned with upholding the school's academic emphasis. The manner in which she incorporated checks to ensure content coverage was interesting. Concerned that the students would not be "shortchanged" in terms of information, the *Jigsaw* strategy was designed using the teacher's compiled notes. In addition, outlines were supplied for each topic. Tests were administered regularly to evaluate students' learning, and oral questioning used in class with the weaker pupils.

The changes she made demonstrate how *Jigsaw* was used according to the context of her school. Three constraints led to the adjustments — limited curriculum time, classroom space and academically weak students. As Sarason (1971) and others have described, instructional innovations are not used as they were originally designed but adapted to fit particular circumstances in the class. Unfortunately, such adaptations can result in the reduction of the method's power (Myers, 1992). Ms L found that it was too lengthy to use all the phases in Jigsaw, and decided to omit the expert discussion phase with the Sec 2 class. Her experiences, particularly with the weaker students, were causing her to "reframe" her conception of *Jigsaw*. In the following comments, she described the events that led her to question the expert discussion phase:

> It depends on the ability of the class. If the class is vocal, eager to learn and enthusiastic, I don't see why the expert discussion should be done away with. Because I think teenagers should carry them out if they can, but I feel that the constraint of space is there. The classroom is pretty tight.

... I had to try to condition the pupils with two kinds of seating arrangement which took more time. For Sec 4A, I knew they had the calibre to do the expert discussions on their own and that was fine. For Sec 2, I couldn't do that because they are not equipped with skills of discussion and they are not strong. So even when I had expert groups, I was very much involved in going to the groups, teaching them. That is why I gave them each a topic and they basically needed to study on their own as I walked around — I felt it was easier for me to handle the pupils. The Sec 2 can't handle two kinds of discussion. They not only have to learn, but they have to teach — you know, that's two different skills altogether.

Ms L's reflections tell a story of her personal journey with cooperative learning. It has similarities to the experiences of other teachers, described by Myers (1992):

In my days as a full-time classroom teacher, I shaped cooperative learning in response to a host of immediate practical classroom concerns. In fact, for most of the time I struggled, as alone as those teachers described earlier, to move from a concept of group work to a fuller notion of those elements which made for effective group learning.

She did not perceive a conflict between cooperative learning and the competitive orientation of the school system. However, her perspective of cooperative learning and the Jigsaw approach now includes "critical conditions" necessary for its use. She has been thoughtful about her practices in the classroom and noted that she has become "more conscious" of what actions were necessary in using the approach. While she remains convinced of the potential of cooperative learning, she has acquired deeper understanding and insights on the basis of her practice. She now believes that simpler structures should be used where students are academically weaker or have not developed information-processing skills.

Ms L's experience in employing cooperative learning has been a somewhat lonely journey. As a sole implementer in her school, colleagial support was absent. The school-based workshop in which she had shared the approach had not stimulated other teachers to use cooperative learning. While still believing that cooperative learning is ideologically desirable, she now admits to a degree of uncertainty about its wider use in her school:

I find that it takes time — it really takes time — and I am already loaded as a HOD [Head of Department] and my time is tight. So if the teachers were to do something like that, I feel it is going to take time from them. It is enjoyable, I am enjoying it and I feel that this is what we should do as teachers. But I can't help but realise that there are always the other constraints and responsibilities that are going to get at us.

I wish there were other teachers trying out the method as well so that it would not be so difficult for me to get the groups going — to teach them skills, group skills and things like that.

Conclusion

The reflections of the teacher's experience in using cooperative learning with her students as revealed in her journal entries and open-ended interviews raises questions on several important aspects of the implementation process. One is that the teachers' philosophical beliefs about teaching and learning are a powerful motivational force in his or her effort in implementing cooperative learning. The teacher in our case study used cooperative learning over a period of several months and even experimented using it with information technology. The use of cooperative learning continued in the face of the constraints of curriculum time, classroom space, student expectations and the lack of information-processing and social skills.

Second, the initial experimentation phase of implementing an instructional innovation such as cooperative learning may lead to compromises of the essential features of the instructional method. These compromises are sufficient for the time being as the teacher attempts to cope with some constraints existing in the realities of the classroom and the school. In this case study, due to lack of curriculum time *Jigsaw* was adapted to exclude the expert discussion phase.

Third, teachers need time to carefully think through what they understand of the various forms of cooperative learning. Time is also needed to prepare cooperative lessons and to teach students the necessary information-processing and groupwork skills for effective use of cooperative learning. Unfortunately, teachers in schools have to contend with many administrative and organisational responsibilities which take away precious time from curriculum development and innovation. Ms L through her participation in this study was committed to set aside time to reflect on the experience she had acquired in the use of cooperative learning. In reflecting on her classroom practice, Ms L became more conscious of some of the problems and difficulties she faced, as well as the adaptations she made to the method and her underlying beliefs about teaching and learning. The issue that remains is — given the many competing demands on their time — whether teachers will, on their own, reflect on their classroom practice.

Implementing cooperative learning in classrooms need not be a lonely journey for teachers. The concept of classrooms as caring and cooperative communities should extend to the whole school community. A community can be defined as "an inherently cooperative, cohesive, and self-reflective group entity whose members work on a regular, face-to-face basis toward common goals while respecting a variety of perspectives, values, and lifestyles" (Graves, 1992, p. 64). A cooperative and caring school community will mean a more comfortable and inspiring work environment for teachers as well as students. Teachers can support each other in their use of cooperative learning with their students; they can collaborate to develop both methods and curriculum materials; they can visit each others' classrooms and provide feedback; they can share ideas and help each other reflect on their experiences.

Nonetheless, it is important to realise that no matter how good a teacher is in creating a cooperative community in his or her classroom, much of this work can be undone when students move to classes with competitive or alienating environments.

References

Cohen E. (1990). *Continuing to Cooperate: Prerequisites for Persistence.* Phi Delta Kappan, pp. 134–138.

Fullan, M. (1991). *The New Meaning of Educational Change.* Toronto: OISE Press.

Graves, L. N. (1992). Cooperative learning communities: Context for a new vision of education and society. *Journal of Education*, 174(2), pp. 57–79.

Johnson, D. W. & Johnson, R. T. (1992). Approaches to implementing cooperative learning in the social studies classroom. In Robert Stahl and Ronald VanSickle (Eds.), *Cooperative Learning in the Social Studies Classroom*. Bulletin no. 87. Washington DC: National Council for the Social Studies, pp. 44–51.

Johnson, D. W., Johnson, R. T. & Holubec, E. (1990). *Circles of Learning: Cooperation in the Classroom*. Minn.: Interaction Book Company.

Kohn, A. (1992). Resistance to cooperative learning: Making sense of its deletion and dilution. *Journal of Education*, 174(2), pp. 38–55.

Myers, J. (1992). Cooperative learning: A personal journey. *Journal of Education*, 174(2), pp. 118–143.

Russell, T. & Minby, H. (1991). Reframing: The role of experience in developing teachers' professional knowledge. In D. A. Schon (Ed.), *The Reflective Turn: Case Studies In and On Educational Practice*. New York: Teachers College Press.

Sarason, S. B. (1971). *The Culture of the School and the Problem of Change*. Boston: Allyn and Bacon.

Sapon-Shevin, M. & Schniedewind, N. (1992). If cooperative learning's the answer, what are the questions? *Journal of Education*, 174(2), pp. 11–56.

Schon, D. (1983). *The Reflective Practitioner*. New York: Basic Books.

Schon, D. (1987). *Educating the Reflective Practitioner*. San Francisco: Jossey Bass.

Vernette, P. (1994). Special section on cooperative learning. *Social Science Record*, 31(2), p. 4.

Group Learning for Doing Case Studies in an Engineering and Technology Management Course

Ziqi Liao

School of Accountancy and Business
Nanyang Technological University
Singapore

Ai-Yen Chen

School of Education
National Institute of Education
Singapore

Synopsis

A reflective group learning model to facilitate the teaching of case studies in the area of engineering and technology management is presented in this case. The model systematically structures a learning process into establishment phase, preparation phase and class phase. It involves rule setting, group formulation, individual study, group discussion, random group sharing, presentation and reflection. Experiments have been conducted by using the model to teach a number of case studies. The results suggest that the students are able to achieve deep learning through cooperative effort. The motivation and involvement of the students have also been enhanced. Furthermore, a systematic structure of the learning process, an encouragement of active participation in group discussion and the supportive role of a teacher are essential for the successful implementation of the model.

Group Learning for Doing Case Studies in Engineering and Technology Management

Ziqi Liao and *Ai-Yen Chen*

Introduction

Case studies are useful to help students realize deep learning since they place great emphasis on training of analytical skills and logical judgments based on facts and findings. Therefore, case studies are increasingly popular in engineering education. However, traditional pedagogy for case studies is usually associated with some problems. For example, students who have not fully digested what they have learned from lectures and textbooks usually have great difficulties in doing case studies. It is also not uncommon that only a few may be actively involved in discussions while the majority are rather passive in a class. As a result, most students may not quite progress from the dualistic stage of learning. Therefore, it is still challenging to motivate students to achieve deep learning through the implementation of appropriate learning approaches.

As far as this is concerned, we attempt to use a cooperative learning strategy to develop a learning model to teach case studies in engineering and technology management. This paper begins with the background in relation to students' learning approaches and cooperative learning strategy. It then presents a reflective group learning model, followed by a description of the experiments in relation to the use of the proposed model. Finally, it suggests several approaches to motivate students to achieve deep learning.

The Background

Students' motive and strategy for learning constitutes a distinct approach to learning and studying. In general there are three approaches such as surface learning, deep learning and achieving learning (Biggs, 1979). The surface learning approach is based on extrinsic motivation in which learning is perceived as a means to passing an examination or getting a job. The motive of surface learning is instrumental because the purpose of study is to meet minimal requirements (Biggs, 1987). Therefore, surface learning is a reproductive strategy. The effort is directed towards achieving certain objectives within limited time and with little stress. It is also usually confined to memorization through rote learning. On the other hand, the deep learning approach is based on intrinsic motivation because it is derived from students' interest in the subject matter of the task (Biggs, 1987). Deep strategy aims to maximize understanding of concepts as well as their meaningful relationships. Deep learners are those who not only are concerned with a burning desire to learn and understand, but will also read beyond the prescribed texts and articles in the pursuit of new knowledge (Chang, 1995). Furthermore, students who adopt the achieving approach are motivated by achievement in their learning and studying, either aiming at receiving higher marks or becoming the best student in the school. Therefore, they would particularly pay attention to efficient time management and effective use of learning environment. However, deep learning is fundamental to training analytical thinking for future achievement.

Extensive researches have been conducted to examine approaches to learning and studying. It is not uncommon that many tertiary students use the surface approach in studies. Some students adopt a reproductive or surface approach to the study of reading materials even in situations where the task requires a clear understanding for meaning (Marton and Saljo, 1976). In 1987, Biggs designed a study process questionnaire (SPQ) and used it to investigate the learning approach of Australian students. He discovered that most students in the colleges of advanced education are surface learners (Biggs, 1987). The SPQ had also been used to examine the learning of Asian students. For example, Kember and Gow (1991) used the SPQ to survey the learning behavior of students at universities in Hong Kong, in order to challenge the anecdotal stereotype of Asian students. Their results suggested that the tendency for reproductive approach to learning would be more a teaching practice than an innate tendency of Asian students. Furthermore, a number of surveys were conducted in Singapore across disciplines in 1994/95. The popularity of the surface approach towards learning and the increased dependency on teachers are found strongly correlated (Chang, 1995). Therefore, it seems to be necessary to improve on the current learning approach.

The rationale and notion of structured group learning approach and participation in learning can be captured in most of the discussions in existing literature. Whipple (1987) defines cooperative learning as a structured form of collaborative learning which provides a practical framework for implementing mutual goals such as promoting active learning, bridging the gulf between teachers and students, creating a sense of community and locating knowledge in the community rather than in the individual. Cooper and Mueck (1989) also suggest that cooperative learning is a structured and systematic instructional strategy in which small groups work together toward a common goal. Therefore, cooperative learning is a structured form of small group work based on positive interdependence, individual accountability, appropriate team formation, group processing and social skills.

Cooperative learning in which students work together in small groups has been recognized as a useful teaching approach. Many educators believe that collaboration in small groups is a major ingredient in learning since it not only has a positive impact on the acquisition of social skills and interactions of students but also has considerable potential for promoting a better quality of instruction and learning (Whipple, 1987; Cooper et al., 1989; Sharan, 1990; Tottle et al., 1991).

First, cooperative learning fosters positive social relations among members through peer collaboration and mutual assistance in small groups. When students worked cooperatively, positive and supportive relationships tend to develop, even among students from different ethnic, cultural, language, social class, ability and gender groups (Johnson et al., 1992).

Second, it enhances students' decision making ability since members need to decide how the group work will be reported to the class as a whole and determine the amount of work load for each individual. Therefore it is helpful to overcome a serious disadvantage of most teaching strategies which is leaving students passive in their learning (Elton, 1988). Cooperative learning could move students from a passive learning mode to an active discussion mode since it requires students to participate actively in their learning, while a lecturer only takes on the role as a facilitator. Therefore, cooperative learning is an intrinsic motivation approach. Research also indicates that cooperation promotes greater intrinsic motivation to learn, more frequent use of cognitive processes such as re-conceptualization, higher-level reasoning and networking, and greater long-term maintenance of the skill learned (Johnson and Johnson, 1993).

Third, cooperative learning provides an opportunity to develop communication skills. Students learn to voice their opinions and substantiate their ideas. They learn to challenge other's ideas when there are disagreements. The cooperative effort enables students to work out solutions themselves (Johnson et al., 1992). As a result, students could develop confidence in their ability to solve problems rather than depend on the instruction of a teacher.

Furthermore, cooperative learning could promote the learning of both academic and team-work skill (Johnson et al., 1992). For example, students could construct and extend conceptual understanding of what is being learned through explanation and discussion. They could also receive interpersonal feedback and social support to take risks in increasing one's competencies. Students would be held accountable by peers to practice until the procedures and skills being taught are over-learned. They could establish a shared identity with other group members and observe the most outstanding group members as behavioral models emulated.

Finally, students working in a group environment are able to learn more, are more satisfied with the classes and less likely to drop out since cooperative learning helps increase group members' motivation (Maier and Keenen, 1994). The achievement is also higher in cooperative situations than in competitive or individualistic ones (Johnson and Johnson, 1990; Lazarowitz and Karsenty, 1990).

However, the achievement resulted from cooperative learning might not be guaranteed all the time. Therefore, a well structured and an appropriate arrangement for a cooperative learning process is essential. Reid et al. suggest a stimulating model of group learning which includes such stages as engagement, exploration, transformation, presentation and reflection (Needham et al., 1992). Engagement is the time when learners acquire information and engage in an experience that provides the basis for, or content of their ensuing learning. Secondly, exploration is the stage that students need time to explore the new information for themselves. Thirdly, transformation is the stage in which students focus their attention on the aspects of the information which represent the desired outcomes of the learning activity. Moreover, students are asked to present their findings to audiences which might be other small groups in a class. Finally, reflection is necessary to help students learn effectively. In our experiment with case studies discussed in the following sections, the group learning approach is used to activate students' learning enthusiasm and to enable them to achieve deep learning.

Reflective Group Learning Model

This section begins with the structure of the reflective learning model, followed by several steps associated with the implementation of the model. Experiments in the use of the model are then discussed as a case study is exemplified.

Model Structure

The systematic reflective group learning model was developed on the basis of the rationale of cooperative learning mentioned previously. It allows an integration of a number of activities in relation to a cooperative learning process. As displayed in Figure 1, the model systematically structures seven activities into three phases. They are: establishment phase, preparation phase and class phase. Hence, students are able to progressively go through the process of engagement, exploration, transformation, presentation and reflection.

Figure 1
A reflective group learning model

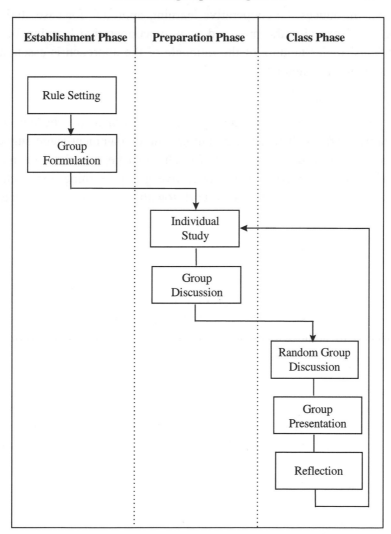

1. *Establishment Phase*

Rule setting

A teacher introduces the cooperative learning approach for case studies to students, and explains the pros and cons of cooperative learning because the students' understanding of the rationale of the approach is essential for successful implementation.

Group formulation

Small groups of four or five students each are formed for the purpose of cooperative learning. This stage resembles the engagement stage suggested by Reid et al. (Needham et al., 1992). This can be organized in the first class after the introduction of the reflective group learning approach. For the rest of the semester the groups work together on case studies assigned.

2. *Preparation Phase*

Individual study and exploration

Students are required to read through every case before group discussion although cooperative effort is suggested in the next step. Individual reading at this stage is necessary because a student can acquire minimum information needed to achieve deep learning. The student can also explore new information and knowledge from reading a case study.

Group discussion

Group members are encouraged to come together sometime before a class to discuss an assigned case study and to prepare for presentation cooperatively. This will help students in both exploration and transformation of information because students would normally participate in discussion in a small group environment.

3. *Class Phase*

Random group sharing

At the beginning of a class, a few students are allowed to randomly sit together in the classroom. They are encouraged to share their opinions and findings in relation to a particular case study.

Group presentation

The pre-arranged groups come to the front of the classroom in turn to present a case to the whole class. Members of each group are expected to tackle at least one or two of the problems associated with a particular case study. If a case is rather long, each group may be responsible for presenting a particular part of the case. They are also expected to be able to answer questions raised by the teacher and the other students in the class.

Reflection

At the end of a class, the teacher should comment on the case study as well as the group presentation. A review of what students have learned and the learning process they have gone through should be helpful for the students to gain a deeper understanding of the fundamental principles associated with a particular case study. Both the students and the teacher are encouraged to reflect upon the experience of studying a particular case. Their reflection should improve their future problem-solving exercises.

The rule setting and group formulation in the establishment phase can be carried out at the beginning of a semester. However, those activities associated with both the preparation phase and the class phase can be repeated periodically depending on the assignments of case studies to the students over the semester.

Experiments

The systematic cooperative learning model had been used to teach at least twenty case studies in the area of engineering and technology management from 1995 to 1996. A Gannt Chart for the reflective group learning process has been developed on the basis of the authors' experience (Figure 2). The model is comprised of three phases: (a) establishment phase, (b) preparation phase and (c) class phase, in which there are a number of activities. The following describes the implementation of the model.

At the very beginning, it took about 20 to 30 minutes to introduce the reflective group learning approach and its potential benefits to our students. Hence, the students appreciated why they were asked to work in groups

Figure 2
Gannt chart of reflective learning process

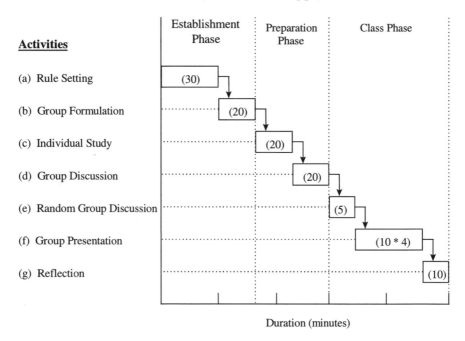

Duration (minutes)

and how group work could impact on their understanding of a particular subject. They were required to work in a small group to master case materials through cooperation. Each group was required to be responsible for presenting a certain part of a case study and answering some pre-determined questions. Preparing an outline on transparencies for presentation was required. It is possible that the students may resent cooperative learning if someone in a group did not contribute to the group. Therefore, everyone was strongly encouraged to participate in group discussion.

Cooperative learning seems to work best when the teacher, not the students, organizes the groups because students learn best from others who are different (Cooper, 1990). Ideal groups should include diversity of gender, ethnicity and academic and social skills. However, students prefer to form study groups by themselves in the light of personal interests and conveniences. Actually, there are 20 to 25 students in a class. The students themselves organize five groups of four or five which are actually task groups. Each group is responsible for a particular task related to a case study. The groups, therefore, are actually task groups.

The time required for the preparation phase and the class phase will vary depending on a particular case study. The following illustrates the process of both preparation and class phases through a case study from Stoner et al. (1995).

Case Study: Manufacturing at Boeing Company

The case study is related to the use of computer-assisted design (CAD) as the major tool in developing Boeing's new 777, an aircraft with more than 3 million individual parts and an overall cost of development somewhere between $10 and $12 billion. To make it as sure a venture as possible, given the massive investment, the company used CAD to help ensure that the airplane would fly at the first try.

Boeing relied heavily on the use of CAD to develop a three-dimensional computerized modeling system. CAD's ability to model in solids allowed the company to design everything from the 777's main cabin to the tools to be used on the craft. More than 1,700 engineers worked on the project together.

CAD worked in a number of ways. First, a proposed aircraft component is generated by the computer. Then, a digitally-generated "human" tries out the component. Throughout the design process CAD is able to guide the designers through the various tests needed to design the aircraft. CAD was also effective in improving the actual construction of the 777. Assembly line workers were aided by CAD by receiving instructions that included detailed graphics and explicit instructions on how to assemble the plane. Overall, CAD had redefined the very nature of building an aircraft. Utilizing CAD technology has enabled Boeing designers to save the company lots of resources. Through CAD, Boeing has developed the 777 in less time with less money and with quality and greater safety.

Our students acquire information and engage in the case study through individual study and group discussion. First of all, they are expected to individually read through the case material at least one time before group discussion. Actually, individual study is not contrary to cooperative learning. Individual practice is usually necessary, and competitive and individualistic activities can be used to supplement and enhance cooperative learning (Johnson et al., 1992).

Group members then get together and spend about 20 minutes to go through the case study and to prepare for presentation sometime before commencement of a class. They are actually required to identify the main ideas and key points of the case through cooperative efforts. They are also required to explore answers in relation to the case questions. Furthermore, they are expected to be able to critically evaluate the case and elaborate further from the information given through an in-depth discussion of the case, which is important to achieve deep learning. Basically, the individual study and group discussion allow them to go through the process of engagement, exploration and transformation of information in a particular case study.

The class phase usually begins with a short random group sharing, followed by a presentation and reflection. At the beginning of a class, students are allowed to sit randomly in the classroom regardless of what self-organized groups they usually belong to. Chairs in the classroom are arranged to form a few circles of four or five students. In terms of time, they are given about 5 to 10 minutes to exchange information before their presentation starts. Such random arrangement is useful because students from different groups have an opportunity to exchange ideas and explore new information related to a case study from members of the other groups.

The students come back to their study group after the above sharing section. Each group is given about 5 minutes to present their findings to the whole class. Every student within a group is allocated 1 or 2 minutes to say something. It is not surprising that their presentation is interesting. Most of the questions they raise are also critical. This is because they already had some idea in mind about the case study. Immediately after the group presentation, there is an open discussion section in which each group is given 5 more minutes to welcome questions and comments from the other groups. The work of each group could be challenged by others. The teacher plays a coordinative and supportive role during the discussion. The students are told that their arguments are always treated as positive contributions to the whole class. Hence, they get rid of the constraint of feeling bad if they are not able to present the questions well or interpret the case correctly. As a result, students are able to give some very innovative ideas. Finally, the teacher debriefs the case study by commenting on each group's findings and opinions.

Discussion

It has been found that the use of the reflective learning model has animated the classroom atmosphere due to the active participation of students. The results of our experiments show that cooperative learning actually not only leads to very meaningful discussion in the class, but also stimulates the analytical thinking of the students. Students can initiate a number of questions apart from answering those assigned questions. In the case study of Manufacturing at Boeing Company, for example, our students are able to not only analytically discuss the provided case itself but also deductively suggest the application of CAD technology in different areas. It has been found that interaction among students is very frequent. The classroom dynamics have been enhanced by cooperative learning since almost all students in the class would actively participate in discussion.

Although some surveys show that many students are surface learners, we should not simply assume that our students are not positively motivated in learning. Instead, we should try to eliminate the constraints that caused surface learning, and explore the mechanism in achievement of deep learning. Based on our experience in using reflective learning strategy, it is not impossible to change students' learning behavior from a surface mode to a deep learning mode. However, since there are a number of variables affecting students' learning, it is important to structure a cooperative learning process systematically. The following suggests the key in relation to the motivation of students.

Firstly, an appropriate structure of a reflective learning process is important since it not only helps enhance students' motivation but also helps achieve deep learning. Generally speaking, students are positively motivated to study at a tertiary institution. After talking to a number of students recently, we found out that if students perceive that a course will be valuable to them in the future, they are likely to be motivated and study hard. Therefore, the selection of case materials must aim to enhance motivation of students. In addition, it is important to structure exercises so that a group has to count on each member to do his or her share. Therefore, from a practical point of view, reflective group learning should be structured in a way that students are able to apply general theories and principles in tackling a practical task cooperatively.

Secondly, encouraging participation is important in cooperative learning in order to achieve deep learning. The model requires students to be actively involved in discussion even when they prepare a case study before presentation. However, they should be given sufficient time and opportunity for relevant activities to acquire knowledge. Cooperative group learning not only enables students to become active, but also makes the learning environment in a classroom become very constructive. Students are motivated by the reinforcement they feel as they demonstrate competence in analysis of a practical case. This is because active participation in group discussion helps to stimulate motivation. As a result, students are able to develop skills they need to perform competently.

Thirdly, a supportive role of the teacher in facilitating students' learning will also definitely add to students' motivation. When a student demonstrates an acceptable performance during the presentation of a case study, feedback confirming his/her performance should be given immediately. In particular, a positive comment on students' presentation could greatly increase the morale of students because they feel good about their competence.

Furthermore, students should be encouraged to feel free to give opinions which may differ from those described in a particular case study. They should also be allowed to make mistakes although a teacher has to correct their incorrect opinions positively and give reasonable explanation. There is little doubt that a constructive comment will prevent students from becoming frustrated. As a result, students will be much more actively involved in discussions in the next class.

Finally, both open-ended and what if questions are useful to stimulate the analytical thinking of students. For example, asking some relevant questions in addition to those assigned questions of a particular case study, or suggesting the students think about a changing situation and any practical implication of the case in other areas would help very much to enhance their motivation and achieve deep learning.

Conclusions

The reflective group learning approach has been explored to teach case studies in engineering and technology management. The benefits from the use of the reflective learning model include the following: First, students are able to apply relevant theories to tackle practical problems through cooperative efforts. As the students question each other, they are forced to think and discuss a particular issue together, which should result in an increased understanding and better retention of information. Second, the small group work could greatly reduce students' passivity due to surface motive. It improves their learning from a shallow mode to a deep learning mode, which is very important to prepare students for problem-solving in the real world. The reflective learning strategy particularly encourages analytical thinking. As a result, students will have confidence in their abilities to apply their knowledge in the future. Third, the model allows students to feel free to share information and to fully participate in group discussion. In particular, the group presentation and the follow-up discussion provide students with an opportunity to reflect their abilities to apply basic theories and general knowledge to critically evaluate a practical case study. As a result, students are able to go very much beyond dualistic stage and achieve deep learning.

Successful implementation of the model requires systematic arrangement of a reflective learning process. Students should be introduced to the basic rationale of reflective learning and taught how to use the cooperative learning strategy. They should also be required not only to actively

222

participate in group work, but also to behave cooperatively in group activities. As a facilitator, the teacher should guide students' presentation, comment on their findings and lead the students to discuss practical implications and future development of a particular issue. Finally, a stimulation of analytical thinking throughout the reflective learning process is definitely necessary to enable students to achieve deep learning.

References

Biggs, J. B. (1979). Individual and group differences in study processes and the quality of learning outcomes. *Higher Education*, 8: 381–394.

Biggs, J. B. (1987). *Student Approaches to Learning and Studying*. Melbourne: Australian Council for Educational Research.

Chang, C. S. A. (1995). Rapport or compliance? Research Paper No. 14, National Institute of Education, Center for Applied Research in Education.

Cooper, J. L. & Mueck, R. (1989). Cooperative/collaborative learning: Research and practice at the collegiate level. *The Journal of Staff, Program, and Organization Development*, 7(3), 149–151.

Cooper, J., Prescott, S., Cook, L., Mueck, R. & Cuseo, J. (1990). *Cooperative Learning and College Instruction. Effective Use of Student Learning Teams*. Long Beach: Institute of Teaching and Learning.

Elton, L. (1988). Student motivation and achievement. *Studies in Higher Education*, 13(2), 215–221.

Johnson, D. & Johnson, R. T. (1990). Cooperative learning and achievement. In S. Sharan (Ed.), *Cooperative Learning*, pp. 23–38. New York: Praeger Publishers.

Johnson, D. & Johnson, R. (1993). What we know about cooperative learning at the college level. *Cooperative Learning*, 13(3), 17–18.

Kember, D. & Gow, L. (1991) A challenge to the anecdotal stereotype of the Asian student. *Studies in Higher Education*, 16: 117–128.

Lazarowitz, R. & Karsenty, G. (1990). Cooperative learning and students' academic achievement, process skills, learning environment, and self-esteem in tenth-grade biology classrooms. In S. Sharan (Ed.), *Cooperative Learning*, pp. 123–150. New York: Praeger Publishers.

Maier, M. H. & Keenan, D. (1994). Cooperative learning in economics. *Economic Inquiry*, XXXII: 358–361.

Marton, F. & Saljo, R. (1976). On qualitative differences in learning. *British Journal of Educational Psychology*, 46: 4–11 and 115–127.

Needham, D, Teomans, B., Dransfield, R. & Howkins, S. (1992). *Teaching Business Studies*, McGraw-Hill Book Company.

Sharan, S. (Ed.) (1990). *Cooperative Learning*, New York: Praeger Publishers.

Stoner, A. F., Freeman, R. E. & Gilbert, D. R. (1995). *Management*, 6th Ed. Prentice-Hall International, Inc.

Tottle, S., Stills, T., Digby, A. & Russ, P. (1991). *Cooperative Learning: A Guide to Research*. New York: Garland Publishing, Inc.

Whipple, W. R. (1987). Collaborative learning: Recognizing it when we see it. *AAHE Bulletin*, 40(2), 3–7.

Wilkinson, J. (1994). Using group-projects in the teaching of mathematics to electrical engineering students. In L. Thorley and R. Gregory, (Eds.), *Using Group-Based Learning in Higher Education*, Kogan Page Ltd.

The Reflection On A Masters Of Educational Administration Programme

Mollie Neville with Terry Fulljames and Shirley Macmillan-O'Rourke

Massey University
Auckland
New Zealand

Synopsis

In February 1994, a Masters of Educational Administration at a new satellite campus for Massey University in Auckland, New Zealand, attracted a wide range of administrators ranging from syndicate and section leaders, principals of primary and secondary schools and heads of departments to registrars in tertiary institutions. The problem was to make the course relevant to this range of participants and to adapt what had been designed as an extramural programme to an internal higher degree programme. Based on the experience of the academics who initiated this course ten years ago, as well as on the continuous reflection of the participants and the writer-lecturer, the course was progressively modified and, more importantly, the participants changed their practice. This case study traces three interwoven cases: that of myself, as the newly appointed lecturer modifying the course and methodology as I and the class critiqued the programme throughout the year, and those of two participants reflecting on changes made to their practice.

The Reflection On A Masters Of Educational Administration Programme

Mollie Neville with *Terry Fulljames* and
Shirley Macmillan-O'Rourke

Background

This case study is really a story, the narrative of the beginning of a new university, a new staff member and 14 inaugural students. It is changing and dynamic in nature. It is something like a 'mystery' unfolding as there was no precedent for the actors. I was responsible for setting up the first, internal course of the Masters of Educational Administration Degree Programme at Massey University, Albany campus in 1994. The course had been initiated by Associate Professor Wayne Edwards and Associate Professor Tom Prebble 10 years earlier as an extramural qualification and has proved very popular, with course places oversubscribed every year. I was one of the first graduates and felt excited and privileged to be chosen to start an internal course in Auckland, the largest city in New Zealand, having one third of the country's population. After obtaining my educational qualifications, I had the privilege of teaching Educational Administration to heads of department at the National Institute of Education, Nanyang Technological University in Singapore.

The New Zealand class comprised 14 administrators: a principal from a country school who travelled 60 minutes each way to attend class; three deputy principals of large urban secondary schools; a classroom teacher; two heads of departments in large urban private secondary schools; a head of syndicate in an urban primary school; two principals of primary schools (one urban and one rural); a full-time university researcher; a senior lecturer from the college of education; a university registrar from another university and the academic registrar of the second largest polytechnic in the country. Three of the participants were male. The age group ranged from early-thirties to middle-fifties, and included among the participants was a senior member of the Pacific Island community. Two students participated in this study as the case study is a portrayal of people reflecting on their action, not on the issues in education, as is the focus in the co-requisite paper, *Theory and Process in Education*. The process of reflective practice examined here applies to one of the two compulsory course papers entitled, *Action and Research in Educational Organisations.*

Theory In Use

Since its inception the course has been based on reflection-in-action, as the course title indicates (Schon, 1983, 1987). The three major assignments encourage students to keep work diaries and reflect on their practice, and to relate theory learned in lectures and readings to action. If necessary the students are expected to modify their practice, implement change and evaluate the effects of this change. The works of Sergiovanni (1992) and Owens (1992) form the core of their reading. The recent rapid move to self-managing institutions in New Zealand has resulted in the influence of Australian writers like Caldwell and Spinks (1988, 1993) on New Zealand administrators. The co-requisite paper has a strong critical theory bias and the influence of the work of Bates (1985), Smyth (1989), Foster (1986) and Codd (1989, 1992) are considerable. During my doctoral studies from 1990–94, I became familiar with Chen's adaptation of Schon's model (Chen, 1993) in her work among student teachers in Singapore. Her model is cyclical, beginning with reflection-for-action in identifying and analysing the problem preceding any action. This is followed by continual interactive process of reflection-on-action and action-on-reflection, reflection-in-action and action-in-reflection during the supervisory cycle and ends with the post-action activity which is once again reflection-on-action. This model seemed to me to be eminently suitable for a course for capable administrators, who although very busy are able to monitor their work practices and relationships and adjust them in action. There is evidence that novice teachers cannot adequately practice reflection-in-action (McIntyre, 1995) but there is no doubt from the work of researchers like Schon (1983) and Schulman (1986) and from my own experience with my mature students over many years, that they are able to engage in profitable reflection before, during and after an event. In other words, reflecting on the theory as content as well as process.

Methodology

The author has spent the last five years in research into school culture using naturalistic inquiry (Lincoln and Guba, 1985). This use of the human instrument to inquire into the natural setting of the institution proved to be the most suitable method of conducting research into reflective practice. Participants kept logs, journals or diaries and analysed the mass of detail of their everyday administrative lives in order to examine it for emergent themes. All three assignments centred on the application of theory and reflection to practice.

Narrative One: A Primary School

Shirley Macmillan-O'Rourke's primary school is situated in an affluent North Shore suburb of Auckland. There are 300 pupils in the school and although she is not a teaching principal, her job description is a demanding one. It includes responsibility for the school's management and professional leadership; implementation of policies and programmes; direction and supervision of teaching and non-teaching staff and directing the day-to-day operation of the school in accordance with the school's Charter.

Macmillan-O'Rourke's analysis of her diaries shows an exceptionally busy leader. As her co-participant Terry Fulljames, a polytechnic registrar, has noted in class on several occasions, although he is busy he does have support staff, whereas his administrative colleagues in smaller institutions have to carry out many of the trivia and menial tasks of administration — such as attending to faulty plumbing and covering for an absent clerical or teaching staff — themselves. In the first day of her diary she initiated 19 interactions and others staff member initiated 22, and she made 17 telephone calls. After itemising a full day — including spending an hour coping with a child that was tearing up books and was greatly distressed, she notes:

> The thing that strikes me most is the lack of time to reflect or even think clearly for five minutes. I must work on that (Macmillan, 14 March 1994)!

The second day she began the day at 7:40 am and finished at the end of the Board of Trustees' meeting at 10:30 pm. On the next day she adds:

> I am constantly aware that my day is broken up by a multitude of variables over which I have little control (Macmillan, 16 March 1994).

One of her major goals as a result of the first reflections was therefore:

> To take care not to try to be all things to all people for fear of role overload and stress. As the school is in a growing stage, the amount of time that clerical staff are available is perhaps insufficient in light of the demands of the extra paper work involved in Tomorrow's Schools and the number of new enrolments that are coming in. To avoid role overload, it may be necessary for me to look at the hours worked by the secretary and teacher's aide to ensure that there is always someone available to do the many trivial technical jobs that I find myself doing (photocopying, dealing with sick children, and answering the phone) (Macmillan, 29 April, 1994).

In her final assignment, she reflects on the whole academic year. She says that her leadership model is now less managerial and more of a transformative and reflective nature. As a result of standing back and examining the major issues in the current educational scene in New Zealand she feels:

> A major task for educational leaders today is to take a stand in rejecting market-driven utilitarianism and in promoting the concepts of social justice and fairness for all in education (Macmillan, September 1994).

At the beginning of the year she admits she had taken up most of her energy with 'managing the firm' but now she has developed a theoretical perspective which she calls 'critical-reflective'. In a practical way she implemented this by encouraging meaningful involvement of participants in important aspects of life in the school.

The 'critical incident' she describes is the decision of the staff to put on an art extravaganza instead of the time-honoured school concert. She decided to become a follower-leader and supported the staff in their ambitious project which ran counter to her own wishes and the traditions of the community. Her process was one of 'reflection-in-action' throughout. The theme of the extravaganza was Maori legends and involved the Maori culture group, sound effects, children reading legends and magnificent works of art. The benefits were the formation of a community of staff instead of one divided according to the age group they taught and 'the acceptance by parents, of things Maori':

> By delegating responsibility to the teachers I took a risk that it would work and that they would feel committed to complete the task to a high standard. Our 'extravaganza' was a complete success (Macmillan, September, 1994).

Narrative Two: A Polytechnic

Terry Fulljames is the academic registrar of a polytechnic with 500 full-time and over 500 part-time staff. The prevailing culture is corporate, (Ball, 1987) with a strong hierarchy led by a leader known as the CEO (Chief Executive Officer) rather than 'director' or 'principal'. Terry records that the single most important event in the year was the process of reflection that began with the first assignment:

> I knew I was always busy working 9 to 10 hours per day. It was amazing to identity how much of that time was spent in meetings, talking to people, telephone calls, responding to and assisting staff. The act of taking time to reflect has been a vital part of the transformational approach I am now taking (Fulljames, September 1994).

Early in the academic year, when the word 'reflection' had only been used infrequently, Terry uses the word again and again. The very process of engaging in the assignment showed him the importance of reflection. His last paragraph reads:

The key to success will be 'reflection', consciously thinking over each activity and evaluating how and why I performed the way I did and consider whether it could have been performed better or not performed at all (Fulljames, April,1994:15).

Like his co-participant, Shirley, he notes the difficulty of taking time to reflect:

> The biggest problem in the job is finding time for planning and reflection...
> My workload is large and I usually spend 9–10 hours per day at work and often take work home (Fulljames, April, 1994:15).

He also notes that in completing the reorganisation of the academic registry throughout 1994, the theory he had studied and influence of class colleagues and lecturers had a powerful effect on this implementation. This involved the reduction of hierarchies, the introduction of three team facilitators with 'total interaction between all three teams, and decision making' left to each team.

In the process of critiquing the appraisal system at his institution and sharing appraisal systems with the other 13 participants, Terry devised a system of continuous appraisal, rather than the annual system used by the organisation. He notes, however, that this system will fit into corporate requirements. He concludes that:

> The sharing together of experiences covering the primary through to tertiary education sectors is helping to broaden my whole perspective and understanding of education in New Zealand (Fulljames, September, 1994).

Narrative Three: Reflection on the Course

- **Andragogy**

  As the course became internal with 28 two-hour lectures in two semesters, it was necessary to modify the traditional lecturer-dominated style, especially as the participants came to lectures twice a week from 4–6 pm when they had already put in a long day in their institutions. The emphasis was first put on the learning environment and attention was focused on the participant's needs, with an attractive seminar room and provision of drinks and snacks as they arrived. This created an encouraging and relaxing environment for adult learners, most of whom had not engaged in formal study for many years. The next step was to adapt the content from an extramural study guide dependency. The author spent two sessions determining the learning needs of the class and working with them to establish evaluation criteria.

As a result, use was made of the widest variety of teaching media possible and as the year progressed the emphasis was increasingly placed on participant involvement and on relating everything to the particular institutions of each participant. As trust developed, the participants opened up about their problems and allowed others to offer support, empathise and perhaps offer advice. Teaching methods used were based on catering to several different learning styles within each lecture. These included lectures with overhead transparencies, debates, buzz groups, devising models and graphics, brainstorming on A3 sheets of paper, videos, datashows as well as role play and simulations. A constant checking on the participants' needs resulted in each lecture averaging at least three different learning styles. The basic principles of adult learning — relevance, honesty, sincerity, encouragement, involvement and ownership — with which the author and several participants were familiar were kept to the forefront.

- **Continuous Course Evaluation**
    a) Verbal feedback times in every lecture, using questions such as 'What have I learned?' and 'What is hindering my learning?'
    b) Verbal feedback in last lecture from each student in the presence of the lecturer and head of department (Professor John Codd), as to strengths and weaknesses of the course.
    c) The official university student evaluation test (SET) which is conducted by a colleague in the absence of the lecturer and sent to the Academic Vice Chancellor's department for interpretation. Results from the final SET indicated an overwhelmingly positive response to the course content, methodology and relevance to their workplace.

Conclusion

The process of 1994 was one of 15 colleagues (14 participants and the lecturer) working cooperatively to support each other's learning. This took place within a trusting, encouraging environment where people were supported in their tragedies, celebrated in their successes and sustained through the bad patches when finishing the course seemed impossible. All participants completed the two papers, and all achieved well when compared with the extramural participants. The continuous adjustment and self-scrutiny modelled by myself and participants together using the Schon (1987) and Chen models (1993) provided an exciting introduction to a pioneering programme. We all believe "there will be no year like this again".

References

Ball, S. J. (1987). *The Micro-Politics of the School.* London: Methuen.

Caldwell, B. J & Spinks, J. M. (1988). *The Self-Managing School.* East Sussex: Falmer Press.

Chen, Ai-Yen (1993). Experienced and student teachers' reflection on classroom practice. *Educational Research and Perspectives*, Vol. 20, No. 1, pp. 46–63.

Codd, J. (1989). Educational leadership as reflective action. In J. Smyth (Ed.), *Critical Perspective on Educational Leadership*, pp. 157–177. East Sussex: Falmer Press.

Foster, W. (1989). Towards a critical practice of leadership. In J. Smyth (Ed.), *Critical Perspective on Educational Leadership.* East Sussex: Falmer Press.

Fulljames, T. (1994). *My Leadership Style: What Has Influenced It and Has There Been Any Change This Year?* Unpublished Masters assignment, September, 1994.

Fulljames, T. (1994). *The Administrator's Work Study: The Academic Registrar, What Does He Do With His Time?* Unpublished Masters assignment, April, 1994.

Macmillan-O'Rourke, S. (1994). *A Leadership Model based on Transformative and Reflective Action*. Unpublished Masters assignment, September, 1994.

Macmillan-O'Rourke, S. (1994). *The Administrator's Work Study: All Things to All People*. Unpublished Masters assignment, April 1994.

Owens, R. G. (1992). *Organizational Behavior in Schools*. New Jersey: Prentice-Hall.

Schon, D. A. (1983). *The Reflective Practitioner*. New York: Basic Books.

Schon, D. A. (1987). *Educating the Reflective Practitioner*. San Francisco: Jossey Bass.

Schulman, Lee S. (1986). Those who understand: knowledge growth in teaching. *Educational Researcher*, February.

Sergiovanni, T. J. (1992). *Moral Leadership: Getting to the Heart of School Improvement*. San Francisco: Jossey Bass.

Smyth, J. (1989). A pedagogical and educative view of leadership. In J. Smyth (Ed.), *Critical Perspective on Educational Leadership*. East Sussex: Falmer Press.

Reflecting On University Teaching Practices

Marnie O'Neill

Graduate School of Education
University of Western Australia,
Australia

Synopsis

In Australia, as in many other countries, academic staff in universities are usually appointed to positions on the basis of the expertise in their subject discipline and their demonstrated or potential achievement as researchers. Those positions normally require at least half-time commitment to teaching comprising a mix of lectures, seminars or tutorials and laboratories or clinical work, depending on the particular subject discipline.

In the early 1990s, it was acknowledged that teaching competence in tertiary institutions could be improved through professional development activities. Programs were initiated by the federal government to provide financial assistance for the development of such activities. This article reports on a project, 'Enhancing the Quality of Teaching and Learning', funded from the National Priority Reserve Fund by the Department of Employment, Education and Training (DEET), Canberra, Australia to produce multimedia packages for professional development of academic staff. Under the terms of the grant, materials had to be generic; although a specific case was used as a basis, the product had to be appropriate for professional development of tertiary teachers from diverse disciplinary backgrounds in collegial learning programs or for private use.

Reflecting on University Teaching Practices

Marnie O'Neill

Introduction

Preliminary research for the development group included participation in a professional development program for tertiary teachers working in large lecture situations. Participants

- identified problems or anxieties they experienced in working in large lecture situations (varying from class sizes of 50 students to 650 in a single lecture setting)
- viewed video taped extracts of beginning, middle and end of two or three large lecture situations, focusing on techniques and strategies used by each lecturer
- reflected on the relevance to their own practice, and shared alternative approaches based on own practice
- refocused on original anxieties etc to see how they might be resolved on the basis of shared reflective experiences of the workshop.

The information collected in the workshop indicated that the competencies required for effective teaching and learning at the tertiary level differed from secondary school teaching more in scale than in kind. More teaching took place in large group settings, making it more difficult for teachers to assess the level of knowledge or competence of the learners both on entry and throughout the course, and making it more difficult for academics to develop a rapport with their classes, and to feel confident about maintaining the interest and cooperation of students in such settings. The key concerns expressed by participants in the professional development program included:

(a) discipline, management and control,
(b) ascertaining students' entry level; activating existing student knowledge,
(c) acquiring and using feedback from students.

Because of the interests in constructivism and cooperative learning shared by the project team, the teaching approach taken in the particular case includes cooperative teaching and learning strategies applicable to large lecture situations.

One of the intentions of the project was to promote reflective teaching practices. The proposition was that, if these are encouraged, the long term effects of the instructional packages would be greater than that of a set of decontextualised exemplars of 'best practices'. Although teaching adults varies somewhat from teaching secondary school children, many reflective teaching practices apply equally well in universities as they do in schools. Certainly the complexity of teachers' work, as described by Richert (1991, p. 132), with its requirement for vast amounts of information about a vast number of things, and the ability to select from and deploy this information 'on the run' is little different. Part of the challenge for this project, therefore, was to find a means of making those complexities available to self-directed learners in ways that they could control the flow of information and select from it what they needed at any particular time.

Method

The research base for the project included effective teacher research, expert-novice teacher research (Livingstone and Borko, 1989; Westerman, 1991; Cole, 1993), collaborative teaching and learning, conceptualisation of teaching and learning, and more recent work on reflective teacher theory. The term 'expert' in the research literature is intended to convey a high level of competence and success as a teacher rather than denoting a hard-edged technocratic view of teaching. 'Expertise' is not necessarily linked to age or experience — as Cole (1993) pointed out, some teachers may acquire both age and experience without reaching the status of 'expert' as recognised by their peers and students or the results gained by students in their courses. Thus, although the term 'expert' is not entirely satisfactory because of some of its technocratic connotations, it was used in this project because no other single word satisfactorily conveyed the qualities shared by the teachers interviewed for this study.

The argument for using modern technology such as digitised video and CD-ROM was based on research on expert–novice teachers, interactive video and computer-based instruction, and modelling in teacher education. In particular, multimedia CDs seemed to offer the opportunity for interactive packages that could provide diverse information (print, graphic and audio visual) which could be accessed selectively and recursively according to the user's individual needs and interests.

Design and development of the program was based on a number of assumptions:

• demonstrations of pedagogical skills are more likely to be helpful if they are illustrated in holistic classroom settings enabling users to become involved in typical student-student and teacher-student interactions.

• understanding of teacher behaviour in classroom interactions will be enhanced if observers have access to the teacher's explanation of his/her decision-making process.

• there is usually more than one effective way of dealing with a problem, so it is useful to have access to a diversity of opinion in which to locate reflections on one's own teaching practices.

• students, being expert teacher-watchers and clientele can offer valuable advice on the ways in which they experience classroom interactions, and their expectations of teaching and learning situations.

• research findings are sometimes contradictory, depending on the specific contexts in which the research was conducted, and cannot be regarded as absolute guidelines; instead they provide a context in which the users of the program can reflect on their own classroom practices, and pursue congruent research findings.

Structure of Program

The program consists of edited video footage of a teaching and learning situation (that is, a large lecture) supported by excerpts of interviews with the teacher, the experts, and students, which can be accessed from the classroom video by 'clicking' on the appropriate icon with the mouse. The equivalent of 40 minutes of real-time video footage is compressed on each disk.

Although first-time users may find it most beneficial to watch the classroom interaction right through, and sample the additional information by clicking on the icons as they come up (Option 1), once users have a feel for it, they can track through for specific information, rather than watching the whole program. Option 2 allows users to select specific sections of the video, and the associated interviews, research and practical advice. Option 3 provides direct access to the research base and practical advice strands to read or print the information required. The structure of the program thus allows users to determine which information they want to access, and how much of it they can take in at any one time.

The teacher presenting the lecture was an acknowledged expert teacher who had thirty years experience and had won a number of awards for teaching. His lecture was a forty-five minute mathematics class for approximately 100 first year undergraduate students, edited to 12 minutes of video time. The teaching and learning interactions in the program were not intended to be regarded as exemplary practices. Rather, they provide opportunities for discussion of what goes on in the context of the teacher's own rationale, the opinions of other experts and students, and research findings. The expectation is that users will relate them to their own teaching practices.

The ten expert teachers had received awards from the university for excellence in teaching and were identified by students as outstanding teachers. They were located in a range of disciplines, including mathematics, geology, chemistry, agriculture, law, French language and literature, Italian language and literature, Japanese language, and teacher education. When invited, they expressed willingness to contribute to the program. Each participated in a video-recorded interview of approximately forty minutes. Although the participants were given a broad indication of the territory of the interviews, they were not supplied with the questions beforehand. Frequently there was a good deal of commonality in their views, but on some issues they offered divergent opinions.

The ten students interviewed were located in a similar range of disciplines. Their university experience varied from first year Arts to final year studies in Agriculture and Law. Like the experts, the students were not provided with the interview questions before being interviewed on camera. Again, not all of the material could be included in the program; representative extracts which relate to the topics of this program were selected.

The selection of material from the interview data for inclusion in the program was made on several criteria, some of which were very pragmatic — visual appeal, succinctness of comment, and tight focus on the specific topic were primary considerations. Equally important was the content of what was said, and where possible, selections were made on the basis of difference, to offer users divergent views or practices which might serve as lenses for reflection on their own practices. If interviewees were in general agreement, then comments which extended or elaborated the shared position were included.

The research abstracts were not intended to be comprehensive, but as a summary of current information in the field. Consequently, the material is eclectic in nature, rather than taking a particular position or orientation in the research literature, and presenting only information congruent with that position. A short list of references was included with each abstract, and was supported by a more extensive bibliography. Although much of the research on teaching and learning cited was conducted in school settings, many of the findings apply equally well to university education (Dunkin and Precians, 1992).

Information in the practical advice strand was intended as a guideline for translating some of the research findings and the advice from the experts into practical strategies for the user's classroom. The suggestions are not infallible. Users are encouraged to reflect on the specific contexts in which they work, and the groups of students with whom they work in evaluating the appropriateness of some strategies to their contexts. For example, although the classroom footage shows students working effectively in pairs in a lecture group of 100+, it is not suggested that the same technique could be used equally effectively with a group of 600. The practical advice strand provides both caveats and guidelines to consider if users plan to apply the strategies in their own practice.

Examples from Program

The examples selected from the program for this paper address the key concerns expressed by the tertiary teachers in the preliminary research. Coincidentally, they are also topics on which the expert teachers offer diverse opinions, depending on their subject discipline and their own practices.

Activating Student Knowledge

(i) Planning phase

Given that university teachers are usually appointed because of their expertise and research in specific subject disciplines, and that one of the roles of university teachers is to induct students into a specialist field of knowledge, it seemed reasonable to assume that most university teachers might be located in the academic tradition of reflective teaching. That is, their reflections and practices might be driven more by subject discipline considerations than, for instance, social efficiency, or social reconstruction, except where those considerations were part of the way in which the subject discipline was constituted. Shulman (1986, 1987) and Buchmann (1984) have emphasised the importance of teachers deliberating about ways in which their subject matter is constructed, and how that might best be transformed for students. Shulman (1986) proposed that for informed decision-making, subject matter knowledge must be integrated with pedagogical content knowledge and curricular knowledge; that is, the teacher must be able to deconstruct the teachability of subject specialist knowledge, and plan a curriculum sequence to make it learnable for students. A teacher should be able to identify alternative routes through the information if the initial approach turns out to be inaccessible for some students. For example, successful teaching and learning might be characterised by the capacity of students to assimilate the new information, resolve anomalies between existing and new information, apply the new information or procedures to different situations, or to generalise from the specific instances to a more general case or application.

A feature of this project was the extent to which the experts consciously considered the ways in which the subject matter information might be made accessible to their students, suggesting that their criteria for assessing the adequacy of their teaching are primarily drawn from their academic disciplines (Zeichner and Tabachnick, 1991, p. 5). At the planning stages, lecturers tended to think about the current state of students' knowledge, how they might best come to terms with the material to be presented, and how to make it interesting to them:

> When I am planning a session, I think about how the students are going to best get this knowledge that I am trying to give them, and the first thing I tend to think about is how I am going to get their interest. You can have all the information prepared so that it is interesting to you, but how are they going to respond to it? So I think the first thing in all my teaching is thinking of what the students' reaction to this material might be. It might be interesting to me, but deadly dull to them. So I think that is where I start.

> One of the ways I decide whether something is going to be interesting to students or not is through experience because you have to try things out and get reactions through time. When I first started teaching, I thought that students would be really interested in the history of how things came to be, and I would tell them all these exciting things about the sequence of events of how we know these things, and they were not very interested in that at all. They were more interested in things that were current and active now; the history did not really attract them, although that may have been the way I was presenting it. But students are interested in things that are relevant and it is easy in Agriculture, because there are a lot of really

relevant things to draw on and so current things that farmers are involved
in now, interactions that I have with farmers; they are all the things that
I can draw on now to make things more interesting for students.

(Lynn Abbot, Agriculture)

I guess I try to see it from the student's point of view, where they are at,
what they have done before, what I might reasonably expect as a starting
point for many. I think I also think about what might be reasonable
challenges for the students to be left with, because I think in the end, the
responsibility is the students' for what they learn, and I certainly don't
think in terms of what I have got to get across. I am totally opposed to
the idea that I am sitting out there transmitting knowledge to them. It just
does not relate to me at all. I think the idea of a lecture is guidance for
what sort of things they need to construct, maybe picking out some
highlights. So that leads me to think well, what the heck *do* they know
now, what sorts of thoughts might they have, how can I get at their level.

(Bob Bucat, Chemistry)

The students in the study indicated that they were not very forthcoming
about what they did know. They were unanimous about the difficulty of
asking questions in large lecture situations, and most said that they would
not, leaving the lecturer to find other means of assessing the knowledge
that students have about a particular topic:

Yes I do ask questions in tutorials. They are different because you have
gone through a lecture, you have semi-understood the material and you are
trying to clear up what you have heard and what you may possibly have
misunderstood, what you have researched, so it is not just material from
lectures, but materials from your research so there is a wider scope there,
basically.

Asking questions in either lectures or tutorials can be embarrassing, but
I have found over the years that asking a question usually does not just
involve you, it involves quite a few other people, it clears up a lot of
matter not just for one person, but a lot of people. Embarrassing yes, but
worthwhile.

(Premela, Science student)

I don't really like asking questions in lectures because of the large size of the group, but in tutorials I find that just by asking a few questions you can really get a lot out of a tutorial session, probably quite a lot more than a lecture because you can clear up things you may find hard to understand.

(Kate, first year Arts student)

In the case used in the project, the teacher attempted to overcome these difficulties in the ways that he engaged students with the mathematics problems:

When I'm teaching, I always encourage students to think about the problems before they actually start writing things down and get carried away with trying to solve it. The first thing is to try and construct an image in your mind of what the general problem is all about. Then you can carry on with filling in some of the details and maybe trying to sort out some of the arithmetic or algebra. But the initial thinking about the problem in a bigger setting and constructing in your mind the way you're going to approach the problem is one of the keys to problem solving, I think...........

One of the challenges in lecturing to large groups — or small groups for that matter — is to get the students to think about the problem at the same kind of level that I'm thinking about it. I always encourage them to think about it, and ask them, "What do you think *I'm* thinking about?" And try to get a communication at that level. When I see them nodding their heads and smiling, and understanding, then I think they are really beginning to understand some mathematics, and that's particularly rewarding.

(Doug Pitney, Mathematics)

(ii) Interactive phase

In the case used in the study, the teacher deliberately attempted to make use of students' existing knowledge, by linking it with applications in the real world and by foreshadowing the ways in which it would connect to work in the short term future. The students had been working through assigned problems for some time; as they reached closure on one, the teacher turned to a brief discussion of application of the kinds of problems they had been working. In his interview he offered a brief explanation:

I think the students can relate to the mathematics if I can set it into a bigger picture. Like in this case I used an example of carbon dating, and there are a host of examples that we will be doing in future lectures. So this also gives students a link from what we're doing now to what we'll be doing just down the road.

(Doug Pitney, Mathematics)

The expert teachers offered a range of views on this issue, seeking to relate material to the life experience of students, to existing subject knowledge, and to leave them with an intellectual challenge to stimulate further thought and reading:

It is always an interesting exercise in teaching literature to try to let the students see a link between the literature and their life experience or their knowledge of reading or films or theatre, and when they make these connections for themselves then it is always very exciting in class. Even if it is not maybe necessarily very useful for their ultimate mastery of the discipline. It is something they have got involved in, and they remember it, therefore, so I think that in teaching a literature course where you are mainly dealing with human emotions and social interaction, there are lots of parallels you can draw with everyday life. Just one example, if there is room for a slight example is that in my teaching Caribbean literature, I can call upon the student's own knowledge of the aboriginal situation in Australia; they are interested in that parallel and they know things that I don't know, so they can contribute towards the learning process in a way that I couldn't.

(Beverley Ormerod, French language and literature)

I think a common strategy for relating to existing knowledge is by presenting either some bit of information that they might be familiar with or doing a lecture demonstration in which there is some sort of conflict, in which there appears to be a conflict with what they might have known before. In other words, the expectation — indeed I might ask them — is that they will make a prediction about some situation that is very common. I guess by the end of most years, most students know that when I ask a question in a particular way, the answer is going to be the one that is not expected. Cognitive conflict is the way I would describe that.

(Bob Bucat, Chemistry)

In trying to activate the students' existing knowledge, there are two aspects to it. One is their existing general knowledge, so if you are presenting an example, then perhaps you try to present examples which would be within their range of experience, maybe sporting, or some kind of industrial process, something like that, and they can imagine how things would work. Mathematically it is a little more difficult because you have to think about what they have done in the past and try to tie what you are doing to it. Quite often that will involve summarising things which they might have done a year or two before — things which they did and forgot about. So if you perceive while you are lecturing that perhaps they are not following what you are doing, quite often it is not the particular issue you are talking about; quite often it is something they did a few years ago which they have forgotten about, so you have to bear that in mind, and perhaps try to summarise very briefly that particular aspect of the problem.

(Graham Hocking, Mathematics)

The students expressed strong views on the ways in which teachers might best relate the new material to their existing knowledge. One aspect which was not picked up by the experts, in this context, although they did identify it as one of the reasons for using small group cooperative learning interactions, was the difference between the level of specialist discourse in which experts felt comfortable, and that which the students had achieved:

They could try and communicate with the student at the student's level. A lot of teachers I find have problems communicating because they just do things like assume the student knows things without verifying if they actually do understand some sort of background, or teachers speak with terminology which they are really accustomed to but the student is struggling with, and that all sort of tends to make it confusing for the student.

(Kate, first year Arts student)

Another student added to this with a plea for structuring large chunks in ways that students could discern the relative importance of different parts of the material:

I think to become better communicators, teachers could possibly first of all realise the capacity of who they are talking to. Like they are talking to students; they are not talking to world experts, so they should first of all realise that and sort of come from there. A lot of the time, especially in my course, the areas that the lecturers are covering are very complex and they encompass large and difficult bodies of information, so the capacity to pick out the important parts and not dwell upon little insignificant things which detract from the important things is important, and not to get too technical because students lose interest if they think they are listening to a lot of information they don't feel is applicable out in the field. That is an important part if the lecturer can bring a practical aspect into what he is talking about. That sort of seems to catch my attention a bit more because I know what he is telling me is not a waste of time as far as future work and research goes.

(Adele, fourth year Agriculture student)

The research abstract available at this point in the program offered a brief summary of main findings, and some directions to relate to their own practice.

Reading Feedback from Students

Reading feedback from students during the course of the lecture was important to all of the experts involved in the project. They used it to make decisions about students' readiness to move on to the next phase of the lesson, approximating to Schon's (1983) notion of 'reflection-in-action'. The teacher in this particular case said:

The way I get feedback from the class, I look at particular individuals. I have four or five people in that particular class that I watch, and I get feedback from them by way of a frown, or I can see their mouths actually answer the question, so that I can see they know how to get going — and some of them outright smile, and I know they have got the idea. I know that their ability is not necessarily very high, but it's also not low, so I can make judgements on the spot as to how much more I have to teach that material, or the class is ready to move on to something new.

(Doug Pitney, Mathematics)

The experts garnered feedback from their students in a variety of ways:

I guess eye contact is one of the ways in which I try to assess understanding, and I can't explain it much more than that. I think there is a sense in which you can look at somebody, and if you catch their eye, they may well give you a slight nod, or there may be a look in their eye that is a look of complete blankness, in which case I think it is time to take some further steps in terms of explanation of the concept.

I certainly do look around for cues from students, particularly if I have been trying to explain what seems to me a difficult point. I will very much look for some sort of acknowledgment of understanding, then I will try other techniques such as asking students questions and trying to get responses from the student group to see if the message has got out effectively.

(Neil Morgan, Law)

.....it seems that I often have six or seven students who, because students often sit in fairly much the same places, I seem to be able to focus on. I don't know what causes them to stand out, and I will often say to them in Labs that I use them as monitors. Perhaps it's because they are more exaggerated in their body language and I continue to notice these people as guides to how I am going. I certainly don't try to get feedback from two hundred and fifty, but I'm very aware of how it is going for these six or seven.

(Bob Bucat, Chemistry)

One of the experts was very aware that some nonverbal feedback may not always be reliable:

Feedback from body language and facial expressions is of several sorts. At one end of the scale is the student who nods in agreement with everything that you have said and after a while you learn not to be flattered by that because the reason is not necessarily that the student agrees with you. The other kind at the opposite end is the student who talks or fidgets at the back of the room, and again that is something that one must try not to take personally. It is not always necessarily that the student does not want to be there, but that the student has something different on their mind that is more important, so I think that learning to cope with that kind of disruption is difficult. Learning to cope with the nodding student is not hard at all, but it is distracting. I try looking for feedback with a group for signs that they are meeting my eyes, that they are following what I am saying, if it is a language that they are looking at the book or they are looking at me, that they are not indulging in too much talking among themselves, but they are with the mainstream of discussion.

(Beverley Ormerod, French language and literature)

One lecturer organised her program to collect feedback systematically from her students and used it as a means of establishing rapport with them:

I like to get feedback from students and I do this in lectures. Every second lecture I get them to fill in little pieces of paper with questions that I have asked them, or I get them to write something that relates what I have been teaching them to the wider world, or to their knowledge of agriculture in general — how does what I am teaching them fit into what they know outside. Because I do this regularly, the students give me a lot of feedback about the way I am doing it; I ask them whether they like the way I am presenting it, and they tell me what they do like and what they don't. I am quite open to asking them bluntly how I am going, and that has been the most useful thing to me because students are very honest. I found that the rapport that I build up with them in this feedback session means that they give me quite honest responses and I can respond quickly. I can respond at the next lecture to something that they have suggested to me.

(Lynn Abbot, Agriculture)

Students were aware that they provided feedback to lectures, some of them more overtly than others:

I think I give nonverbal communication to a lecturer if I get along with the lecturer. If I don't care about the lecturer or what is going on, then I am not very conscious of maybe my facial expressions and everything else, but otherwise I have had lecturers who will kind of look to me for approval or look at me to see if I am interested and I give them that sort of nonverbal communication, like nod of the head, or a smile or something to make them think that you are still listening or interested.

(Shannon, third year Arts student)

Others were a little more sceptical about the possibility of influencing the teacher in a large lecture situation:

> I don't think the lecturer is going to do very much about it because he or she is faced with anything from 100 to 200 students in there, and unless everyone is displaying some kind of negative feedback it is not going to click with them that there is a problem happening here. Some lecturers are very perceptive and they are very particular about the noise level and use that as an indicator of what is happening in the class. If the noise level goes up suddenly, they say something like, "So what is happening, is there a problem? Have I done something stupid or not, are you bored, or whatever?" And that is a point to stop and get things clarified, but otherwise they just sort of rattle on with whatever they were saying.
>
> (Maria, Mathematics student)

Cooperative Learning Techniques

The case teacher, Doug Pitney, held the view that students need to construct knowledge for themselves, and to promote articulation of the ways in which they were shaping their knowledge, used a variety of cooperative learning strategies. In the lecture, the teacher set a highly specific task for students to work on in pairs. Immediately after clearly setting the task, he moved around the class, making sure that each student had a partner with whom to work, and that no-one was left obviously and uncomfortably stranded. His rationale for using cooperative learning techniques with students was clear:

> I try to group students up in pairs as much as I can, because I think when they're discussing the ideas with each other, they consolidate the ideas in their own minds, and that is the key. So when I ask them to think about these things, that's an individual activity, and when they talk about it with their partner in their group, they can consolidate what they're thinking about, and hopefully get an idea of what's going on.
>
> Another way I use groups in large lectures is just to have the students turn to their neighbour, and discuss their approach to the problem, or how they think they're going to start the problem with their neighbour. Sometimes

it is a little more difficult to get the students to come out of their groups because they sometimes want to continue to chat. I find that if I'm firm at the beginning, they understand that what I'm trying to do is encourage them to think about it individually, and explain it to their partner, they really enjoy doing it that way, and they stop talking as soon as I say, "OK work on it on your own."

I find that when I put students into pairs, they discuss the problem at their own level with words and language they understand, because basically they're all in the same boat. When they run into a problem, then of course I can intervene, but I find that if they discuss it in their own terms, they actually will come to some understanding very quickly.

(Doug Pitney, Mathematics)

One of the expert teachers was engaged in preservice teacher education. Part of her attention was directed to providing demonstrations of strategies appropriate for secondary school classrooms, but she found that the strategies equally suited students in tertiary studies:

In terms of school classrooms it is important to have kids talking in small groups because they learn well when they hear the language from their peers and when they use the language themselves. If I stand at the front of the class and deliver information, the students won't really understand that information unless they have the chance to process it in some way. They need to be encouraged to talk about it with someone who talks at the same level as they do and to explore it a bit further to share ideas with their peers and come to some conclusions of their own. The same thing is very appropriate at the university level...... I do divide them into groups, but not using the content level that school students would use; I give them appropriate adult content level, and it is interesting to note that the process they go through is just as valid.

(Di Gardiner, Teacher Education)

Neil Morgan used buzz (discussion) groups as a means of increasing student involvement without having to direct questions to a specific individual (a practice that most students indicated they hated in large lectures):

I would certainly divide the group into buzz groups or discussion groups at times, and certainly ask questions in lectures. If I don't get any response,

I will ask people to talk amongst themselves for a while and think about the answer, and then call on people or ask for volunteers. I will do that even in small tutorials if I find that the discussion is not going.

In terms of buzz groups, I organise them rather informally, in that I simply ask students to talk in a group of about five to ten — depends on the size of the class and class dynamics. I certainly don't formally divide people up into buzz groups; it depends on where they are sitting in the lecture. I find generally speaking that it works if you do it from the start of the course. If you wait until you are two thirds of the way into the year, and people have got used to a certain form of behaviour in lectures, then it doesn't work so well.

(Neil Morgan, Law)

The students in this study generally regarded their peers as valuable resources for learning:

When there is a small group of people you can't expect other people to answer the questions for you, you have no choice but to learn the material and answer it for yourselves. I think pairing up with someone is great. I have had lots of friends and people who have study groups, and they learn ten times more. I learn a lot when I can bounce things off somebody else, and when you can study together, and learn together, prepare for things together you learn a lot more, it makes you remember things more. I think I learn a lot from other students because they see things I might not have seen, or they read things I would not have read, and they have got different opinions. I mean talking to more people gives them more information, really. If you assume that they know what they are talking about, then you can get information from them as well.

(Shannon, third year Arts student)

Some students found cooperative learning situations so effective that they were prepared to organise them outside the formal class structures:

I find small groups are very useful for studying and learning because you can all have your own say; it is not like a lecture where you have got to sit and listen to one lecturer, you can all put in your own bit and together you can form an opinion on a matter which you didn't understand before. It happened last year when I was doing contract law, when I used to get together, just ourselves as students into groups of about six or seven. If we didn't understand an area of law, we all used to sit down and give our opinion on what we believed that area of law was, and then we sort of came to a conclusion about what it actually was. I found that very useful.

(Duncan, second year Law student)

Group work was not totally endorsed by the students. One student drew a distinction between work that was designed to facilitate learning, and work which might count for assessment:

Collaborative group work I find useful in a way because you get other people's feedback and their ideas, so it is useful in that sense, because you are not just concentrating on your point of view which could be too narrow; you get feedback, you can get some understanding of how broadly you are thinking, so that is quite useful.

Pairing up with other students I think is a bit of a bad idea. It is good in a way, because you can get another person's point of view and ideas coming in, but it can lead to one doing all the work and one not being interested, so it can be a waste of time as well. It depends on the sort of area you are covering and the situation.

(Adele, fourth year Agriculture student)

The research abstracts provided a brief rationale for use of cooperative learning techniques, followed by more detailed reporting of research findings for lecturers who wanted to pursue particular issues. This information in the research strand was supported by practical advice on group size.

From the preliminary research, lecturers seemed to have two fears about group techniques, especially in large lectures: loss of control, and inability to recall students once they had been 'let loose'. The approach in this study gives users the opportunity to see a lecturer using paired strategies in a large lecture situation, to hear fairly explicit explanations from expert teachers about ways in which they employ the small group techniques, as well as some caveats and endorsements from students, together with practical advice to consider before they put themselves at risk in their lecture room. The program can also provide some starting points for reflection on the way that their attempts went, and in what ways they might be improved.

Disruptions and Deviations

One of the most pressing anxieties of the teachers in the preliminary
research workshop was the fear of disruptive behaviour, and doubt about
their capacity to deal with it effectively. In this research two dimensions
of disruption were dealt with: off-task noisy disruptive talk or throwing
things, and challenges to the content of the material being presented.
Because teaching can be an activity relatively isolated from colleagues, it
can be difficult to seek help (especially on control of disruptions) without
feeling a failure; equally, even if colleagues are aware that an individual
lecturer is experiencing discipline problems, they may be reluctant to offer
unsolicited advice in case it is seen as critical or patronising. All of the
experts admitted to encountering disruptions quite recently in their careers;
they were also equally quick to insist that the problem had to be dealt
with, and could not be ignored in the hope that it might go away of its
own accord:

> Disruptions range from people just chatting about the weekend, talking
> amongst themselves to actually throwing things. On the two occasions
> when people have thrown things I have not had any hesitation in evicting
> them from the class. One rule I have in lecturing is that nothing gets
> thrown; if it happens and you have made that statement, you have to be
> prepared to carry out any threat you have made. Rather than pointing out
> someone at random and saying, "You get out," I will say, "Will the person
> who threw that object leave." Then I will stay there until they do leave,
> but if they don't leave then I am quite prepared to leave myself. That is
> a major disruption and it happens very rarely. Excessive talking, I will
> sometimes just ask them to be quiet, and that usually works.
>
> (Graeme Hocking, Mathematics)

It happened in a lecture course more recently and for three or four weeks
at a time I tried to suppress it by gazing at the offender in the course of
the lecture. That had only a temporary effect, and the fourth time it
happened I was really furious and I said in the middle of the lecture, "I
would like to see you at the end of the lecture," whereupon everyone in
the room turned around and looked. At the end of the lecture I was very

angry and tried very hard to remain calm, and said to the student, "If you are going to talk in the lecture, I'd rather you didn't come." So the student did not come the next time, but returned the time after, and it was all right from then on. But that is a trying experience.

(Beverley Ormerod, French language and literature)

The students displayed interesting ambivalences in their responses to disruptions, both holding lecturers responsible for disruptive behaviour by students, but also expecting them to deal with it effectively and justly, without offending either the protagonists or the innocent bystanders:

I think the most effective way for a lecturer to handle disruption is not by intimidating the student and making a fool of whoever it was causing the disruption, but just trying to put themselves on the same level and just say, "Hey we are trying to do this thing together, Do you want to help and participate?" It makes the people who are causing the disruption think that rather than being a nuisance, they should pull their weight so every one can learn together.

I am not sure what a lecturer should do, if someone was really being disruptive..... I suppose they could always tell them that they are welcome to leave if they are obviously not interested in the lecture at all, because by being disruptive they are really stopping everybody else ....Telling a student to leave the lecture often puts a huge gap between the students and the lecturer, so that it is probably the type of thing that you would do (only) if the case got really bad. But I think you should try to avoid that if possible.

(Kate, first year Arts student)

Last year in Human Biology we had a lecturer who was extremely quiet; she wouldn't speak up very much, very timid, so you tended to find these big bulky guys who used to sit at the very back of the lecture. They made paper aeroplanes and threw them down, annoyed the lecturer and generally made a lot of noise. The material was interesting, but you couldn't hear what she was saying, and if you can't hear something you might as well not be there in the first place. Most of the students wanted to pass, and wanting to pass and not being able to even know what you are going to study for your exam doesn't help. I suppose they were being disruptive basically to get the idea that you are not doing the job you are meant to do, and if you want us to start being attentive, then pull up your socks and actually start lecturing us properly.

Basically she dealt with it by ignoring them, then she got angry and told them to leave the lecture. After that she sort of got the idea that there was something wrong here, and her lectures definitely started improving. They became louder, you could hear what she was saying and she started giving out guidelines which really helped.

(Premela, Science student)

The teacher in the case used in the project, preferred to defuse potential disruptions before they affected the entire lecture group:

Another advantage of putting students into groups is that I can move through the class and actually approach people in a very quiet informal way — maybe they're falling asleep, and I suggest perhaps they should go and get a cup of coffee. Other students may be talking and a minor disruption will occur. I can actually get to that group of students and discuss it very quietly, so the rest of the class is not bothered, and it almost always brings people back into line. And, of course, I'm getting feedback all the time, because sometimes when they're talking in class it's because they don't understand. When I find that out, I can go back to the front and maybe clarify it for a large group of students.

(Doug Pitney, Mathematics)

However, preemptive interventions are not always possible or effective, and among other information the practical advice strand in this section of the program offered highly specific suggestions for teachers to reflect on possible causes of disruptive behaviour, and some suggestions for tackling the problem (See Table 1).

Conclusion

The availability of multimedia technology has provided the opportunity to present cases in ways that enrich case data by locating it within other sources of information. The case presented in this paper might properly be regarded as the video material of the lecture (the teacher working with his students) and subsequent interviews with the teacher. In a first encounter, one might want to limit it to that, in order to focus more closely on the individual teacher, and the students with whom he was working.

As an instructional package, it is more than that. The opportunity to include the reflections of other teachers offers to users confirmation from

Table 1
Reflections on disruptive behaviour. (Extract from Practical Advice Strand, CD program)

POSSIBLE PROBLEMS	POSSIBLE SOLUTIONS
Is your voice audible to all students throughout the lecture?	a) use a microphone b) practise voice projection – get some professional help if necessary c) ask a colleague to sit at the back and signal to you if your voice drops too low
Are your overhead transparencies legible i.e. clearly presented and large enough, neat enough to be read?	a) use a word processor to produce printed OHTs in large bold type b) have them prepared by your media support centre c) if diagrams must be hand done, draw them on paper and have them converted rather than drawing directly onto plastic film
Do you: talk about the OHTs while students are frantically trying to copy them down? flash up complex OHTs and take them off before students can absorb them?	a) give students time to copy the OHT and then talk about it b) provide students with a printed copy to annotate as you talk c) place copies of OHTs from each lecture in the library or support centre and let them know that before you begin the lecture
Do you: read pages of lecture notes verbatim without pause, or making eye-contact with students? present complex information at a pace too fast for students to understand it?	a) summarise your lecture on palm cards or into a set of headings and key points and talk about each in turn b) use an OHT of main points and maintain eye-contact with your audience as you talk c) break up dense presentations with small student activities – a sample problem to do; a particular question to discuss; a list of examples to build in pairs; reflection or personal or real-world example.

other experts the effectiveness of the technique employed. They also suggest alternative ways of thinking about and responding to the same problem. The practical advice strand extends and makes more explicit the teaching strategies referred to by the experts, especially for novice users who may have had no formal teacher education. For those who wish to pursue any aspect beyond the limitations of the instructional package, the research abstracts and references offer starting points for exploring new fields.

The structure of the program has several advantages in promoting reflexivity. A stance that was deliberately non-prescriptive was taken, to promote openness of discussion among user groups and to avoid promotion of the teacher as a technician. There are, of course, absences — nothing about skills and drills, rote learning, or transmission approaches to teaching, which might suggest that teaching competence is a collection of skills or techniques that, once acquired can be applied in any context. What it does offer are successful teachers demonstrating the ways in which they think about teaching, who, despite being 'certified' as skilful still identify problems in their teaching, acknowledge difficulties that they experience, and the ways in which they attempt to solve them.

Users can be highly selective about which information and how much information they engage with at any time. If they choose they can follow a single theme or topic throughout the package, rather than watching the whole program. It is also possible to review, in order to cross check or to interrogate the material more closely. Because the program contains a great deal of interview material, the program should have greater immediacy for users than the same material might have presented in print form. In the formative trials, users, especially in collaborative groups tended to respond with examples from their own experience which were confirmed or challenged by the material in the program. The tacit invitation is there to try something from the program in the next class, in order to share it the next time the user group meets.

Although the multimedia package described in this paper was designed for use by university teachers, the methodology and the media are neither subject nor context bound. They could be applied quite effectively to a range of educational levels or subject disciplines. From a professional development perspective, whether for teachers, policemen, health workers, or any other field of industrial, commercial or professional enterprise, the technique has two significant advantages. First, it is portable and can be used by individuals or small groups at sources of need. It eliminates the necessity of bringing large groups together for intensive instruction. Second, and perhaps more important, by allowing learners to control the focus of instruction, it encourages reflection upon their performance in the context of information and resources outside the usual range of their direct experience.

Reflections and Reservations

Having argued in the previous stages of this case for the advantages of presenting a case in the way described, it may be useful to deconstruct it in terms of the problems which the project team saw in the process of construction. (We expect to learn about the problems of which remained ignorant through feedback solicited from users of the program). The program described in this chapter has had only limited formative trialling in a Western Australian university context. As with the production of any learning package, choices and compromises have to be made.

There were tensions in the structure of the program. For example, the decision to use a mathematics class for the case may suggest to (potential) non-mathematics users that this program has little to offer to them. The attempt to make the particular case generic by locating around it interview material from teachers in other disciplines could be regarded as a rationalisation rather than a resolution of this tension. The alternative, using excerpts from several different classes and disciplines, may have led to fragmentation that degenerated to a perception of idiosyncrasy, rather than promoting the view that there are some shareable practices, approaches and strategies that might be applied to or modified successfully in different contexts.

An objective in producing this package was to promote reflection on both the content of the package, and the theoretical framework and practices of users. Thus it is not the intention that the program should be regarded as an instance of exemplary practice; however, the nature of the medium may be such that it will be regarded by some users in that way, which is bound to lead to disillusionment if practices recommended by contributors to the package do not work in other contexts. It is inevitable that some aspects of the package will not travel well; the case was developed in a specific cultural context in which participants had particular expectations about the roles and conduct of both teachers and learners which are not necessarily explicit in the program. A further limitation to the program is that although the preferred use would be in cooperative learning situations where shared discussion might promote reflection on practice, the fact that it is on CDs means that it can be networked or used in isolation, where benefits from shared use will not accrue.

In construction of any case, whether in print or multimedia mode, there is also the issue of selectivity. In a postmodern world, it is impossible to claim that any text is value neutral, or 'objective'. In preparing this package, far more material was collected than could be used in a single program; as indicated in the discussions above, some selections were pragmatic rather than ideological, but others were not. For example, one student related with considerable enthusiasm a story about the way in which his second year group of law students had deliberately set out to harass a lecturer, on the basis of information from previous students, and in the knowledge that they could 'get it out of the book anyway'. After much discussion, that comment was not included — a form of censorship based on the belief that the comment might do more to destroy than promote confidence in possible user groups. In a different way, there was a bias built into the program by the shared belief of the project group that interactive lecturing strategies should be promoted. Although we had a colleague who was a successful exponent of the lecture as a virtuoso performance, and who would not tolerate any attempts by students at interaction during his lectures, that was not an approach about which information was sought during the interviews with the successful teachers who contributed to this study. Views that they may have had about lectures as virtuoso performances were not excluded at the selection and editing stage; they were never sought during the interview, because the focus of the program developers was on interactivity.

Inclusion of the two print strands — research and practical advice — was also problematic. With the exceptions of the film producer/director and the computer programmer, the project team were teacher educators. The problem of specialist discourse (or jargon) dogged the construction of the two print strands (and this paper). Successive rewriting of the print strands, especially the research information has not solved the problem. In fact, it may have produced a different problem — research abstracts that are so reconstituted that they are little more than 'motherhood' statements which will offend teacher educators and others in different kinds of ways. A similar tension exists in the practical advice strand: how can advice be offered which is practical and useful to beginning university teachers without being made inaccessible by teacher-educator jargon? Conversely, can such advice be offered in print mode (or any other?) without it sounding patronising?

Cases are constructed versions of reality. As with any other text, variant readings of case data are possible. One of the issues in both construction and use of cases is to make that explicit in such a way that the particular case itself becomes problematic, rather than an exemplary instance. Elliott's (1995) suggestion that rather than presenting finished cases, what should be provided is case data, has its attractions but the practicalities of handling the bulk of such data in class situations is mind-boggling. The most manageable alternative may be promotion of the practice of seeking alternative explanations of case texts in relation to the contexts of production and reception.

References

Anthony, H. M. & Raphael, T. E. (1987). *Using Questioning Strategies to Promote Students' Active Comprehension of Content Area Material* (Occasional Paper No. 109). E. Lansing, MI: Michigan State University, Institute for Research on Teaching.

Brophy, J. & Good, T. L. (1986). Teacher behaviour and student achievement. In M. C. Wittrock (Ed.), *Handbook of Research on Teaching*. 3rd Ed. pp. 328–376. New York: Macmillan.

Buchmann, M. (1984). The priority of knowledge and understanding in teaching. In L. Katz and J. Rath (Eds.) *Advances in Teacher Education*, Vol 1, pp. 29–50. Norwood, NJ: Ablex.

Chen, A. Y. (1993). Experienced and student teachers' reflection on classroom practice. *Education Research and Perspectives*, 20(1), 46–63.

Cole, P. G. (1993). Expert and novice teachers compared: A comparison of their roles and functions with implications for teacher education. Inaugural professorial lecture, Edith Cowan University, Perth, Western Australia.

Colton, A. B. & Sparks-Langer, G. M. (1993). A conceptual framework to guide the development of teacher reflection and decision making. *Journal of Teacher Education*, 44(1), 45–54.

Dunkin, M. J. & Precians, R. P. (1992). Award winning university teachers' concepts of teaching. *Higher Education*, 24(4), 483–502.

Eddinger, S. S. (1985). The effect of different question sequences on achievement in high school social studies classes. *Journal of Social Studies Research*, 9: 17–29.

Elliott, J. (1995). Researching and writing effective cases. Paper presented at the international seminar on using cases for effective professional education, Singapore, 1995.

Gall, M. D., Ward, B. A., Berliner, D. C., Cahen, L. S., Winne, P. H., Elashoff, J. D. & Stanton, G. C. (1978). Effects of questioning techniques and recitation on student learning. *American Educational Research Journal*, 15: 175–199.

Lemke, J. L. (1982). *Classroom Communication of Science*. Final report to NSF/RISE, April (ED 222346).

Lemke, J. L. (1987). *Using Language in the Classroom*. Burwood, Victoria: Deakin University.

Livingston, C. & Borko, H. (1989). Expert-novice differences in teaching: A cognitive analysis and implications for teacher education. *Journal of Teacher Education*, July-August, 40(4), 36–42.

Redfield, D. L. & Rousseau, E. W. (1981). A meta-analysis of experimental research on teacher questioning behaviour. *Review of Educational Research*, 51: 237–245.

Reynolds, A. (1992). What is competent beginning teaching? A review of the literature. *Review of Educational Research*, 62(1), 1–35.

Richert, A. (1990). Teaching teachers to reflect: A consideration of programme structure. *Journal of Curriculum Studies*, Vol. 22, No. 6, pp. 509–527.

Richert, A. (1991). Case methods and teacher education. In B. Robert Tabachnick and Kenneth M. Zeichner (Eds.) *Issues and Practices in Inquiry-Oriented Teacher Education*. London: The Falmer Press.

Rosenshine, B. (1976): Classroom instruction. In N. L. Gage (Ed.), *The Psychology of Teaching Methods*. Chicago: University of Chicago Press.

Schon, D. (1983). *The Reflective Practitioner*. New York: Basic Books.

Shulman, L. (1986). Those who understand: Knowledge growth in teaching. *Educational Researcher*, 15(2), 4–14.

Shulman, L. (1987). Knowledge and teaching: Foundations of the new reform. *Harvard Educational Review*, 57: 1–22.

Westerman, D. A. (1991). Expert and novice teacher decision making. *Journal of Teacher Education*, 42(4), 292–305.

Zeichner, K. M. & Tabachnick, B. R. (1991). Reflections on reflective teaching. In B. Robert Tabachnick and Kenneth M. Zeichner (Eds.), *Issues and Practices in Inquiry-Oriented Teacher Education*. London: The Falmer Press.

Section
FOUR

Educating
the
Larger Life

Educating The "Larger Life"

Lori Breslow

Sloan School of Management
Massachusetts Institute of Technology
United States of America

Synopsis

The students are alive, and the purpose of education is to stimulate and guide their self-development.

— Alfred North Whitehead

The incident upon which this case is based took place in the MBA course in communication skills at a leading business school in the United States. For one of the assignments, students were asked to create a 10-minute presentation illustrating business communication practices in a country other than the U.S. One of the presentations dealt with the relationship between men and women students. The instructor led a discussion about that presentation in the next class; following that discussion, one of the women students received an anonymous note that was critical of her comments and attitude during the discussion. The instructor attempted to use these incidents as an opportunity to teach students to communicate responsibly and sensitively.

Educating The "Larger Life"

Lori Breslow

For the past five years, I have taught a course called "Communication for Managers," a required first-semester class in a two-year MBA program at a leading business school in the United States. The course is devoted primarily to improving the students' ability to write and make oral presentations. It covers both informative and persuasive communication within a variety of formats. We begin the semester by discussing a series of guidelines, or "best practices," that underlie effective managerial communication, but because skills are best learned by practicing them, the bulk of the course is spent on assignments and in-class exercises done both individually and in groups. The students receive extensive oral and written feedback on the work they do, not only from the instructors and teaching assistants assigned to the course, but from each other as well.

Besides being proficient in writing and speaking, a manager must also know how to communicate well interpersonally. This requires another set of skills, which includes, for example: how to listen; how to empathize; how to frame a message so that it accomplishes its aims; how to give feedback effectively; how to listen for gaps between the intent and the interpretation of a message; how to correct misunderstandings when they occur; how to negotiate; how to motivate; how to compromise. Although our students are required to take an organizational processes course which focuses on these interpersonal skills, many are an integral part of our course as well.

During the five years I taught "Communication for Managers," I had created a repertoire of instructional tools and techniques, as well as a style of interaction, that had defined my approach to teaching these skills and helped to fashion the way I functioned in the classroom. This is not to say that my teaching had become rigid or standardized — at least I hope not. But it is to say I had a sense of how the material needed to be presented, how students would react to it, what problems we would encounter, and what questions would arise. I had a set of strategies to accomplish the objectives I laid out for my teaching, which served me well. Taken together, this was the "knowing-in-action" that I brought into the classroom.

The incident upon which this case is based called into question that knowledge and my familiar methods of operation. In both *The Reflective Practitioner* and *Educating the Reflective Practitioner*, Donald Schon explains that we are challenged as professionals when the assumptions and actions we usually call upon to do our job fail us. As he writes:

> In such cases the practitioner experiences a surprise that leads her to rethink her knowing-in-action in ways that go beyond available rules, facts, theories, and operations. She responds to the unexpected or anomalous by restructuring some of her strategies of action, theories of phenomena, or ways of framing a problem; and she invents on-the-spot experiments to put her new understandings to the test ...
>
> (Schon, 1987:35)

I was faced with just such a "surprise" when a student role play depicting the treatment of businesswomen in Latin America angered and insulted a number of my female students. Because I was used to approaching the material I taught and the students I taught it to with a certain degree of objectivity and detachment, when I was suddenly confronted with strong emotions in my classroom, I was at a loss at how to deal with them. As I have said, one of the purposes of this class is to teach future managers how to communicate with empathy and understanding. But when I found myself in the midst of a situation that gave me the perfect opportunity to teach that lesson in real time, I discovered I had neither the strategy nor the skills to do it. In a similar vein, prior to this incident I saw much of what I taught as relatively value-free. But in time I came to realize I would need to take a moral stand on what had happened, and thus I struggled, too, with how to bring an ethical perspective to my teaching.

As you will read, over the three-week period in which this incident occurred, I did much reflection — both "in action" as the events were happening and "on action" after they took place. Writing this case in what Schon (1983:61) might call the "relative tranquility of the postmortem," I have come to see even more. In order to share with you the nature of those reflections, let me begin by describing the context in which the incident occurred, re-create the situation as best as I can, and, finally, lay out the lessons I learned and their effect upon me as a teacher.

The Context

Besides covering the topics I identified above, our course also touches upon several more specialized areas, one of the most important of which is intercultural communication. Because of the diversity of our students (approximately 40% come from other countries outside the United States) and because of the trend toward global-scale business, we feel it is important that our students receive some exposure to the norms associated with business communication in other countries. But on a deeper level, we also want them to understand how culture, in the broadest sense of the term, affects how people view the world, and how, in turn, those world views influence the way business is conducted.

The centerpiece of this part of the course is a group assignment that culminates in a short presentation, usually about 10 minutes long. These presentations have started as early as week 5 of the course; however the semester this incident occurred, they weren't begun until week 10. (While we would prefer to cover this topic sooner rather than later, sometimes the logistics of the course make that impossible.) The three-class sequence on intercultural communication begins with the instructor's introduction to the topic and the assignment, followed by time in-class for the students to work on the presentations. These presentations are then given during the next two classes, and our treatment of this topic ends with a debriefing and the instructor's synthesis of the material that has been covered.

For the assignment, the students form themselves into groups of four or five with the non-American students evenly distributed among the groups. One of the international students in each team then becomes an "informant," whose job it is to educate other team members generally about his/her culture and, more specifically, about the business communication practices that exist in his/her country. On the basis of that discussion, the group creates the presentation, which begins either with a description or re-enactment of a particular business situation (groups usually choose to do some kind of skit or role play), and then proceeds to an analysis of the business communication practices that are exemplified in the situation. We have had presentations, for example, on job interviews in Italy, negotiations to bring MacDonald's to India (talk about a clash of cultures!), and a business lunch in Argentina among potential joint venture partners. Time is left at the end for questions, and there are usually many. Often the international student, who is the "authority" in the group, answers most of the questions, so that the whole exercise becomes a good way to get some of the shyer foreign students to participate in the class.

A number of insights emerge from the presentations and the debriefing that follows. For example, the international students consistently depict American businesspeople as, at best, hurried and pressured, and at worst, ill-tempered and insensitive. They want their American classmates to know that in their cultures, business dealings arise out of solid relationships built between people over time. Typically, students also learn something about the relative importance of hierarchy in different cultures, that perceptions of time and space differ worldwide, and that definitions of success — both personal and organizational — vary from place to place. The other issue that often crops up in these presentations is that of gender: the relative rigidity or flexibility of gender roles, how easy or difficult it is for women to enter the world of work, and the norms that dictate how men and women interact with one another in the workplace. Although this is often a sensitive issue, it is usually — but not always — handled with diplomacy and care.

As I have explained, the incident I would like to describe began with a presentation that illustrated the relationship between business men and women in a country in Latin America. What began as a seemingly harmless skit jumped off the stage to become a viable presence in my classroom; a real here-and-now interaction between students — fraught with a degree of misunderstanding, confusion, and ill will — that made it the perfect vehicle for teaching students how to interact with one another, how to communicate with one another, and how to value one another..... if only their instructor could lead the class in a way that accomplished those goals.

In the Classroom: The Problem

That year I had done something new in introducing the *intercultural communication exercise*. I gave the students a list of about 25 questions to help structure their initial conversations with one another. Although I had intended the questions only as a guide, I noticed as I went around to observe the groups at work, that many of them were using the list in interview style. However, that seemed to be eliciting some good discussions, and after class several of the students told me that they had learned a great deal when the international students answered the 25 handout questions. So I was optimistic that the presentations would be especially good ones. Unfortunately, when they began the next week, I was disappointed. The work of the first two groups was fairly typical; their presentations were the usual combination of humorous exaggeration, hints on business etiquette, and a tidbit or two of useful insight.

The third presentation depicted contract negotiations in a Latin American country through the use of a role play. Antonio,* one of the Latin American students, portrayed a businessman who was about to give out a contract to one of three bidders: a man from the U.S.; a Latin American woman (played by Joan, who was actually an Anglo); or a Latin American man, who was Antonio's brother-in-law. First Antonio met with the student playing the North American; their conversation illustrated very little about cross-cultural dialogue. Then he called Joan into his office so they could talk about the contract. They weren't very far into the conversation when

---

*I have changed the names of all my students throughout this narrative.

Antonio began to act in a way that can only be described as inappropriate. He commented on Joan's clothes, suggesting, for example, that her skirt could be shorter; broadly hinted that they see each other socially; and made references to how her responses to him could influence his decision. I subsequently found out that Antonio was ad-libbing these lines; they hadn't been in the script the group had used during rehearsal. So besides being offended by Antonio's behavior, Joan was completely unprepared for it, and was struggling to find an appropriate way to respond under the gaze of 25 of her classmates.

In the meantime, the women in class were becoming increasingly incensed over what was happening. On one hand, I wasn't particularly disturbed by what was going on in the skit, which as I'll discuss in a moment — was problematic. What the women saw as sexism, I interpreted as a depiction of the reality of doing business in that part of the world. I felt Antonio was delivering an unpleasant, but nonetheless realistic, warning: If you are a businesswoman in Latin America, be prepared to meet with prejudice in the workplace. The women students, on the other hand, didn't see Antonio's message as merely informative; they believed he was an advocate for the position he was representing. I'm still not certain whether the women were misinterpreting Antonio's behavior or I was, but I think that is beside the point. The problem was that I was out of touch with the emotional response of a significant number of my students.

The last presentation represented business practices in Japan. I can't remember the exact subject matter, but I do remember there were only indirect references to the role of women in Japanese business. But because the women were already upset over the previous presentation, they began to question Shigeki, the "informant" for this group, closely about sexism in Japanese business. He tried to be diplomatic, but he made it clear that, in his experience, women were not to be found in the upper echelons of Japanese management. One of the women asked him directly, "What would you do if you had a woman boss?"

"A woman would never be my boss," he answered, but it was impossible to tell from this response whether he was describing the situation as it existed for women in his particular industry, or whether he was expressing his own feelings about working for a woman. The women asked more questions to try to get Shigeki to clarify what he meant, and he began to look more and more uncomfortable as he struggled with a language he didn't know very well and with the increasingly antagonistic tone of the questions.

By that time, it was apparent that feelings were running high in the room — so high I simply couldn't ignore them. I struggled to find the right thing to say; the problem was I didn't know what message I wanted to send. Did I want to give the women students an opportunity to vent their anger more openly? Did I want to move away from the specific interactions that had been occurring to talk more generally about the problems of gender in the workplace? Or would it be better to try to distract the class from what was going on and then return to the topic at a later time when people's emotions weren't quite so palpable? Without having a clear objective in mind, I was finding it impossible to frame an effective response.

Suddenly, one of the male students in the audience, attempting to break the mood in the room through humor I suppose, asked Shigeki if he allowed his wife to drive. (In other words, was Shigeki at least "liberated" enough to grant his wife that degree of freedom.) To my surprise, Shigeki answered a sheepish, but definite "No." To say that that answer did nothing to improve the situation is a tribute to understatement.

At that point, there were only a few minutes left in the class, and I felt compelled to say something to bring about closure. I had decided there was so much tension in the room, I didn't want to say anything too pointed for fear those tensions would ignite, and I wouldn't be able to control them. I knew, of course, there were lessons to be learned in what had happened, yet in the pressure and confusion of the moment I couldn't settle in my own mind what these lessons were... So I simply acknowledged that many powerful issues and feelings had emerged, which in part, was the purpose of this exercise, and that we would deal with them next week in the debriefing. As I look back on those closing remarks, I think they were weak, but I knew that at least they would allow me to open up the topic for discussion the next time the class met.

People began to file out of the room, but the group of women who had been so upset remained, congregating in one place. I went over to them immediately because I felt it was important for me to make contact. "Did you hear all that?" one of them asked me. I said I did. I think they wanted me to express the outrage they were feeling, but I hung back because even at that point — and this is something that I had to work through over time — I sensed that if I sided with the female students against the male students, I wouldn't be able to help the male students with what they needed to learn. So I again acknowledged that we would deal with the incident in next week's class, and then I asked the women this: *Would they please think about what they wanted to say to the men in the class the next week and, in particular, would they think about how they could say it so their male colleagues could genuinely hear what they thought and how they felt*. With that said, I found that I had discovered a theme that would become central to the lessons I wanted to teach.

The Week Between: Reflection

I came back to my office and sank into my chair. I was still shaken by what had happened and disappointed with the way I had handled the situation.

Why had my responses to Antonio been so out-of-sync with those of my women students? Why was I so willing to shrug off, in hindsight, what I now saw clearly as inappropriate behavior? And when the anger and frustration were so obviously present, why had I been at such a loss as to how to deal with them?

As I struggled over the next week to try to understand my own reactions, several things become apparent.

First, I think there was a simple explanation for why I missed what was going on in the room: My attention had been divided. Whenever there are student presentations, I am always simultaneously evaluating the performance of both the individual and the group, digesting the content of the presentation to see what is lacking or what can serve as a springboard for discussion, and keeping an eye on the time to make sure things are moving along.

With so much to do, I just wasn't as aware as I should have been of the reactions of members of the audience.

Second, my opinion of Antonio colored my response. I liked Antonio, and I think I knew him well enough to know that while he might have been guilty of poor taste, he wasn't consciously being sexist. Even now I believe his actions were misunderstood.

Third, because of the particular topic, I shrank back from what was going on in the classroom for the obvious reason that gender can be a minefield for a woman faculty member teaching in a male-dominated field such as Management. The men in her class are likely to assume (and sometimes rightly so) that she comes to the issue from a perspective that may not be entirely in sympathy with theirs. On the other hand, her women students may see her as their "champion" even if she doesn't necessarily perceive herself that way. (I had certainly gotten the feeling from my female students that they wanted me to take on that role.) I have always tried to treat both sexes equally in my classroom, but since the issue had become so volatile so quickly, I was afraid that the fact of my own sex might make it impossible for my students to see that I was making every effort to be fair. (I do realize, of course, that a man finding himself in the position I was in would have his own set of challenges to confront.)

While all of these explanations have validity to them, as I have reflected on this incident, I have come to see that even taken together, they don't completely account for my shortsightedness in the situation; something else was at play. In order to explore this point, I'd like to digress for just a moment to describe another incident — eerily similar to this one — that had taken place in this same course three years before.

This incident had also occurred during one of the intercultural communication skits; again it had to do with the portrayal of the relationship between men and women in a business setting. This role play depicted a meeting among four Italian businessmen. In this skit the sexism was even more blatant. For example, one of the women students had taken the part of a secretary. She had come into the room to serve the men coffee, and as she turned to leave, one of the male students slapped her in a playful, but suggestive manner. This was followed, after she left the room, by several comments about the woman's appearance. Then, as the meeting was ending, one of the men took a piece of woman's underclothing from his suit pocket and twirled it around his finger as he closed the deal.

At that time, in that class, I said nothing. I thought these antics were in bad taste but, mistakenly I now see, I chose not to comment on them. I rationalized this by telling myself they were simply childish pranks that showed poor judgment on the part of the students involved.

Although I had decided to let this pass, my students were not so forgiving. I later heard this occurrence was the talk of the social hour that is held at school each week. Not only were many of the women offended, but many of the men were too. (Evidently, the Japanese male students were particularly embarrassed by the display of undergarments in public.) It wasn't until two of the women students came to me a full week later to discuss what had occurred that I was aware of how serious the reaction had been.

Here was a pattern. The first incident I tossed off as no more than a bad joke that had gone too far. The second I came perilously close to ignoring again until it was almost too late.

I finally came to realize — out of my own embarrassment, my own unwillingness to deal with unpleasant situations, and my own reluctance to confront the emotions that had surfaced in the course of what had occurred — I had made an unconscious decision not to confront these incidents. I acted as I did because it was the easiest, most comfortable thing to do. In making that decision, I failed my students because I neither championed those who were offended nor used what had happened as a way to educate.

As I look back on my life as a teacher before the incident that is at the center of this case, I know there was a part of me that held my breath and hoped I wouldn't have to deal with things like emotions and feelings in my classroom. I saw these as potential booby traps that could sandbag all but the most careful of instructors. I was happy to work with my students on how to evaluate arguments, create strategies, and analyze positions, because as an intensely private person (as I believe many academics are), I could do so without revealing too much of myself. I wanted to stay on safe ground, to stay detached and above the fray. In his book, *The Aims of College Teaching*, Kenneth E. Eble describes me perfectly when he writes:

> College teachers find it too comfortable to apply the supposedly value-free character of their special investigations to the lives they affect. At an extreme, such a teacher draws back, not in humility, but in comforting blindness, from claiming to affect the student's larger life.
>
> (Eble, 1990:154)

In untangling the motivations, feelings and fears that led me to act as I did, I began to reassess my role as a teacher. I began to see I needed to be with my students in their anger and their frustration, just as I hoped I could be with them in their triumph and their joy. I had always believed, in theory at least, that I had a responsibility to develop my students, as Carl Rogers puts it, into "fully functioning persons." (Carl Rogers, 1969: 279–297, in Eble, op. Cit.: 154). What I don't think I ever really understood was how much of myself I had to bring into the classroom in order to achieve that. So even though, I must admit, I continued to be reluctant to grapple with this issue and even though I sensed the obstacles that would hamper my attempts to deal with it successfully, I became committed to exploring what had happened in those two presentations the next time the class met.

Therefore, I began to focus my thinking on three questions:

- First, how could I best use the feelings and issues that had surfaced as a vehicle for learning?
- Second, what did I want the students specifically to learn? and,
- Third, what did I have to bring of myself into the classroom in order to make that learning successful?

The Week Between: A Plan for Action

In response to the question of pedagogy — how would I do the teaching — I decided on three things:

First, of all the points that could be made in response to what had occurred, I needed to identify in my own mind the two, three, or at most, four crucial ideas I wanted the students to take away with them. I knew from my reading in cognitive psychology that learning is more successful if the number of ideas introduced in any one class is kept to a minimum; there was no reason why this class should be an exception to that rule.

Second, I felt my proper role was that of facilitator, helping the students to learn from one another. I wanted the class to be a living laboratory where they could practice — in real time — some of the concepts they had been exposed to in our course and in their organizational processes course. It would be counterproductive to their learning if I became the "final authority," who knew precisely the right answers to the questions they were struggling with.

Further, as part of my role as facilitator, I felt it was my responsibility to be as supportive of each person as I could. I once took a master class in teaching with Professor Chris Roland Christensen of the Harvard Business School, who is an authority on using discussion as a teaching tool. Chris began that class by telling all of us that no matter what any one of us said during the course of the ensuing discussion, our comments would have his support. Such was Chris' way of making his class a safe environment in which we could express our ideas without fear of being judged. I'm not sure I have quite cultivated Chris' generosity of spirit — I could easily imagine myself cringing at some of the comments my students might make — and I'm not sure that we do our students a service by uncritically embracing every point of view, but I knew I needed to listen and keep myself quite open during the discussion just as I expected my students to be open to each other.

Thirdly, I did not want the class to turn into a "therapy session," nor did I want it to become an opportunity for gender bashing. I felt that to the extent I could guarantee that neither of those things would happen, I could do so by rooting the discussion firmly in what a *manager* needed to know or what skills he/she had to develop to handle problems associated with gender in the workplace.

Having decided upon these general principles, I then needed to determine the main points I wanted the students to learn. Limiting myself to three, I came up with the following:

- Successful communication begins with an understanding of who your audience is. Even if you didn't intend to be offensive, you may well be if you don't have a sense of what may be an affront to members of the audience. I still firmly believe that the men in my class did not intentionally set out to anger or insult their female classmates; yet they managed to do so, I suspect, because they simply didn't stop to think about how their words would be perceived.
- Once you have identified the characteristics of your audience members, think about how to frame the message so that they interpret your meaning in the way you intended it to be received. This was the "assignment" I had given the women at the end of the class. I was anxious to see how well they did with it.
- The relationship between men and women in the workplace continues to be a source of conflict. I wanted the students to think about how they could further educate themselves on this subject, so that they would be better prepared to deal with it when they entered the business world.

The other thing I needed to think about during that week was how to reintroduce the subject of what had happened in class. I hoped that one of the students would bring it up because I felt that would be the most natural entree. But if that didn't happen, I had to find a way to broach the subject so that the discussion wouldn't be biased or curtailed in any way. I eventually decided I would simply be as descriptive as possible, commenting only that certain issues had arisen in class the week before that I thought merited more exploration.

Finally, in attempting to learn from my mistakes of the past, I realized I had to be committed to the possibility that strong emotions would surface during a discussion of this sort, and I had to be prepared to deal with them. I spent time during that week imaging the emotions that might emerge, and how I would respond to them. Like an athlete trying to visualize his/her performance before the actual competition, I rehearsed how it would feel to be with the students in class talking about these issues.

In *Educating the Reflective Practitioner*, Schon has a passage describing what happens when a "practitioner reflects in and on his practice", enumerating the variety of things that may become the object of that reflection. He writes:

> [The professional] may reflect on the tacit norms and appreciations which underlie a judgment, or on the strategies or theories implicit in the pattern of behavior. He may reflect on the feeling for a situation which has led him to adopt a particular course of action, on the way in which he has framed a problem he is trying to solve, or on the role he has constructed for himself within a large institutional context.

> (Schon, 1983:62)

This was the experience of my own process of reflection during the week I have described.

In the Classroom: Reflection into Action

I came into that next class with an uneasy feeling about what would unfold during the following hour-and-a-half. I had practiced how I would reopen the topic if I had to do that; I had written out the three key points I wanted to make; I had thought about the personalities in the class and what reactions I might encounter from particular students.*

---

*I should mention that, in general, I found this class, which had 26 students in it, to be an amiable group. If there were tensions that existed among them prior to this incident, I was unaware of them based on their classroom behavior during the first three-quarters of the semester.

There were two members of the class whom I thought of as somewhat "difficult personalities." One sometimes acted in a fairly outrageous manner; the other, I felt, didn't have much respect either for me, the subject matter of the course, or both. (This was the student who asked the Japanese fellow about his wife's driving privileges.) I made it clear to the first student that while I usually enjoyed his sense of the dramatic, he had to keep himself under control in class, which he did. The second student and I had an uneasy truce; he did nothing publicly to challenge or confront me although my sense of his disapproval was sometimes unnerving, and I had imagined what feelings might come up for me during the discussion.

We still had two more presentations to see, which I was thankful for since I felt they would get us back into the spirit of things. Both were innocuous enough. After the second one had finished, I worked my way down from where I had been sitting in the back of the room to the front of the class. When I got there, I announced I wanted to take some time to debrief, so that we could identify common themes and draw conclusions from the six presentations we had seen.

I began the discussion with an open-ended question ("What have you learned from this exercise?") to give the students as much latitude as they needed to direct the conversation. For the most part, they talked about the points of etiquette they had picked up, which is a fairly typical response to this exercise. But after a few minutes of this level of discussion, when the students were still not making more insightful observations, I asked a narrower question that forced them to think in a more sophisticated way about the material (e.g., "What have you learned about the role of hierarchy in different cultures?" or "What do you now know about cultural differences in the perception of time after watching these presentations?").

We worked at this deeper level of analysis for a period of time, but then I could tell the discussion was winding down. No one, it seemed, was going to open up the subject of what had happened the week before: I was going to have to do it. And so, finally, I said, "I felt some tension in the room last week about issues having to do with gender in the workplace. I'd like to talk about that."

There was dead silence; the kind of seemingly never-ending silence that only a teacher standing in front of a room full of students can know. Not one person raised his or her hand. I looked around the room and sensed from the way most of the students were looking at me (or more importantly, *not* looking at me) that either they hadn't the faintest idea of what I was talking about, or they had no interest in the subject at all. What had happened? Had they had so many problem sets to do, so much reading to digest, so many papers to write that they had long since moved away from the events of the last class?

I remembered something I had learned from Chris Christensen about leading a discussion: If you want to heat things up, make your questions more personal. That bit of advice should have led me to ask someone to comment specifically on what she/he felt or thought about some aspect of either the Latin American or Japanese presentation. But for some reason my instincts told me that was the wrong thing to do. Even though people looked as if they were completely distanced from the topic, I guessed they weren't responding because they were uncomfortable. So rather than "heating things up," I decided I needed to make the discussion more neutral, more impersonal. I asked, "What do you think are some of the problems men and women face as they deal with one another in the workplace?"

That helped. One of the male students said he felt men were in a no-win situation. Even if they tried to treat women at work in a fair and honest way, that goodwill either was misinterpreted or went unnoticed. Another male student said he felt sympathetic towards women and the problems they had in organizations, but he didn't know how to make things any better.

These were nice sentiments, and I was happy to hear them, but they weren't giving me an entry into the discussion I wanted to have. I was also very disturbed by the fact that not one woman had yet made a comment. *Not one.* I tried to make eye contact with some of the women who had been most vocal after the previous class, but it didn't seem to have an effect. I began to feel betrayed by them, a feeling that surprises me even now — given my strong stand that my male and female students were equal in my eyes — as I look back on it. Evidently, it's difficult to overcome primal loyalties, even if you want to.*

Then finally, Vinay, an international student, made an observation that gave me the wedge I was looking for. Vinay typically did not talk very much in class, but when he did, his comments were thoughtful and articulate. What he said was this, "You Americans get so caught up in these dilemmas. You are so worried about being 'politically correct.' In my country, we value the unique contributions and characteristics of each

---

*If I remember correctly, there were perhaps four or five comments by women over the course of the entire discussion, which probably lasted 40 minutes, and those comments were by the women who had seemed the least upset the class before. I never challenged the other women about their lack of participation, and I still wonder if I should have done so.

gender." And then he asked rhetorically, "Why do you people waste so much time and energy on these things?"

I canvassed the room as quickly as I could to see how people were reacting to Vinay's comments. It looked as if many of the American students were taken aback by his sweeping condemnation of "you Americans." I decided I would choose the person who would respond to Vinay because I wanted someone who I thought would be level-headed in his/her reaction. I chose Charles, in part because he looked more surprised than dismayed by what Vinay had said. (I should note that in our school, "cold calling," or asking students to answer a question even if they haven't volunteered to do so, is considered acceptable.)

I asked Charles what he thought — and felt — when he heard Vinay's comments. He said he didn't like them very much, but his tone was diplomatic rather than confrontational, which is just what I had hoped for. What ensued was a conversation between Vinay and Charles in which I tried to get Charles to say in a way that Vinay could hear that he felt stereotyped by — and therefore, resentful of — Vinay's depiction of Americans, even though he realized Vinay had not intended to be insulting. I orchestrated this conversation by restating points, asking questions, and reframing comments. I forced Vinay and Charles to talk to one another, not to me. (I find students are reluctant to speak to one another directly; they feel they need to go through the instructor much as two people who don't speak one another's language rely on an interpreter to help them communicate.) When other people wanted to join the conversation, I invited them in as long as they contributed to the topic at hand, which I saw as the process of the dialogue. When comments went to content, I asked that they be held. I tried to be a one-woman Greek chorus, commenting on what was being said and attempting to get the rest of the class to observe carefully what was going on.

Throughout the discussion, I tried to monitor my own internal state. If I felt myself shrinking back from something, I pushed myself forward. If I found myself reacting negatively to something said, I questioned the source of that feeling. If it was a subjective response on my part, I kept it to myself. If I decided I had identified something that was getting in the way of effective communication, I brought it to the students' attention and asked them to work on it. I remember that during most of the discussion, I felt torn by a desire to make sure my three main points were brought out and by my promise to myself to only play the role of facilitator. I think there is a fine line here: We want students to be in charge of their learning, we want to be flexible enough to allow for points to be raised spontaneously, but still we have an agenda to cover. I haven't yet determined how to reconcile these two goals successfully.

By the time the class was over, I was exhausted. Looking back on it, I give myself no more than a "C" on my performance. I know there was some confusion in the room as to what I was trying to achieve. Vinay ended up apologizing to the class, telling everyone he meant no disrespect. I blame myself for his discomfort. Although I said several times during the discussion that I knew he had no intention of being critical, and that, in fact, generalizations of the kind he made were important tools in human communication, I had not protected him well. I sent him a note afterwards telling him how grateful I was that he allowed me to use him as an example (not that he had much choice in the matter), and how much I generally appreciated his presence in class.

Also, I never did get to my third agenda item, the more general discussion of how the relationship between men and women in the workplace can be improved. Finally, although I attempted to put the whole discussion into perspective at the end of class, I don't think I linked this discussion very well to what had happened in the earlier class. Nonetheless, we had made a start.

The Week After: A Test of New Found Knowledge

It was late in the afternoon several days following that class. I was in the office doing paperwork. I had put the events of earlier in the week out of my mind because I simply had too much work to do to dwell on them.

Susan appeared at my door. She had been one of the students most upset by the Latin American and Japanese presentations yet she had said very little the following class. I thought perhaps she might want to talk about the situation now in the privacy of my office.

She sat down and told me that something had happened, and she needed to talk to me about it. With that, she handed me a piece of paper. On it, in large type, was a nineline message that criticized Susan's behavior in class and warned that her attitude could have a negative impact on her relationships with her classmates.* The note was unsigned, and Susan told me she had found it in her mail folder.

I was furious, but I wanted to keep my own feelings from Susan until I assessed how she was feeling. I told her, of course, how sorry I was that this had happened. I assured her that her responses in class had been perfectly justifiable. I asked her if there were other people she had shown the note to, and if they were giving her some support. As we talked, it became clear to me that Susan was more angry than hurt by the letter.

Then I asked Susan what she wanted to do about the situation. I think the question surprised her. She told me she had assumed nothing could be done, and that she had come to me simply because she wanted me to know of the letter's existence. I told her I thought we had another option. While protecting her identity, I could inform the class of what had happened and publicly condemn the act. I let Susan know I thought it was very important there be an "official" response to the letter, but I made it clear to her that the decision about what to do next rested in her hands. In other words, if she preferred not to pursue the matter, I would respect her wishes. We agreed to talk in two days after she had time to think.**

As I sat in my office after Susan left, I felt enraged, defeated, and scared. Enraged because I was witness to an act of cowardice that I considered indefensible. Defeated because I feared that all my efforts to educate my students about the importance of sensitive, tolerant communication had come to no more than this. Scared because I was going to

---

*Susan has preferred that only a few people have access to the note, and she has requested that its specific contents not be made public.

**Although I intended to keep Susan's identity a secret, we both knew that given the small number of students involved and how closely they worked with one another, it was unlikely she could remain anonymous.

have to take an even more public stand on this issue than I had up to that point.

While Susan was debating what to do, I informed my program chair, the head of the master's program, and the university ombudsperson about what had occurred. I wanted to find out if there were any legal factors that needed to be taken into account in the decision about how to proceed, and I wanted to make sure that Susan wouldn't be in any danger if we brought the issue out into the open.

I was assured on both counts, and so the decision about what to do next was in Susan's and my hands.

Susan came to see me the next day and told me that she was prepared to let me "go public." She saw this as a way to take a stand against what she felt was a transgression against her, her female classmates, and the principles in which she believed. We talked again about how it would be unlikely that she could remain anonymous. We imagined the different responses she and I were likely to encounter after people learned about the note, including the possibility there would be little reaction at all because everyone was so exhausted from the work of the semester.

There was one other problem: I wasn't going to meet with the class for another two weeks, and when I did, it would be the last class of the semester. Although I preferred to have another in-class conversation about this latest turn of events, I didn't want to wait two weeks for that to happen, nor did I want to have that discussion in the last class when most of the students' attention would be focused on getting through their exams. So I decided I would write a letter to be distributed in people's mail folders. It was a less-than-perfect solution, but the only one I felt I had available to me. I asked Susan and my teaching assistant to review the letter before I distributed it.

As I sat down to write the letter, I struggled with some of the same problems I had faced in thinking about how to approach the class discussion. Now, however, there was another issue to consider: I felt the appearance of the letter brought a heightened ethical dimension to the situation. Where Antonio had blundered, in my opinion the writer of the letter had performed an unconscionable act. But I wondered if it really was my responsibility to teach morality in my classroom. Who was I, anyway, to impose my ethical framework on this group of students just because they happened to register for my section of communications?*

But I had not backed down when I was faced with the challenge of working with the students' emotions, and as I looked back on that decision, I felt it had a positive outcome. As Schon writes, experimentation often leads to further experimentation. Perhaps it was time to expand my role and repertoire of actions again.

The first letter I wrote was a hellfire-and-brimstone sermon. But when I reread it after letting it sit for a day, my instincts told me it was too strong. I tried to follow the guidelines I had been preaching all semester — begin with where your audience is — and I sensed that letter might turn off those students who most needed to hear what it had to say. So I created another letter that was more subdued in tone, but one that was quite clear and firm in its stand.

The final version of the letter began by complimenting the students on their "attempts to grapple with the difficult issues that have come up in class discussion," a compliment I felt they deserved. It went on to say that "unfortunately an incident occurred following the second class" that upset me. I explained a member of the class had been the recipient of an anonymous note that commented on the way this person had reacted to class discussion. I made the point that "while the content of the note upset me, the fact that the writer chose not to reveal his/her identity was especially disturbing."

---

*If I am to be honest with you, I must tell you there was another factor in this debate I was having with myself. I had a suspicion that at least a certain number of my students would react negatively if I responded too harshly to the letter. I anticipated that a contingent of them would think I was making a "mountain out of a molehill" or getting on an ethical high horse. I guessed that since most of them would know the recipient of the note was a woman and they would likewise assume (as I admit I did) the writer was a man, I might be charged with strident feminism if I criticized the note's author too severely. I was afraid, then, that in taking a strong stand, I would be swamped by a backlash of some proportion that would affect my evaluations. Although I wish I could tell you I was not concerned about this, in fact, because I teach in a school where student ratings carry a great deal of weight — and because I'm not tenured — faculty evaluations are quite important to me.

I explained why I believed this kind of communication was so harmful. "By sending the note anonymously," I wrote, "the writer robbed both himself/herself and the receiver of the opportunity to communicate." I went on to elaborate why I thought it was important that managers engage in open, clear, honest communication, and that I knew the ability to communicate in that way would serve them well throughout their careers. I ended by inviting anyone who wanted to come talk to me to do so.

The letter went out one week before the last class. I heard indirectly that generally the reaction was favourable. I subsequently found out that even before the letter appeared, many of the students knew it was coming, and I correctly guessed that at least some of my male students had assumed it would be critical of men. From what I heard, these students were particularly complimentary of the tone and substance of the letter.

I wish I could tell you that throngs of admiring students greeted me when we came together for that last class of the semester; in fact, as I had anticipated, *not one* initiated any discussion about what had occurred over the previous three weeks. My guess is all they wanted to do was get through their finals and — get some sleep.

I wish, too, that I could end the story here, but I can't. After Susan and I went public with her note, we found out that beginning even earlier in the semester, other students had received anonymous letters that had been critical of them in some way. Then in the week following the incident with Susan, after a discussion in a different class, another women received an even more hateful letter. The issue then became schoolwide. Susan, of course, is to be congratulated for the actions she took. Because she was willing to come forward, other students found the courage to do the same, and thus we have begun a conversation that is still going on about the kind of community in which we want to live.

The Aftermath: Change

I entitled this case "Educating the 'Larger Life'" because as I have contemplated these events, I have come to see they forced me to reassess my role as a teacher of things beyond the scope of what is normally considered "managerial communication." As I have written, I always believed — at least in theory — that as teachers we have a responsibility to instruct our students in something more than the discipline in which we have been trained. I'm not sure exactly how to categorize this other kind of pedagogy. I suppose it might go under the label of "human development" or "character building" or "social relationships." I am loath, actually, to use any of those terms because they sound so ponderous and old-fashioned; they conjure up images for me of imposing, humourless figures lecturing in front of legions of half-comatose students on unyielding principles of ethics and morality. Yet it is hard to dispute the fact that in every class we teach — whether it is on 17th Century English literature, quantum mechanics, or the history of Russia — we are also showing our students something about the way human beings interact with one another.

As I lived through the incident I have described, that abstract principle — that we must "educate the larger life" — came alive for me. But in writing this case, I discovered another life has been educated, and it is mine. I have identified several lessons I have learned from all this, which, if I can use Schon's terminology, revolve around the norms that underlie my judgments, the strategies and tactics implicit in my behavior, my feelings for (and I would add in) the situation, and the roles I have constructed for myself. For now, those lessons include:

1. *Communication is best learned when students are given the opportunity to practice the principles of the discipline.* In the 15 years I have taught courses in Communication, I have become convinced that the challenge in teaching this material is to make the principles we espouse real for the students. For example, it's easy to talk about the techniques one can use to become an effective listener; it's harder to create the experience of effective listening in the classroom. We can often come close, but any exercise I have used always has some degree of artificiality to it. In the discussion between Vinay and Charles, however, the students could observe the problems associated with listening actually being played out. They could see two people trying to get past prejudices and preconceived notions; searching for language to give form to their thoughts; trying to grasp how words that seemed innocent enough could hurt or

anger; and rephrasing ideas as they struggled to be understood. I believe that lesson was more vivid than anything I could have passed on to my students in a lecture, and I need to try to create more opportunities for that kind of learning to take place.

2. *Teachers must pay attention not only to content, but also to relationships and process.* There is an axiom in communication theory that says all communication takes places on both the content and relationship levels (Watzlawick, Beavin, Jackson, 1967:80–83). In other words, an interaction between instructor and student or between student and student may not only be about course material ("Is it proper to end a sentence with a preposition?" or "How can I create compelling overheads for my oral presentations?"), but may also be about the relationship between the two parties ("Who are you that I should believe anything you tell me about prepositions, or overheads, or anything else for that matter?"). If we are to teach well — and if we are to help our students learn something about how they can best manage their interactions with others — we would be wise to pay attention to the relationship level of the communication.

A corollary to this is that instructors need to keep their fingers on the emotional pulse of the class. Had I been more aware of how upset my students were getting during the intercultural presentations, I might have been able to intervene earlier, so we could have dealt with the issues more quickly and directly.

3. *The proper balance between the role of facilitator and the role of "authority" is hard to achieve.* In his book *Education for Judgment*, Chris Christensen (1991:106) asks, "What is a discussion if not a voyage of exploration, with the leader as both captain and crew member?" I am still struggling with how to shift back and forth between those two roles: If you impose too much of yourself on the discussion, you run the risk that students will become passive or disinterested bystanders in the subject at hand. (And then we blame them for not being attentive to or involved with the course material.) We need to keep ourselves fluid enough to see where the class is going and to follow its lead.

But if the crew has no captain, the ship may well wander off course, or worse, run aground. I have watched or participated in a number of discussions where I thought the instructor's presence — or, more importantly, his/her expertise on a particular subject — was so diminished that it was virtually nonexistent. More often than not, these discussions take on a rambling quality and lack the form or structure I think is needed for successful learning.

4. *Instructors are responsible for balancing the interests of subgroups in their class, as well as balancing the needs of individual students against the rights of the class as a whole. In other words, instructors must be fair.* After reading this case, one of my colleagues pointed out that in bending over backwards to make sure I was fair to the male students in class, I had placed an unfair burden on the female students. For example, she pointed out that when I talked to the women directly after the presentations, I asked them to think about how to frame a message so that the men in the room could genuinely hear what they were saying. Yet, I didn't ask my male students to do the same. I think my colleague is right; I overcompensated. Our own attitudes, preferences, and beliefs may get in the way of our ability to be fair, so we have to be extraordinarily vigilant in this regard.

5. *Teaching is a moral act.* (ibid: 117) Although issues of morality may not often seem present in the classroom, in fact, they exist virtually all the time. The cases we choose, the way we treat students, how we balance the needs of the individual against the needs of the group all have a moral dimension to them. In this case, the appearance of a letter sent from one student to another anonymously required me to comment directly on an issue of ethics.

I still have not resolved how to do that well. I am not an ethicist or philosopher, therefore, I don't feel I have the ability or the right to teach ethics *per se*. In the final analysis, then, the only thing I felt qualified to say was: "Here I stand" In that way, I was clear that I was not trying to foist my values on the students (although perhaps I should have been doing just that), but in my role as their teacher, as well as a member of the community in which they live and work, I had the right to condemn what I saw as an immoral act.

6. *Teachers must admit to and share their humanity.* If there is one overriding thing I have learned from this case — and in its writing — it is that the more we can bring of ourselves into the classroom, the more our students will benefit. "I teach not only what I know," Chris Christensen writes, "but what I am." We must also help students to learn who they are, and we do that, in part, by living with them through uncomfortable situations, tense interactions, and the experiences that force them to bring their own selves to us and to each other.

In an article entitled, "Teaching Like It Matters," Jane Tompkins, a professor of English at Duke University, writes:

> The classroom is a microcosm of the world; it is a chance to practice whatever ideals we may cherish. The kind of classroom situation one creates is the acid test of what it is one really stands for.
> (Jane Tompkins, August 1991:26)

Living through the incidents I have described in this case gave me a chance to practice the ideals I cherish, and the opportunity to see if I could put into action the things I believe in. Yet in introducing this list of lessons I learned, I wrote that these were the lessons I have learned "for now." I wrote that because I have no doubt that there are still lessons to be mined from this case — as there will always be lessons learned as long as I continue to teach. I am still in the process of creating my classroom, still testing what it is that I stand for and discovering who I am.

References

Christensen, C. R. (1991). Every student teaches and every teacher learns. In C. Roland Christensen, David Garvin and Ann Sweet (Eds.), *Education for Judgment. The Artistry of Discussion Leadership*, p. 106. Boston: Harvard Business School Press.

Eble, K. E. (1990). *The Aims of College Teaching*, p. 154. San Francisco: Josey Bass Publishers.

Rogers, C. (1969). *Freedom to Learn*, pp. 279–297. Columbus, Ohio: Merrill, as quoted in Eble, op. cit., p. 154.

Schon, D. A. (1983). *The Reflective Practitioner*, p. 61. New York: Basic Books, Inc.

Schon, D. A. (1987). *Educating the Reflective Practitioner*, p. 35. San Francisco: Josey Bass Publishers.

Tompkins, J. (1991). *Teaching Like It Matters*. August 1991, Lingua Franca: p. 26.

Watzlawick, P., Beavin, J. & Jackson, D. D. (1967). *Pragmatics of Human Communication*, pp. 80–83. New York: W. W. Norton & Co., Inc.

Solving Problems In A Saturated Dental Curriculum

Lum-Peng Lim

Faculty of Dentistry
National University of Singapore
Singapore

Synopsis

The Dentistry course at the National University of Singapore has traditionally been a demanding course involving the acquisition of a variety of cognitive and psychomotor skills. To enhance independent life-long learning, changes made in the dental curriculum include problem-based learning (PBL) and expanding project work into the current assessment system. Feedback on these learning strategies was favourable although PBL received a higher rating than project work. To meet future challenges in educating a reflective practitioner, there is a need to modify the current learning environment.

Solving Problems In A Saturated Dental Curriculum

Lum-Peng Lim

Introduction

There has been increasing emphasis in reflective teaching and educating a reflective practitioner in higher education. This would encompass the development of intellectual and imaginative powers, problem solving and creative thinking skills and the ability to link relationships across disciplines (Gibbs, 1992). Active learning strategies have been advocated to enhance the development of these skills. These activities include problem-based learning (Barrows and Tamblyn, 1980; Kaufman et al., 1989); cooperative project work (Johnson and Johnson, 1991; Meyers and Jones, 1993; Garvin et al., 1995); case studies (Cox and Ewan, 1982; Meyers and Jones, 1993); and computer-assisted learning (Boud, 1988). The Bachelor of Dental Surgery Course, National University of Singapore, is a 4-year course and consists of a combination of didactic and clinical sciences. The basic sciences like Anatomy, Physiology, Biochemistry, Pathology, Microbiology and Pharmacology are taught in the early years of the dental course, while the medical sciences like Medicine, Surgery and Pediatrics are taught later in the course. Clinical dental disciplines like Preventive Dentistry, Periodontics, Children's Dentistry, Orthodontics, Restorative Dentistry, Oral Surgery or Oral Medicine are taught from the second year extending to the final year of study. The essential skills required are a combination of cognitive, kinesthetic, visual, verbal and interpersonal skills.

Reflective Thinking in Dental Education

The Faculty of Dentistry is currently in the process of introducing a new curriculum. To reflect upon the current and innovative learning strategies in dental education, the Reflective Thinking and Collaborative Inquiry Model by Chen (1996) will form the framework for discussion of reflective teaching strategies. The framework consists of 5 stages: Reflection, Recognition, Realisation, Response and Resolution. Reflection refers to reviewing the current system; Recognition is identification of the problems and the contributing factors; Realisation is recognising the potential of certain learning strategies; Response involves implementation of a new strategy; while Resolution is reflection and evaluation of the situation, and the cycle continues. Upon reflection, several problems have been identified with the current traditional educational system which pre-empted such a move. This includes a lack of integration of the basic sciences into clinical dentistry and also across disciplines in view of the tendency to compartmentalise the various disciplines. The teaching tends to be teacher-orientated or teacher-directed. The curriculum has also been generally considered to be rather saturated giving little allowance for students to consolidate the concepts and to explore more deeply into certain areas of study. As a result it has been perceived that the traditional system does not appear to encourage critical thinking skills but rather a rote learning approach. In a survey conducted by the Ministry of Education on employers in the workforce, it was noted that new graduates from tertiary institutions in Singapore tend to need a lot of hand holding and are lacking in creative thinking skills (The Straits Times, September 1996). The Vice-Chancellor of the National University of Singapore, Professor Lim Pin, in a convocation ceremony last year, reiterated the need for more creative thinking activities in university teaching and advocated a trimming of the curriculum by at least 20% to give allowance for more self-study and reflection (The Straits Times, August 1996). In response to some of the problems identified, the Dental faculty has introduced PBL as a new mode of learning into the curriculum. Although project work had in the past been implemented, the impact of these projects on learning has been questionable.

To reinforce the importance of project work, it has been incorporated into the assessment system for the past year.

One may question whether the development of critical thinking skills has direct relevance in a course like dentistry which has generally been perceived to be rather mechanistic in nature involving manual dexterity skills. In reality, if one considers dentistry as a clinical profession in medicine, successful practice would include not only the manual dexterity skills which undoubtedly are essential, but equally important is the ability to understand the underlying problems and to manage them in the most efficient way. There is yet another feature which has received increasing attention, that is the interpersonal relationships. Empirical evidence suggests that many of our successful practitioners succeed not only because of their clinical competence but also their analytical and interpersonal skills such as the ability to communicate to patients and to reduce anxiety. Let us take a case scenario of a patient with gum disease, who is a diabetic and a smoker. Management of the patient's problems not only includes the treatment of his gum disease. The type of treatment delivered and predictability of the outcome also depends on the patient's oral hygiene and medical status. This would entail ability on the part of the practitioner to motivate the patient to be aware of risk factors such as diabetes and smoking. Collectively, the management of the case incorporates clinical skills, communications skills and knowledge in medicine.

Problem Based Learning (PBL) & Project Work as Modes of Learning

The objectives of introducing PBL and project work into the curriculum is firstly to promote critical thinking and problem solving skills by giving students exposure to 'real-life' problems and authentic tasks. Secondly, to enhance self-directed learning as well as collaborative learning skills.

Problem-based learning has been defined by Barrows and Tamblyn (1980), one of the pioneers in the problem-based approach to learning, as learning which results from the process of working towards the understanding of, and resolution of a problem. One important feature of the learning is the student seeking solutions to 'real-life' problems. It is an approach which is gaining popularity in medical education. One of the earliest proponents of PBL is the McMaster Medical School in Hamilton, Canada (Neufeld and Barrows, 1974). Since then, various medical schools have implemented PBL into the curriculum. In certain schools like the University of New Mexico and the Dalhousie University, PBL has replaced the traditional mode of lectures. PBL was introduced as a pilot project into the dental curriculum in 1996. The Dalhousie COPS (Case Orientated Problem Stimulated) Model was adopted (Kaufman et al., 1989). It always begins with the presentation of a problem followed by the identification of problems and relevant facts. The students are expected to generate hypotheses of causes and mechanisms of problems. The hypotheses are ranked, prioritised and tested using available data or by requesting for new data. This will be followed by management of the problems which would again raise certain issues and hypotheses. Students in the process of discussion would be challenged to the edge of their knowledge. Learning issues are expected to be raised throughout the learning process. These learning issues are discussed when the students reconvened for subsequent sessions.

Learning through projects, especially cooperative projects, has become the major learning activity in many courses in higher education. Morgan (1983) defines such a form of learning as "an activity in which students develop an understanding of a topic through some kind of involvement in an actual (or simulated) real-life problem or issue". They have some degree of responsibility in designing their learning activities. Project work can be divided into four fundamental types of inquiry: literature review, information search by making use of available data, empirical research and design project (Henry, 1994). The type of projects relevant to dentistry would be the literature review and empirical research. In reviewing the various elements of PBL and empirical project work, there are some similarities in the learning process which consists of: (i) Identification of problem (ii) Generating hypotheses (iii) Collection of relevant facts in order to find the solution to the problem (iv) Ranking and testing of hypotheses and (v) Management of problem. These various stages in fact also fall in line with the various stages of the Reflective Thinking and Collaborative Inquiry Model of Chen (1996) elucidated earlier. Both forms of learning are student-centred with varying degrees of emphasis on cooperative learning skills. While the literature review is a central element in project work, this is not necessarily the case for PBL.

Reflection of PBL & Project Work as Modes of Learning in Dental Education

To reflect upon PBL and project work as modes of learning, feedback was received from third year dental students who participated in the PBL pilot study and final year dental students who were involved in project work. Informal feedback was also received from staff. The effects of PBL and project work will be viewed from various aspects based on the taxonomy of learning objectives (Bloom et al., 1956; Krathwohl et al., 1964; Harrow, 1972).

Perceived effectiveness on cognitive skills

There were some differences in the responses of both groups of students on perceived cognitive skills. While over 80% of students from both groups felt they had achieved better understanding of a subject, a lower proportion of the project group felt the learning experience helped them to think critically, reinforced learning and developed problem solving skills.

Perceptions on affective & psychomotor skills

On the affective aspect, while the participants in the PBL course were generally very positive on the interactive aspects of PBL and the interest generated, the amount of enthusiasm was less evident in the project work. It was disappointing that less than 20% of subjects in the project group indicated having developed an interest in research work. On the psychomotor aspects, over 80%–90% in the PBL group were positive of having improved communication and reasoning skills as compared with only one third to two thirds of positive responses in the project group. The appreciation of collaborative learning were less well received by both groups of students.

Perceptions of effects of non-cognitive & environmental factors

While participants in the PBL group were very satisfied with the learning environment, the project group in general found the situation more stressful. Both groups of students indicated the time-consuming nature of the work as an aspect least liked by the students. The difference in responses from both groups of students could be attributed to several factors: stress levels, structure of the programme, learning environment and the time factor. The PBL sessions were better organised, and the students received standard materials. Therefore, interpersonal conflicts and tension was likely to be less, as the dependence on one another was less crucial in PBL as opposed to project work. Furthermore, the project group was in their final year of study, where work tension was supposedly heavier as students rushed to complete their clinical schedule, which resulted in more negative responses. The nature of the research projects were also markedly different. For example, certain groups of students were involved in the literature reviews only, as opposed to some who were involved in some form of clinical or laboratory research. More positive responses were received from those who participated in an experimental project due to the more involved nature of the work and the greater sense of achievement. Another point to note was that the choice of the project was usually directed by the supervisor, which may partially account for the lack of enthusiasm.

It is evident from the feedback from students that several areas of improvement are needed in PBL and project work if we are to foster a deeper approach to learning and a greater commitment to these modes of learning in dental education. This includes time being allocated for self-study; cooperative learning skills should be reinforced by providing some training in basic core skills; autonomy in learning by allowing students to choose some of their own research projects; and more structured guidance in project work by providing students with the basic core skills relating to project work.

Looking Towards the Future

Upon reflection of the two active learning strategies introduced, PBL was generally perceived to be more interesting, enjoyable, less stressful and better able to stimulate critical thinking skills. However, there is a general lack of appreciation of the collaborative learning experiences. Although it is premature to draw any definitive conclusion at this point in time, the realisation of some of the inherent problems through formative evaluation helps to shape learning opportunities. To enhance the learning experience, changes and modifications to the programme are necessary. This would include timing of the courses, allowance being given for self-study in the timetable and staff development programmes for teaching staff to be up-to-date on the paradigm shift in higher education. With an explosion of new knowledge in dental technologies and techniques, the dental profession needs to keep abreast of changes through independent life-long learning. The understanding of the basic principles of research and problem solving would help the future practitioner to critically review some of these new developments applicable to their individual practices.

Sternberg (1996) listed three essential aspects of successful intelligence: creative, analytical and proactive intelligences. All these qualities are applicable in the nuturing of our dental profession. Creative intelligence is essential to allow individuals to see connections; analytical intelligence allows one to analyse and evaluate ideas, solve problems and make decisions. These could be fostered through the problem solving activities we have introduced. The third aspect of practical intelligence is the ability to translate theory into practice. A balance of these qualities is necessary for the training of a successful practitioner. Collectively, the changes in different aspects of the curriculum along with changes in the assessment system and through reflection would hopefully take us through a more relevant curriculum for the practitioner. We should surely look towards fulfilling our goal of "providing adequate training for a dental graduate to practise sound general dentistry and to instill a commitment to life-long learning".

References

Barrows, H. S. & Tamblyn, R. M. (1980). *Problem Based Learning: An Approach to Medical Education.* New York: Springer Publishing Company.

Boud, D., Keogh, R. & Walker, D. (1985). *Reflection: Turning Experience into Learning.* London: Kogan Page.

Boud, D. (1988). *Developing Student Autonomy in Learning.* London: Kogan Page.

Bloom, B. S., Englehart, M. D., Furst, E. J., Hill, E. J. & Krathwohl, D. R. (1956). *Taxonomy of Educational Objectives: Handbook I: Cognitive Domain.* New York: Longman.

Chen, A. Y., Chan, C. M., Lee, S. K., Liao, Z., Ravinthran, U., Wan, Y. S., Wong, C. T. & Zhou, W. (1996). *Towards Exemplary Teaching Through Collaborative Inquiry Into Curriculum Redesign.* Paper presented at the ERA/AARE Joint Conference in Singapore, 25–29 November 1996.

Gibbs, G. (1992). *Improving the Quality of Student Learning.* Bristol: Technical & Educational Services Ltd.

Harrow, A. J. (1972). A taxonomy of psychomotor domain. *A Guide for Developing Behavioral Objectives.* New York: Mackay.

Kaufman, A., Mennin, S., Waterman, R., Duban, S. et al. (1989). The New Mexico experiment: Educational innovation and institutional change. *Academic Medicine,* 64: 285–294.

Krathwohl, D. R., Bloom, B. S. & Masia, B. B. (1964). *Taxonomy of Educational Objectives: The Classification of Educational Goals Volume 2: Affective Domain.* New York: Mackay.

Meyers, C. & Jones, T. B. (1993). *Promoting Active Learning: Strategies for the College Classroom.* San Francisco: Jossey Bass.

Neufeld, V. R. & Barrows, H. S. (1974). The McMaster philosophy: An approach to medical education. *Journal of Medical Education*, 49: 1040–1050.

Schon, D. (1988). *Educating the Reflective Practitioner*. San Francisco: Jossey Bass.

The Straits Times, August 28 1996.

The Straits Times, September 6 1996.

The Straits Times, May 20 1997.

A ccounting For Manufacturing: Reflecting On The Grading System

Fred Kofman

Sloan School of Management
Massachusetts Institute of Technology
United States of America

Synopsis

This case was prepared as the basis for class discussion among participants of a MIT Leaders For Manufacturing Program in 1994. Though the focus was on a new grading policy for group performance, it was a means of giving the participants a personal experience of the impact of performance measurement systems on group behavior with particular emphasis on team learning. It is not meant as an illustration either on effective or ineffective handling of an administrative situation.

Accounting For Manufacturing:
Reflecting On The Grading System

Fred Kofman

This case was prepared as the basis for class discussion rather than to illustrate either effective or ineffective handling of an administrative situation.

At 10:30 am on Monday, June 10, 1991, 41 students in MIT's Leaders For Manufacturing (LFM) program walked into their first class together, *Accounting for Manufacturing*. They received a syllabus that would impact not just what they studied in the course, but how they studied it. Buried on page 2 was a section on grading policy, which read:

> We have organized you in seven groups.... Every member of the group will get the same grade, and that grade will be the minimum grade of the individual members of the group.

> We understand that this is a slight departure from traditional grading methods. We have adopted it because it will give you a personal experience of the impact of performance measurement systems on behavior and because it will encourage the group to learn together.

In class that day, the course instructors explained:

> Our metaphor for this class is the "play-within-a-play." We use readings, cases, and problems to learn about performance measurement systems and how they influence behavior. But simultaneously we will live and breathe this performance measurement system and observe first-hand, in real-time, how it influences individual and group behavior in this class. You are not only the spectators of this play, but are also the actors in it.

Background

The Leaders For Manufacturing (LFM) programme is an educational and research partnership among twelve major U.S. manufacturing firms and the Schools of Engineering and Management at MIT. Its overall goals are to identify new paradigms in world-class manufacturing and develop a new generation of leaders dedicated to manufacturing excellence. (See the mission statement in Exhibit I.)

About 40 LFM fellows are selected each year to participate in a graduate programme that integrates engineering and management and awards two masters degrees. The educational experience extends beyond the walls of the classroom to include many guest speakers, plant visits, and a 7-month internship working at one of the sponsoring companies. Thus the programme's educational goals involve a multi-disciplinary approach to manufacturing that provides students with solid academic and practical experiences.

In order to complete their two degrees in two years, the LFM fellows take a full semester of classes during the summer before the traditional fall matriculation date. There are five summer classes teaching the fundamentals of engineering and management; all of them are specially tailored toward manufacturing and the LFM programme. Every student takes the same five classes together, meeting for eight hours every day in a sort of "boot camp" spirit. All the students carry the same heavy load of commitments and assignments, and a camaraderie develops among them as they help each other with classwork and discover a shared sense of purpose. In short, the summer experience is 10 weeks of hard work, both theoretical and applied, where the students come together to understand the guiding mission and principles of the LFM programme.

One of the fundamental disciplines taught during the LFM summer semester is Accounting. Prior to 1991, the course had focused solely on the mechanics of Accounting without broadening its scope into manufacturing implications and the impact of performance measures. In response to feedback from students and programme sponsors, the 1991 course was completely redesigned to emphasize this expanded context.

Two professors, Charlie Fine and Fred Kofman, under a grant from the Alfred P. Sloan Foundation, jointly developed this new course called *Accounting for Manufacturing*.

Because neither professor had ever taught Accounting before, they brought new perspectives to the discipline. Charlie came with a broad exposure to manufacturing issues as a professor of operations management, and Fred brought a strong background in Economics and incentive systems. As Fred said, "We decided to reclaim ownership of the language of Business and create a radically different course — a course after which leaders in manufacturing would not yield to finance types for lack of technical background."

As part of this "radical" change, the course included some non-traditional topics. In addition to financial statement analysis and book-keeping, the course also covered topics such as the impact of Accounting on decision-making time horizons and also the role of performance measurements in quality, cycle time reduction, and organizational learning. (See Exhibit II for a summary of the syllabus.) To complement the unconventional material, Charlie and Fred also used unconventional teaching methods. For instance, they taught the course side-by-side, openly working out their differing viewpoints. However, the new teaching method that affected the students most was the novel grading system.

The Grading System

The grading system provides incentive for group learning and to focus attention on the "bottleneck person" on each team. Evaluation was based on performance along several dimensions including individual vs. group, concrete test problems vs. subjective participation, and absolute vs. relative standards. Because the class was dedicated to studying performance measures, the grading system in a sense became "a-play-within-a-play," a living and breathing example of what the students were studying.

The grading system divides into two parts: the mechanics of assigning the grades and the support structure surrounding those mechanics.

As for the mechanics, the professors divided the students into seven groups of six students each. The students did not choose the groups themselves, but rather the professors assigned them before the first class meeting. The groupings maximized diversity based on several characteristics from the students' admissions applications, including:

- sex
- age
- race
- work experience (if any)
- geographic origin

The grading process required four inputs from the students: two group-work items and two individual-work items. The two group-work items were:

- A multi-week problem set (25%)
- A final case write-up (25%).

The multi-week problem set covered the fundamentals of Financial Accounting which were studied in the first half of the course. The final case write-up required a set of six essays on the topics of performance measurement, management control, incentives, and other topics in management accounting. For both of these assignments, each team handed in just one copy and received just one group grade.

The two individual-work items included in the grade were:

- A mid-term in-class examination (25%)
- Class participation (25%)

The mid-term examination was two-and-a-half hours long and emphasized financial accounting principles. Class participation grades were based on the professors' subjective evaluation of the quality of comments and questions. Every student in the class received a separate grade for each of these two items.

At the end of the term, once the four items to be graded were complete, the professors determined what letter grade (e.g., A, B, C, etc.) each *individual* would have received. This grade was based on group items (the problem set and the final case write-up) and individual items (the mid-term and class participation) using equal weightings.

The final step was the critical one. The *minimum* individual grade in each group became the grade that everyone in the group received.

A key part of the grading system was the "support structure" surrounding it. The first aspect involved fostering group development. On the first day of class, the professors gave each group a copy of *The Team Handbook* and recommended that students looked over several especially important chapters in it. None of the groups interviewed (later) actually completed this informal reading assignment. Also, each group had one of the professors designated as its team advisor and was required to meet with that advisor (over a free lunch) within the first two weeks of the course and as often as they wanted to thereafter. Despite these team encouragement efforts, there was no explicit group dynamics training nor any discussion during the class on how exactly to "help" others on the team. However, the students quickly realized that they must identify and help, in whatever fashion was deemed useful, the "bottleneck" student (or students) on each team.

The second part of the support structure for the course was a daily feedback system for rapid response and continuous improvement. After each class, the professors asked the students to hand in comments about any aspect of that class or the course in general on "post-it" notes (pink for strengths and blue for weaknesses). Then at the beginning of each class, the professors distributed printed handouts summarizing the feedback from each class and providing responses to whatever issues had been raised. This "rapid feedback" system also fit into the "play-within-a-play" theme since one topic in the course related to the importance of rapid feedback in manufacturing via the information systems.

The "pinks and blues" — as they became called — provided an on-going forum for discussing the grading system and created a permanent documentation of responses to each class. (See Exhibit III for an example day and Exhibit IV for a history on the number of comments per class.)

Relevance to the LFM Programme

The concept of grading based on team performance fits well with the ideals and goals of the programme. The grading system reflects the reality of the manufacturing world where more and more work requires team effort. Future competitive demands are driving firms toward group work because team efforts often yield superior results compared to individual efforts. The result of this trend is that measurement of outcomes is traceable only to group responsibility, not to individuals. If team work provides more effective performance, then measurement systems must encourage subordination of individual efforts to raise the level of the group. The intent of the accounting course grading system was to demand this kind of team work and provide the LFM students with an opportunity to learn important group skills.

Besides being relevant to the future trend in manufacturing team work, the grading system also fits the character of the LFM summer session. During their first summer, the students are isolated in an environment where the programme tries to instill a sense of purpose toward change and improvement in U.S. manufacturing. Making changes involves taking risks, and the LFM programme itself is no exception. The programme is only four years old, and it is constantly evolving in an effort to represent the world-class principles that it strives to teach. Therefore, in a course that focuses on changing traditional corporate performance measures, it makes sense to challenge traditional classroom grading procedures. The summer session dedicated to LFM students provides a supportive environment for taking this kind of risk.

Key Events in the Course Over the Summer

The first deliverable for the course was the group homework. Charlie and Fred assigned a few problems along with each lecture during the first third of the summer, and then the full problem set came due all at once on 2nd July. The homework was too extensive to complete right before the due date, so it provided the first test of how well the groups could work together to plan ahead and reach consensus on their answers. About halfway through the summer, the homework grades were returned, and the groups received their first feedback from scores that ranged from 135 to 150 out of 150. The instructors did not perceive this result to represent significant variability. Essentially all the groups demonstrated a similar level of mastery of the material at this point.

The second deliverable was the $2^{1/2}$ hour mid-term exam on 26th July. The exam provided the first individual grades in the course, and the class average was an 85 out of 150, with a low of 45 and a high of 129. At this point, the potential "bottlenecks" had been revealed. Now it was up to each team to decide how to respond.

The instructors offered an opportunity to take another mid-term exam for the six students who scored below the minimum passing grade of 60 and for anyone else who wished to take it. The chance to re-take the test was designed to remove some of the stress associated with being a group's bottleneck, and only the better of the two scores would count. The cost of re-taking the mid-term for the LFM students was the additional studying time required during a busy mid-term period, with tests or projects due in every class. This cost fell disproportionately on those students who were already having trouble keeping up in other subjects. The instructors suggested that the people who did well on the exam could coach their team-mates in preparation for the re-take, since everyone's grade depended on the "bottleneck resource." Now 41 students, each of whom had succeeded most of their lives by being standouts as individuals, were faced with finding appropriate behaviors within a very different reward system.

One group took this team concept to its ultimate extreme, and in a show of solidarity with a team member who had to re-take the exam, the entire group studied together and re-took the exam. The team undertook this effort despite the fact that several of the members had scored very high on the original exam.

When the students who were re-taking the exam arrived at the appointed hour, there was a message on the blackboard which read,

> *"90% of life is showing up"*
> *– Woody Allen*

They were given the exact same exam again. Needless to say, everyone who re-took the exam did extremely well. In fact, 8 out of the 9 scores over 125 came from the re-take exam.

As a result, the mid-term re-take effectively raised the relative grading standards for the rest of the class. The one group who had all taken the re-take in support of their team-mates now had a minimum team score that was one point below the original high individual score. On the other hand, students who had performed relatively well on the original exam and who had decided not to re-take it suddenly found themselves at the low end of the curve. In essence, they were penalized for not re-taking an exam that was meant to be optional and for low scorers. This conflicting outcome from the mid-term re-take left a difficult question: how to reward the students and the team that successfully re-took the exam without penalizing those who performed relatively well on the first try.

The next key event was a series of heated in-class discussions about the grading system triggered by the tensions surrounding the mid-term. The most controversial issue involved the inequities raised by the shifting relative standards. Over the next six hours of class, two hours were devoted to discussing the pros and cons of bottleneck grading and the idea of Fred and Charlie providing mid-term feedback on class participation. At the time, many students felt that the grading system was in fact changing or could be changed midstream. In the end, Charlie and Fred did not alter the grading system, and they provided interim class participation feedback only to groups that requested it in person.

The final key events occurred at the end of the course. The final case write-ups were handed in and graded with scores ranging from 104 to 128 out of 150. The two professors and the teaching assistants (TA) evaluated class participation. They synthesized their general impressions and evaluations of student performance in each class to arrive at scores ranging from 80 to 136 out of 150.

To calculate the final grades, the professors used a relative standard and agreed that, based on performance and demonstrated level of effort, everyone deserved at least a "B". Next, they put all the students together as individuals and looked for the biggest gap at the low end of the range.

At that gap, they drew a line below which were five students who received B's. Then they put the groups together and found the minimum grade in each. Three groups totaling 17 students received B's, and four groups totaling 23 students received A's. (See Exhibit V for the detail of grades.)

Class Responses to the Grading System

Two student comments from the final Accounting course evaluations illustrate the range of responses to the grading system. The first comment reads:

> The grading system was well-constructed — a good experiment despite all the bickering. I learned a lot from the group and about the group.

And the second comment reads:

> What bothered me most was the instructors' total unwillingness to change once it became apparent that the class was uncomfortable, learning was being compromised, and morale was in the tank.

Although this variety of opinion was present throughout the summer, a generalized evolution of the class responses can be traced. For instance, in the beginning of the summer, students voiced opposition to the system both inside and outside of class. Some claimed that it violated traditional academic paradigms and contradicted our capitalistic culture of rewarding the individual. One blue feedback slip (for weaknesses) actually called the grading system "a communist plot." For other students, the system triggered grade stress intrinsic to high achievers who had always earned top marks. On the other hand, several students who were enthusiastic about trying the grading system felt uncomfortable about showing their support in front of all their new classmates.

The next stage in the evolution of the class response was gradual acceptance or resignation. Not only did the two professors stand firm about their system, but also most (but not all) of the groups found working together on the mechanical homework helpful. (Of course this cooperation and benefit is quite possible in conventional grading systems.) The

Accounting course was not returning any individual grades at this point, and the students had many other concerns during the busy summer term.

All that changed when the mid-term exam was returned. As some groups realized they had failing grades, the initial tensions resurfaced. Emotions flared during in-class discussions and on feedback notes, and a few individuals became very vocal in their opposition. Exacerbating the situation was a tension surrounding class participation and how it would be graded. Class feedback included comments such as:

> Intense nervousness by some who are called on and embarrassed. Is it all right to get an answer wrong?

> Several weeks ago you said an enemy of learning is 'looking good.' Does this 'enemy' pervade our class?

Thus, anxiety levels were running high at this point because "bottleneck" individuals were feeling pressure from mid-term grades and class participation performance. On top of this, group dependence was raising stress levels, and other classes were having tests or projects looming. At this point in the summer, the Accounting course and the grading system in particular became a scapegoat for many of the students' frustrations.

By the end of the summer, the class response was directed more at the content of the Accounting course, rather than toward the grading system process. In comments from the final course evaluation, only 15 of the 40 students even mentioned the grading system, and only 2 of those were altogether negative. (See Exhibit VI or a pareto chart of final course evaluation comments.)

Group and Individual Responses to the Grading System

Benefits Realized

As the final course evaluation comments suggest, the majority of students felt that team learning was one of the biggest benefits of the grading system. While students might have studied together in the course without any elaborate performance measurement scheme, the assigned groups and group grading forced even the troubled groups to collaborate most of the time. Every team felt that they had learned from each other on several dimensions, whether positive or negative.

At the simplest level, the groups taught each other the fundamentals of Accounting by doing the homework together and by studying for the mid-term exam together. Everyone interviewed agreed that discussing Accounting issues with their groups enriched the learning both for the stronger members who did most of the explaining and for the weaker members, who did most of the listening. Although, under a traditional system, stronger students might have been willing to help explain Accounting to others, the group grading system promoted and reinforced this interactive behavior.

In addition, the groups learned how to take advantage of the different strengths that team members brought to the table. One group had a very meticulous member who became the designated number checker, and they had another member who had expertise on the computer and could quickly format all their homework problems. Moreover, many groups learned to take advantage of their diverse backgrounds and experiences from before the LFM programme. More than one group met before every case discussion to review the reading, and often found themselves sharing related work experiences about unions, managers, and organizations.

Another benefit of the grading system was that it provided a living experience to learn about teamwork. Every group experienced an evolution of establishing culture and norms. Over the summer, the team members took on different leadership and maintenance roles, and they even learned mundane but useful skills such as setting agendas and discussing expectations. One group learned how a culture can develop into a problem. One member gradually took on the leadership role and always came prepared, but then when the other members began to skip the work and rely on her, feelings of resentment started to divide the group.

Also, the teams learned how to make group decisions about what level of cooperation and individual effort would work best for them. One team found that working through problems as a group required more time but produced better answers, so throughout the summer they focused on improving their efficiency when working together. Another group decided that "divide and conquer" worked best for them, and they avoided holding meetings until everyone had prepared something on their own.

The final major benefit of the grading system was that the teams actually experienced the effect of performance measurement systems on behavior. One student who was particularly frustrated with the grading system said that the one thing he could really take away from the experience was an appreciation for the power and importance of incentive systems. Another student said that she learned the most about performance measurement systems when the Accounting class had problems.

> I learned that you first need a goal before you put in an incentive system. [The Accounting class] treated the system as an end in itself, and then we lost sense of its purpose. And also, you need to look at the big picture and anticipate everything the system will effect.

Costs Realized

Although many aspects of the grading system were beneficial and provided the expected benefits, many other aspects of the system had negative effects.

In some cases, the grading system fueled conflict within groups by artificially forcing students together who could not contribute to each other's learning. The first divisive issue that arose for many groups was unshared grade ambitions. Some students gave grades a low priority because they had families or had jobs assured with their sponsoring companies. On the other hand, many high achieving students accustomed to earning nothing but As in their work wanted to put in extra effort to get a better grade. As Fred puts it, "This created a clash of cultures. The A-seekers were pitted against the B-satisfieds." In this system, the B-satisfieds have the upper hand.

This grade conflict proved especially divisive for one group. In the beginning of the summer, only one member of the group admitted that he really wanted an A. However, he felt that "it was wrong to impose on the others and demand what I wanted," and the group agreed that a B would suffice. This initial conflict flared up later after the group received mid-term grades (some of which were lower than Bs), and in one member's opinion, "the grades were far more precious than anyone wanted to admit."

Another way the grading system fragmented several of the groups was through its emphasis on the "bottleneck" resource. After the mid-term exam, (a fairly intensive and lengthy test for students who had been out of school as long as 10 years), the students who received the low grade in their groups faced a double stress. Not only had they done poorly on one of the first tests of their new MIT career, but also they faced spoken or unspoken pressure from their groups who were depending on them for their grades. In one group, the student who had the low grade said,

> I lost all my confidence and felt like I wasn't going to make it here. One person in my group called me a liar to my face for saying I thought I knew the material.... My self esteem sank to the level of the group's opinion of me.

In another group, the student who received the low grade felt that even after he had done well on the re-take exam, his group had "lingering resentment that they were stuck with [him]." At that point, he just gave up on the course and towards the end he barely even read the cases.

On the other side of the fence, some of the stronger students who were good at the Accounting found that the grading system was de-motivating. They felt that they could slack off, knowing that their performance would not impact their grade. Instead of channeling their efforts into helping the group's "bottleneck" resource, they concentrated on their other summer courses where they could control their grades. One strong student reasoned,

> Well, if you're going to saddle me with this system, I'll take full advantage of it. It is supposed to be shaping my behavior, isn't it?

The students also faced a problem knowing how exactly to help each other. Although the professors handed out a team-building book and offered opportunities for the groups to meet with them, they never raised the issue of group dynamics in class. Furthermore, the students were not familiar with each other and felt uncomfortable both giving and receiving help from people they were still trying to impress. One student who had just graduated from MIT as an undergraduate said,

> The biggest hurdle was that you feel like you're putting upon others for help. It's much easier to give than receive. Plus, I'm used to MIT where you are in a cut-throat environment.

With all of these pressures, some groups became divided and hostile. One student felt so threatened, he tried to find excuses to skip meetings, which of course only made things worse. Another student became so upset during a session when the group was editing her final essay, she had to leave the room. In one case, a student who was not his group's bottleneck felt "outside of the incentive system." Because his particular team was so divided, he felt absolutely no pressure and no desire to take leadership for it. Even today, he does not know what he could have done differently to improve his group, and he believes that the grading system is harmful when group members refuse to participate.

In addition to the negative group experiences, another cost of the system was the opportunity cost of learning Accounting this way. As the final course evaluations in Exhibit V show, many students wished they had learned more Accounting. Discussions of the grading system consumed a tremendous amount of the limited class time. Moreover, strong students were expected to put their efforts into helping team-mates rather than into advancing their own skills to a high level of expertise. One student felt that the cost of "bottleneck" grading was "regression toward the mean or lower."

Despite these costs to the grading system, almost all the students agree that the experience taught them important lessons about teamwork and incentive systems. In fact, many of the teams learned the most when they had problems. One student summed it up well when he said,

> Our group took a risk. We kept an open mind and admitted our weaknesses. And now we're that much better prepared to face challenges in the workplace.

Views of Other Partners in the Programme

Professor Thomas L. Magnanti, co-director of the LFM programme and
George Eastman Professor of Management Science at MIT, expresses a
high level of enthusiasm for the novel approach the whole *Accounting for
Manufacturing* course took. He supports the curriculum which "reaches
beyond book-keeping to examine how performance measures can affect the
manufacturing firm of the future." Moreover, he feels the grading system
is worth the effort because "it provides a first-hand appreciation of incentive
systems and can drive students towards team work."

Dr. Douglas Braithwaite, Digital's programme manager for manufacturing leadership and a member of the LFM operating committee, compares
the grading system to his days as a marine corps officer:

> In basic training and throughout the USMC, we had a 5-mile race where
> the time for the whole platoon was the time for the last guy to cross the
> finish line. I was one of the so-called "body bearers" who physically
> carried the slowest man after he could go no further. The most successful
> platoons were those where everyone helped the weaker members early.
> This is real life, in the Marines and in industry.

He is excited to see the LFM programme take a risk on "stretch goals"
instead of "resting on its laurels." His feeling is that industry wants to
reward team work but doesn't know how, and the accounting class represents
an important experiment.

Mr. Bryan G. Eagle, an industrial engineer with Alcoa and a member
of the LFM operating committee, feels that the Accounting course addresses
"one of the biggest challenges of future leaders — managing teams to
bring out the best of the whole." He points out that the grading system has
several important differences from real life, especially because the student
teams were not created to have special expertise and because many aspects
of the grading were outside the students' control.

Dr. Roger C. Shulze, manager of Chrysler's technical development
area and also a member of the LFM operating committee, believes the
grading system is dealing with real world issues, but that parts of it are
artificial. For instance, group "grades" are common at Chrysler, but not on

individual efforts. He feels that all the Accounting grades should be based on group efforts instead of the lowest grade on exams because that is more realistic. However, he praises the goals of the grading system saying,

> Single contributions are rare. There is more benefit to American industry to have team excellence rather than individual performance at an exceptional level.

Views of the Professors

Charlie and Fred were not satisfied with the way the incentive system worked in their accounting course. They had hoped that the grading system could quickly establish an atmosphere of cooperation and teamwork during the summer. By viewing the grading system as a means rather than as a support, they feel that they concentrated on the action and not on the context in which it took place. As Fred explains,

> Originally, I envisioned a class where, people were motivated to do the right things and where the grades did not get in the way. However, I think I fell for the idea that the grading system was enough to drive behavior and that I didn't need to spend time working on a collaborative culture. Charlie and I focused on the controllable (the grading system) instead of the important (developing a set of skills that would let the students learn as a team).... Maybe we were expecting too much in too short a time. It takes a while to develop the trust to discuss embarrassing or difficult issues.
>
> If I have learned one thing in this summer course, it is that every action has both a bright and a dark side. Which one prevails is a function of the context of the action. Group grades can foster teamwork (by everybody helping the weakest link) or destroy it (by everybody fighting and blaming each other for poor performance). Relative performance can reassure the class (by assuring that the professors will set realistic expectations) or it can fill it with anxiety (by forcing a distribution curve that will assign Bs to a fixed percentage of the students).
>
> My own blindness was to concentrate on the action and not on the context in which it took place. Maybe by working more on the cultural context

of the class, we could have achieved our goals even with an ordinary grading system.

One student echoed this theme in a final course evaluation that read,

The group learning experience was a good idea, but the grading system as a means to force it wasn't necessarily the best way. I don't like the idea of trying to use peers to force me to study or re-take an exam.

Despite their dissatisfaction with several aspects of the Accounting incentive system, both professors agree that they learned a great deal from the experience. Charlie summarizes his current feelings about the summer and the grading system this way:

In part, because of the difficulties, I believe we learned a great deal from this experiment. I cannot regret the course of events too much. I now have a deeper understanding of this interplay among infrastructure, practice, and incentives. We have a lot to learn about how to teach Accounting to manufacturing students. The "play-within-a-play" philosophy is just one part of it.

Fred also feels the experience taught him new insight:

What I think I have learned from this experience is that the incentive system can go along with or go against the desired goals, but you can't really expect it to "drive" behavior in a productive way. If the incentives ever become the overarching concern for acting, what one will create is a situation of "game playing" where people are only trying to look good according to the measurements, regardless of what they think is the proper thing to do. In the long run, this creates a situation of low self-esteem and anxiety.

Both professors demonstrate their learning from the course in their enthusiasm for continuous improvement. They can scarcely discuss what happened last summer without reeling off a string of ideas for ways they could teach it better. Charlie says:

Of course, much improvement is possible, and I'm looking forward to improving our system continuously. I think the greatest opportunities for this may lie in developing the team processes to support the team incentives.

If I could revisit one decision from last summer, I would veto the students' decision to use different teams for the summer LFM *Total Quality Management* class and our class. The TQM class complemented ours in many ways such as providing significant exercises and infrastructure for team-building. All the potential synergy was destroyed when the class chose to reverse our design of using the same teams for both courses.

Fred, too, has targeted specific areas for continuous improvement:

How to do it better next time? In terms of the team-building process, we will own up to our role of team facilitators more fully. With some support and guidance from our expert colleagues in the area, we will take a more active stance toward group dynamics. We will make the team assignments more regular (homework will be due at every class), and we will think of "common tasks" that can better help to build the teams.

In terms of the measurement system, I am less clear. We could follow Deming and avoid rating people at all; let them experience the pride of their work without evaluating their performance based on nosy observations. If we do away with grades, however, people who are not intrinsically motivated would check out completely. Besides, the other courses are still assigning grades. When the time comes to make hard choices about what to study, if one course is grading performance while the other isn't, the incentive to focus on what will be measured is too strong to resist.

Conclusion

As the professors reflect on the results of the summer, they realize that there is plenty of room for improvement and learning. Nevertheless, they remain convinced that the group "bottleneck" grading concept represents an important experiment in learning how to motivate and evaluate team performance.

Not everyone, though, endorses the "weakest link" model of group behavior. Other minor modifications might be possible such as group mean or median grading. Perhaps other types of group incentives are possible outside of mathematical combinations of individual grades. The key issue becomes "Does the performance measurement system align behavior behind the desired goals without unanticipated effects?"

As Charlie and Fred contemplate the summer and their grading system, they return to their original goals and purposes and ask the fundamental question:

How do we let people do what they consider is right, give them feedback about the appropriateness of their actions, but not measure them in a counterproductive way?

References

Crosby, P. B. (1979). *Quality is Free*. New York: McGraw-Hill

Crosby, P. B. (1988). *The Eternally Successful Organisation*. New York: McGraw-Hill.

Juran, J. M. (1989). *Juran on Leadership for Quality*. New York: The Free Press.

Deming, W. E. (1986). *Out of the Crisis*. Cambridge, MA: MIT Center for Advanced Engineering Study.

Hoyt, D. P. (1965). *The Relationship Between College Grades and Adult Achievement*. Iowa City: American College Testing Program.

Link, H. C., Ph.D. (1919). *Employment Psychology*. New York: Macmillan.

Peter, T. J. & Waterman, R. H. (1982). *In Search of Excellence*. New York: Warner Books.

APPENDIX
Views from the Literature

The Accounting for Manufacturing course addressed a topic, performance measurement systems, that is extensively covered in the literature. With the growing emphasis of work teams in American industry, experiments such as the LFM Accounting grading system represent important new areas of research.

As early as 1919, researchers recognized the importance of evaluation systems and began to analyze how they operated in industry. One of the first issues they encountered was subjectivity in measurements of individual performance. This same conflict arose more than 70 years later in the LFM Accounting course when the class had heated discussions about how to measure class participation grades. The poetic descriptions from 1919 sound remarkably similar to the students' objections from last summer:

> The promotion and retention of individuals depend very often upon momentary consideration and fleeting impressions. In fact, one of the mysteries of management is the way in which individuals progress through the various ranks of occupation and salary. Their comings and goings are as inexplicable as traditional coming and going of the wind.
>
> (Henry C. Link, 1919:321)

Even today, many of the respected quality "gurus", who have commented on almost every aspect of business, recognize the difficulty of performance measurement. For example, Philip Crosby cannot offer any concrete alternative to subjective evaluation when he laments,

> The measurement of job performance in most jobs is subjective, revolving around energy, attitude, and output. The only ones who are compared objectively are those in direct production, and that isn't always accurate. This lack of measurement is not due to the absence of data; it is due to the absence of tradition. Managers just aren't used to that sort of thing and don't really know what to look for.
>
> (Philip B. Crosby, 1988:30)

The quality experts are also surprisingly quiet on team-based incentive systems. For instance, Joseph Juran, who is known for his work at Xerox and Texas Instruments, admits that he knows of no other system but "supervisory judgment" when he writes:

> A further problem in evaluation relates to the performance of individual team members — how to evaluate each individual's contribution to a team project. As of the late 1980s, there was no consensus on how to do this. Until new ways are evolved, this evaluation must be left to supervisory judgment.
>
> (J.M. Juran, 1989:70)

Comments such as this one demonstrate the great need for experiments like the Accounting grading system.

W. Edwards Deming, who is widely credited with helping to catalyze the Japanese quality revolution, takes a totally different approach to evaluation systems, arguing that they should be eradicated like a disease:

> One of the "deadly diseases" is the evaluation of performance, merit rating, or annual review.... [Evaluation by numbers] nourishes short-term performance, annihilates long-term planning, builds fear, demolishes teamwork, nourishes rivalry and politics.
>
> (W. Edwards Deming, 1986:98 and 102).

[Charlie wanted to include a quotation here from Peter's (1982) book: "Forces of destruction begin in childhood."]

Deming continues on to say that evaluation systems often reinforce undesired behavior toward risk-taking:

> Merit rating rewards people that do well in the system. It does not reward attempts to improve the system. Don't rock the boat.
>
> (Deming, 1986:102)

This issue becomes especially problematic in the context of the LFM programme where one of the key operating principles involves leadership through risk-taking. To encourage students to become true leaders and innovators, the programme strives to question the existing systems and "rock the boat" when necessary. In fact, the Accounting course grading system exemplifies this whole risk-taking spirit. It represents an experiment which goes outside of the conventional individual performance-based grading norms and challenges the basic American classroom culture.

Despite his extensive comments on the dangers of performance measurement, Deming can suggest no alternative for measuring team performance. Like many other quality experts, he merely points out the difficulty of the issue, saying,

> Evaluation of performance explains why it is difficult for staff area to work together for the good of the company. They work instead as prima donnas, to the defeat of the company. Good performance on a team helps the company but leads to less tangible results to count for the individual. The problem on a team is: who did what?
>
> (Deming, 1986:107).

Closely related to the whole issue of performance evaluation in the workplace is grading in the classroom. The literature describes how grading, just like incentive systems in the workplace, can be demotivating if it is used as a threat:

> Repeated negative reinforcement..... results in frenetic, unguided activity. Further, punishment does not suppress the desire to "do bad." The person who has been punished is not thereby simply less inclined to behave in a given way; at best, he learns how to avoid punishment.
>
> (Thomas J. Peter and Robert H. Waterman, Jr., 1982:68).

Recent studies also support the Accounting professor's arguments for risk-taking in the classroom because grades are not particularly important indicators of future performance. For instance, an exhaustive statistical study by Donald Hoyt concludes,

> Present evidence strongly suggests that college grades bear little or no relationship to any measures of adult accomplishment. Academic achievement (knowledge) and other types of student growth and development are relatively independent of each other.... We encourage instructors to grade on the basis of multiple considerations.... and substitute a "profile of student growth and development" for the present transcript of grades.
>
> (Donald P. Hoyt, 1965:1 and 48).

Perhaps one of Philip Crosby's sayings best summarizes the current state of thinking on performance measurement systems:

Most things don't work like they are supposed to work.

(Philip B. Crosby, 1979:132).

Exhibit I
Accounting for Manufacturing

Leaders For Manufacturing Vision Statement

The *Leaders for Manufacturing* Programme is a partnership between MIT and twelve US manufacturing firms to discover and translate into teaching and practice principles that produce world-class manufacturing and manufacturing leaders. This partnership is motivated by our shared belief that excellence in manufacturing is critical to meeting the economic and social needs of individuals, firms, and society, and that the health of US-based companies operating in global markets is essential to the nation's well-being.

Mission Statement

The purpose of the *Leaders for Manufacturing* Programme is to identify, discover, and translate into practice the critical factors that underlie world-class manufacturing in a way that:

- attracts potential leaders with a global perspective and develops them to bring about world-class manufacturing
- establishes and verifies a new set of principles and practices for manufacturing
- stimulates new and innovative modes of operation for academia and industry
- achieves a high level of cooperation between academia and industry to integrate the technical, managerial, human, and organizational dimensions of manufacturing
- establishes on-going collaborative processes for problem identification, discovery, and knowledge transfer

Exhibit II
Accounting for Manufacturing

MIT Sloan School of Management   Charles Fine and Fred Kolman
Leaders for Manufacturing Programme   Summer 1991

15.515 - Accounting for Manufacturing
Class Schedule Summary

Pre-	arrival	00		Background Readings	Essentials of Accounting
M	06/10	01	CF	Accounting bores you? Wake up!	Yesterday's Accounting Undermines Production
T	06/11	02	F	Overview of Financial Reporting. The Accounting Process	DSW Chs. 1 and 2
W	06/12	03	C	Income Statement	DSW 3
F	06/14		M	Tutorial	
M	06/17	04	C	Accrual basis for manufacturing costs and revenue	DSW 4
M	06/17	05	F	Statement of Cash Flows	*DSW 5*
T	06/18	06	C	Inventory Valuation	DSW 7
W	06/19	07	F	Long-Lived Assets	DSW 8
T	06/25		M	Tutorial	
T	07/02	08	F	Liabilities	DSW Appendix: 707-730
W	07/03	09	C	Shareholder's Equity	Top Management's Incentive to Invest in New
M	07/08	10	F	The Stock Market: rational, myopic or rationally myopic?	Shareholder Trading Practices and Corporate
T	07/09	11	F	Integrate Exercise: Financial Statement Preparation	Chemlite, Inc, HBS Case 177-078
W	07/10	12	C	Financial Statement Analysis	Harnischfeger Corporation.
F	07/12		M	Tutorial	
T	07/16	13	F	Cost-Volume-Profit Analysis	Bill French, Accountant. HBS Case 104-039
W	07/17	14	C	Relevant Costs	Great Lakes Diversified Corporation:
F	07/26		M	Tutorial	
F	07/26			Mid-term Exam (2:30 - 5:00)	Classes 1-12
M	07/29	15	F	Cost Allocation. Introduction to Activity Based Costing	Seliram, Inc.: Electronic Testing Ops.
T	07/30	16	F	Product Costing, ABC	John Deere Component Works (A)
F	08/02		M	Tutorial	
M	08/05	17	C	Strategic Product Costing	Mueller-Lemkuhl GmbH
T	08/06	18	C	Budgets and Responsibility Accounting	Del Norte Paper Company (B)
F	08/09		M	Tutorial	Broadside Boats
M	08/12	19	C	Variance Analysis and Performance Evaluation	Uncle Grumps Case (Handout)
T	08/13	20	F	Performance Evaluation and Incentive Schemes	Analog Devices, Inc. (A)
W	08/14	21	F	Strategic Measures and Incentives in Advanced	Analog Devices
W	08/14			Final Exam Case will be handed out	
F	08/16		M	Tutorial	
M	08/19	22	C	Decentralization and Transfer Prices	Bultman Auto
M	08/19	23	C	Capital Budgeting	HWC 3 (Hand-out) - KA 12
T	08/20	24	C	Discussion of final case (Absolute deadline at 10:30 AM)	
W	08/21	25	CF	Accounting for Manufacturing and Competitiveness	

C = Charlie,   F = Fred,   M = Maureen

Exhibit III
Accounting for Manufacturing

15.515
Class Sessions 4 & 5
Student Comments & Responses

Note: Student comments are in plain type, and professor' responses are in italics.

19   Very helpful to do examples and problems in class, good discussion.
       OK, we'll keep doing it.
3   Rushed at the end, too much discussion on some issues, need more direction from
       professors.
2   Too much reading and preparation work.
       This is MIT
2   Grading class participation may be bad.
       We'll discuss how we grade.
1   Intense nervousness by some who are called and embarrassed. Build class rapport.
       Is it all right to get an answer wrong?
       Distinguish playfulness from sarcasm.
1   Outlines are very helpful.
1   Not enough time for lunch.
1   Provide answers to questions that are skipped (e.g. last few letters of 4-12).
       Go to section.
1   A little confusing about what order you do statements in.
1   Problem today with students not being prepared.
       Yeah, the class suffers if people don't prepare.
1   If we can't run our companies on financial accounting, why can't/don't we focus
       on more of cost or internal accounting?
       Fred will address this.

Exhibit IV
Accounting for Manufacturing

Number of Student Comments Submitted by Class

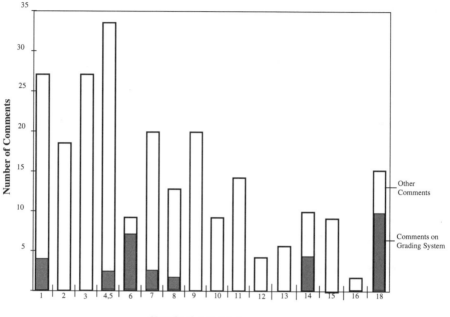

Class Session Number

Notes: There were 41 students in the class through session 7, and 40 students thereafter. Students could submit more than one comment per class. For some classes, feedback was combined, or data was unavailable. There is no data on which comments were pink (strengths) or blue (weakness).

Exhibit V
Accounting for Manufacturing

Final Course Grades

Team	Homework	Mid-Term Exam	Class Participation	Final Write-Up	Sum	Grade
A	150	142*	138	117	547	A
A	150	142*	122	117	531	A
A	150	128*	124	117	519	A
A	150	147*	94	117	508	A
A	150	141*	95	117	503	A
B	150	118	136	120	524	A
B	150	106	127	120	503	A
B	150	116	104	120	490	A
B	150	99	120	120	489	A
B	150	90	126	120	486	A
B	150	88	108	120	466	A
C	150	122	125	120	517	A
C	150	144*	95	120	509	A
C	150	136*	96	120	502	A
C	150	98	134	120	502	A
C	150	93	133	120	496	A
C	150	104	88	120	462	A
D	135	147*	93	128	503	A
D	135	104	134	128	501	A
D	135	122	115	128	500	A
D	135	109	118	128	490	A
D	135	104	112	128	479	A
D	135	89	100	128	452	A
E	150	129	133	106	503	B
E	150	90	128	106	501	B
E	150	114	93	106	500	B
E	150	104	102	106	490	B
E	150	91	109	106	479	B
E	150	91	97	106	444	B
F	150	118*	112	104	484	B
F	150	100	117	104	471	B
F	150	122	89	104	465	B
F	150	100	104	104	458	B
F	150	102	98	104	454	B
F	150	104	83	104	441	B
G	141	123	125	113	502	B
G	141	103	117	113	474	B
G	141	116*	80	113	450	B
G	141	81	104	113	439	B
G	141	83	85	113	422	B
Avg	147	112	110	115	484	
Std Dev	6	19	16	8	28	

*Denotes score on mid-term exam re-take

Exhibit VI
Accounting for Manufacturing
Final Course Evaluation Comments

Number of Comments

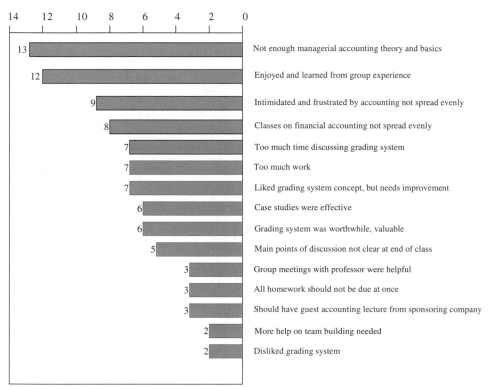

13	Not enough managerial accounting theory and basics
12	Enjoyed and learned from group experience
9	Intimidated and frustrated by accounting not spread evenly
8	Classes on financial accounting not spread evenly
7	Too much time discussing grading system
7	Too much work
7	Liked grading system concept, but needs improvement
6	Case studies were effective
6	Grading system was worthwhile, valuable
5	Main points of discussion not clear at end of class
3	Group meetings with professor were helpful
3	All homework should not be due at once
3	Should have guest accounting lecture from sponsoring company
2	More help on team building needed
2	Disliked grading system

Reflection On 44 Years Of Teaching

Howard Mehlinger

Center for Excellence in Education
Indiana University
United States of America

Synopsis

Howard Mehlinger, currently Director, Center for Excellence in Education, Indiana University in Bloomington, U.S.A., shared his two major concerns as a teacher at various levels of education throughout his teaching career of 44 years. He was concerned about whether he knew enough about the subject — world history — he taught as a teacher as well as whether his students were learning what they needed to know.

Howard Mehlinger shared how his perspectives changed during his career: first, as a high school world history teacher, later as a director of curriculum development projects, and finally as a university professor and dean, School of Education at Indiana University. His perspectives changed not only because of his professional position and status but also because of the different learning approaches and educational theoretical stance adopted, from behavioral to the cognitive to the constructivist. Despite the changes in learning perspectives, the essence of being a teacher is being a learner and helping others to learn effectively.

Reflection On 44 Years Of Teaching

Howard Mehlinger

I began my teaching career in September, 1953, as a high school world history teacher; I concluded my career in June, 1997, as an Indiana University professor of social studies education and Russian history. Throughout that 44-year career I struggled to find answers to two fundamental questions:

1) Do I know enough about the subject I am teaching that I can fulfill the role of teacher? and

2) Are my students learning what they need to know?

Every teacher must answer these questions. Although I taught at various levels of education and very different courses over my career, these two questions remained constant; only the answers changed.

In the beginning, the first question — Do I know enough about my subject — seemed to be more important. I was certain that once I knew what I needed to know, my students would easily learn what they need to know. As a recent college professor, I wanted to be like them. Only later did I become more interested in the second question — Are my students learning what they need to know. While the relative importance of these two questions has changed over time, both remain primary teaching concerns for me.

In the paragraphs that follow, I shall share how my perspective changed during my career: first, as a high school world history teacher, later as a director of a curriculum development project, and finally as a university professor.

World History Teacher (1953–63)

The first lesson a young world history teacher learns is that it is impossible to be a specialist on the entire history of human kind. In the United States, the high school world history course typically covers all of the history of the world from early man to space man and every culture and region of the earth in one school year. Few colleges or universities attempt to teach such a course; yet we routinely expect high school teachers with much less training to teach the history of the world in one year.

In September, 1953, I accepted a position as a tenth-grade world history teacher at Lawrence High School in Lawrence, Kansas. I had received my bachelor's degree only three months earlier. I had been a history major and felt adequately prepared to teach Greek, Roman, Modern European and American history — all courses I had studied in college. I knew little or nothing about the rest of the world.

There are at least two ways a world history teacher can cope with knowledge gaps. He can concentrate on those aspects of world history for which he is best informed and ignore other topics; or he can teach from the textbook and attempt to learn world history along with his students. At various times, I used both approaches.

I also decided that I must become a better educated world history teacher. I began graduate study leading toward a Ph.D. in Russian history. (I wanted to earn a doctorate in world history, but the history department at the University of Kansas said it was impossible to pursue a doctoral degree in world history.) Nevertheless, it did not take me long to realise that whatever pleasure I may gain from my graduate courses in Russian, Chinese, Japanese, and British Empire history, they would not contribute directly to my world history classes. The information I was acquiring was too detailed to be of great value to 15-year-old high school students. Even if I were eventually to become an expert on the history of the world, my expertise would be of marginal benefit to my students unless I found a way to make my knowledge useful to them.

I began to think more about what my students knew and how they came to know what they knew. In the beginning, I was mainly interested in whether my students were able to recall information I provided in the class, either by means of the textbooks and other reading assignments or by my own presentations. My focus was on their ability to recall information — e.g. memorisation. I remember that the main choice for me when preparing examinations was whether I would use "short answer" (i.e. true/false, multiple choice or matching items) or essay questions. The short answer variety took more time to prepare but were much easier to grade; essay questions required less time to develop but much more time to read and evaluate. I remember I also had to consider how difficult I wished the examination to be; if the exam distributed student scores widely, it was easier to justify a range of grades.

I don't recall that I was guided by any particular theory of learning. I suppose I had some crude notions about learning transfer in mind. I assumed that the information provided to students in my class would be stored somehow in their brains, much like paper is stored in a file cabinet; someday, when the facts were needed, the students would access the appropriate "files" in their brains.

I vividly remember a revelation I had one day. I was teaching a lesson about inventors during the Industrial Revolution and had just finished teaching it for the fourth time that day. I remember feeling grateful that I had good notes for my lecture, because I had trouble remembering which inventors had invented certain products and practices. Then it occurred to me: If I have taught this course for at least six years and the same lesson for at least four times each year and I cannot recall the information without my notes, how can I expect my students to retain the knowledge from one brief exposure?

During the last two years I was at Lawrence High School, we created a team teaching program in which three teachers, a part-time secretary, and a grader-assistant who was a teacher-in-training at the University of Kansas assumed responsibility for four sections of world history and five sections of American history — a total of 400 students! The team had access to new facilities that included a lecture room that held up to 77 students at a time; two regular classrooms that were divided by a sound-proof folding partition that together held 60 students comfortably; and a small seminar/ conference room that could accommodate 10 students.

The team teaching project was launched initially to support specialisation among the faculty. We thought that one person could lecture to 60 students in the lecture hall as easily as he could to thirty. By deploying our faculty across large lecture sessions and discussion groups, each faculty member could specialise in particular topics — it was no longer necessary to know all of world history; it also meant that each teacher was likely to find several hours of preparation time during the week.

Ironically, while the team teaching project was originally conceived to help the faculty become more specialised and provide more preparation time, it eventually led us to be more concerned about what students were learning. We soon recognised that meeting students in the large lecture room discouraged student participation; we had to find other ways to engage students in their own learning. The rooms established for group discussion became more important to us. Discussion sessions took place during at least two and often three of the five class sessions each week. Students met in groups of eight around octagonal-shaped tables to discuss pre-arranged topics linked to the course syllabus. The fact that these were student-led discussions placed more responsibility on the students to prepare and to share their ideas. The seminar/conference room was another place where a faculty member might engage in intense discussion with a few students around a book that had been assigned for all to read.

The small group discussions provided better indicators of student understanding than either essay or short answer examinations. Increasingly, lectures were used more to clarify issues and reduce misunderstandings that had been demonstrated in the discussion groups. Gradually, what we teachers knew became less important and what the students knew and understood became more important to us.

Curriculum Developer (1966–71)

From 1966 to 1971, I directed a federally-funded project called the High School Curriculum Center in Government (HSCCG) at Indiana University. HSCCG was one of many curriculum development centers in social studies education at that time, all directed at producing new kinds of instructional materials for use in American elementary and secondary schools. The Indiana University center I directed was charged with the development and testing of new kinds of instructional materials for high school civics and government.

My task as director of HSCCG was quite different from the one I had experienced as a high school world history teacher. Not only was the academic discipline different — political science rather than history — but I had no students of my own. The course materials I would eventually develop would be used by hundreds of students throughout the United States, but I would never meet these students or teachers.

The challenge to my own knowledge presented by this new assignment was both easier and more difficult to overcome than had been teaching world history. The scope of knowledge associated with American government is much less than the history of the world; it is possible to imagine acquiring knowledge competence in American government. Furthermore, I had also taught American government at Lawrence High School and had earned a minor in political science while working on my Ph.D. From that perspective, the task I faced in 1966 was less daunting than the one I confronted in 1953.

The knowledge challenge came from expectations the public had toward federally-funded projects. Such projects were expected not merely to treat the traditional subject matter better than in the past; they were to represent leading thought in the academic disciplines. Therefore, it was not enough to present solid political science in the form of a high school course; the expectation was that we would create a new kind of course, one not previously used in schools and representing the best research in political science. That was a challenging task for someone who was not a political scientist!

In the 1950s and 1960s, a behavioral (social science) approach represented the leading edge in political science research, although courses in behavioral politics were largely restricted to graduate students. At that time, few colleges and universities offered a behavioral approach to American government at the undergraduate level; there were no high school American government courses organised around a behavioral perspective. Traditional high school courses were organized around legal/ institutional approaches to the study of American government.

One of the leading educational theorists during this period was Jerome Bruner, a Harvard University psychologist. He had popularised the notion that the most important job of the schools was to introduce students to the key concepts and modes of inquiry of the academic disciplines. According to Bruner, if students acquired the intellectual tools of the best scholars in an academic domain, they would begin to see society in ways like the academic scholars. Furthermore, Bruner argued that such ideas need not be restricted to scholars; if properly presented, even young children could grasp them.

Thus, the task for us was to design materials for secondary school students that would use the key concepts and methodological approaches of the behavioural study of politics. The result after five years of development and testing was a high school course called *American Political Behaviour* (APB) that was eventually published by Ginn and Company and used in schools throughout the United States.

I overcame my knowledge deficiencies in behavioural politics by securing the advice and support of political scientists who employed behavioural perspectives in the study of politics. They directed me to books and articles that supported my own education and reviewed drafts of materials written by my partner, John Patrick, and I. The major problem we faced was how to overcome the knowledge deficit teachers would feel when confronted by our course. Very few would have studied American government from this orientation; presumably, they would be hesitant to teach a subject from a radically different perspective than the one they had used in the past.

The solution was to devise a comprehensive teacher's guide to accompany the student materials. The guide provided an introduction to the behavioural study of politics; it also provided details about how each lesson could be taught successfully; we also provided a wide range of "ancillary material" — work sheets, transparencies, games, and simulations — that a teacher could use with the course. We assumed that the teacher would "learn" the course along with the students; however, we provided ancillary materials for the teacher that were not given to the students directly without an intervention by the teacher. In this way, we hoped to teach the students *through* the teacher while strengthening the teacher's capacity.

During that period, there was a great deal of discussion about curriculum developers who tried to "teacher proof" the courses they designed. We were never so arrogant to think we could control what teachers did with the course; we did think, however, that we could deliver a course to students that represented a knowledge domain unfamiliar to the teachers. Good teachers would surely adapt the course to fit their own students and improve upon it in many ways. It was also true that the course would do poorly in the hands of weak and ineffective teachers. Nevertheless, we learned that a strong teacher's guide can help overcome knowledge gaps experienced by teachers.

We were also interested in helping APB teachers learn what their students knew from the study of politics. We were much impressed by Benjamin Bloom's ideas regarding mastery learning. In brief, Bloom's idea was that students showed greater range in the speed at which they acquired new knowledge than in their ability to eventually comprehend it. What needed to be done was for teachers to master the new concepts and skills. Examinations should serve as further opportunities to demonstrate applications of knowledge.

We designed the lessons for the APB course in such ways as to support inquiry and application. The first lesson to introduce a new concept or method and to launch a sequence of instruction was always presented as a problem or issue that could inspire an investigation by students. Then, students were provided information enabling them to acquire command of the new knowledge and subsequently apply it to new case studies or situations that had not been part of the original instruction. By organising the content around concepts and skills, it was relatively easy to judge whether students were acquiring the knowledge expected of them and whether they could apply it appropriately in fresh circumstances.

We also developed examinations based upon mastery learning principles. Each examination that followed a section of the course was designed to provide fresh applications of the knowledge covered in that section. The tests were not designed so some would succeed and others fail, if instruction had been successful, all students were expected to succeed. We also provided "back up" tests with similar items to the first test and directed to the same course objectives. When students failed to achieve "mastery" on the first exam, we suggested to teachers that they review problems students may have had on the first test and then allow them to re-take the examination using the back-up test. If they were successful on the second test, the teacher should consider that they had mastered the material.

APB marked a change in my attitude about what a teacher needs to know and what students need to know. As a world history teacher I was concerned that I know everything there was to know about world history and that I somehow transfer my detailed knowledge to students. As an APB designer, it was more important that teachers have a grasp of the behavioural approach to the study of politics and that they have the abilities to help students acquire the key concepts and skills. Remembering specific, factual details was less important for students than applying their new concepts and perspectives to real political events occurring around them.

Professor of a Doctoral Seminar in Social Studies Education (1992–97)

During the last five years I have been teaching an advanced graduate course on "The Nature of the Social Studies." This course is a capstone course for doctoral students in social studies education. It is intended to ensure that doctoral students have knowledge about the individuals who have influenced the field of social studies, that they are aware of the main theories and beliefs that undergird the field of social studies, and that they are capable of articulating their own view of social studies while drawing thoughtfully upon the leading ideas of the field. The course usually draws eight to twelve students and meets once each week during a semester in a seminar setting.

If my task was to be an expert in all that has been said or done in the field of social studies since its origin, it would be a daunting task. But, the task of the seminar is to focus on what the students know and do not know. Furthermore, each of the students bring information and skills to the seminar that are not possessed by other students. Therefore, my task as seminar instructor is to guide the seminar participants across a pre-arranged set of topics and themes and then ensure that knowledge is brought to bear on these topics. The sources of information may come from books and articles read by all, from reports of investigations by individual seminar participants, by guest speakers, or by information and perspectives I provide. Clearly, the knowledge task is not for me to convey all that I know about the field of social studies education; the seminar serves as a learning organisation where each person presents and accepts information and knowledge.

Finding out what the student has learned is a relatively simple matter. Each week, every student is expected to contribute substantially to the seminar's work; I can judge the quality of contributions on a weekly basis. Seminar members accept certain investigations to perform on behalf of the seminar; the written results of these investigations are shared publicly and easily assessed.

The seminar participants have a common, culminating assignment. They are asked to behave as if they are members of a curriculum planning committee for a local school district. They are expected to design a social studies program that ranges from kindergarten through grade twelve and to justify their scope and sequence decisions according to the perspectives they have gained from the seminar. The final product is presented in the form of a written report and presented in an open meeting to which are invited other members of the Indiana University social studies education faculty.

This assignment requires that the participants find practical expression for their theoretical ideas. It also demands that they work collaboratively, sharing ideas and seeking common ground. The presentation of this joint report before the faculty makes the task more authentic and leads the students to take the assignment more seriously.

The theory of learning that undergirds the seminar is mainly constructivist. Students are encouraged to construct their own understanding of the social studies field and to share their perspectives with each other. My role is to guide the discussion but not impose my own views. I am merely one of many sources of information to be employed in the seminar. The focus is on what students understand and can perform with their understanding rather than what I know.

Conclusion

When I began my career as a teacher 44 years ago, I was mainly concerned with what I knew about the subject I taught because I believed that what I knew would determine what students would know. I feel the same way today, but there is a difference. While it is necessary that I be knowledgeable about any subject I teach, it is because I must guide my students along useful paths and toward valuable sources of information. I no longer believe that they will eventually know exactly what I know regardless of my success as a teacher. What they know and understand will be determined in large measure by their own experience. Furthermore, I no longer care that they know what I know, exactly as I know it. It is more important that they be able to reflect on what they know and use their knowledge in constructive ways.

I no longer feel anxiety about what I don't know. I understand much better than I did 44 years ago that I shall continue to learn — on my own and depending upon others, including my students. I have learned that being a teacher is not possessing a body of knowledge that is passed authoritatively to others; being a teacher is being a learner and helping others to learn effectively.

The Continual Dialogue On The Reflective Spin

Ai-Yen Chen

National Institute of Education
Nanyang Technological University
Singapore

John Van Maanen

Sloan School of Management
Massachusetts Institute of Technology
United States of America

Recent economic and political turmoil in some parts of the world have caused great stirs among the business, communication, industrial and transportation communities. The dramatic shifts in financial and power bases have compelled many world leaders to quickly review their understanding, re-examine their problems and reframe their policies, often leading to a revision of their espoused beliefs and theories, and a transformation of ways of learning, working, even living as fulfilled, achieving human beings.

Professionals and organizations that are keeping pace with the developments of world events and market forces will undoubtedly have a cutting edge over the rest of the communities of practitioners. How do we learn to reflect before taking action in cases where established theories and conditions do not apply? Teachers of professionals can no longer teach standard scientific theories and humanistic strategies and well-rehearsed techniques to solve common problems. They can no longer claim a permanent knowledge base and a body of competence that are required for a particular profession. As the knowledge explosion causes many to reel, teachers of professionals today are compelled to respond very quickly to the current situation. They are forced to reflect on their own practices and to be prepared to equip future professionals with the essential knowledge, the thinking skills and values necessary to deal with difficult and unpredictable problems of the real world.

Writers of *The Reflective Spin* have generously shared their concerns, struggles, knowledge and insights about learning and teaching in higher education with our readers. The spin-off is the conviction that all who read will benefit from this *sharing of a **new** reflective experience* in a multi-layered, multi-faceted, and multi-perspective context — the book in print or in cyberspace. The secondary spin-off is the belief that all who are actively engaged in this integrated and extended dialogue and reflection will scale new heights and experience peak insights, even if they went through the marshland of doubts, uncertainty, even chaos and turbulence of the emotional, psychological, intellectual and social nature.

Notes on the Contributors

CHEN AI-YEN

Chen Ai-Yen is an Associate Professor and former Head, Division of Instructional Science, National Institute of Education, Nanyang Technological University, Singapore (1991–1998). She is also the coordinator of the Postgraduate Diploma of Teacher in Higher Education Programme. Ai-Yen has been a secondary school teacher, a curriculum developer, an educational television producer and a consultant in higher education in Singapore, China and the United States. Ai-Yen has written extensively in the area of educational media and technology and their use and impact on learning and teaching, teachers' development and reflective practices in professional education in international journals and books. She is the Associate Editor, Journal of Information Technology for Teacher Education and Educational Action Research, UK.

JOHN VAN MAANEN

John Van Maanen is the Erwin Schell Professor of Organization Studies in the Sloan School of Management at the Massachusetts Institute of Technology (M.I.T.). He has published a number of books and articles on the general area of occupational and organizational sociology and qualitative research methodology. He is the author of *Tales of the Field* (University of Chicago Press, 1988) and, most recently, *Qualitative Studies of Organizations* (Sage, 1998).

S. GOPINATHAN

S. Gopinathan is Professor of Education and Dean, School of Education, National Institute of Education, Nanyang Technological University, Singapore. He is also Head, NIE Centre for Educational Research. A specialist in comparative education, his research interests include education and development relationships, language policy, planning and bilingualism and higher education. Gopinathan has published extensively in such areas as the development of education in Singapore, language policy formulation, language in education, values education and on textbook publishing in developing countries. His publications include *Towards a National System of Education in Singapore, 1945–1973* and as co-editor, *The Revival of Values Education in East Asia.* He is an ex-President of the Educational Research Association and Executive Editor, *Asia Pacific Journal of Education.*

EDGAR H. SCHEIN

Edgar H. Schein is the Sloan Fellows Professor of Management (Emeritus) at M.I.T. He studies organizational culture, process consultation and organizational change and learning. He has recently published *Strategic Pragmatism: The Culture of Singapore's Economic Development Board* (MIT Press, 1996) and *The Corporate Culture Survival Guide* (Jossey Bass, 1999).

CHRISTINE BENNETT

Christine Bennett is Professor of Curriculum and Instruction: social studies at Indiana University, U.S.A. She is the Director of Research Institute on Teacher Education and Project TEAM: A program to recruit minority students into teaching positions. She specializes in social studies and multicultural education and has published articles in teachers' perspectives and teachers' knowledge.

LORI BRESLOW

Lori Breslow is a Senior Lecturer in the Sloan School of Management and Director of the Learning Laboratory at M.I.T. Her research interests center on academic, intercultural and managerial and professional communications. She has recently created a pilot program at M.I.T. to develop teamwork skills among undergraduate majors in mechanical engineering.

D. JEAN CLANDININ

D. Jean Clandinin is an Associate Professor of Education and Director of the Centre for Research for Teacher Education and Development at the University of Alberta. She was a former teacher, counselor, and school psychologist. She has published extensively in the area of classroom practices, the reflective practitioner, and narrative studies of teachers. Together with F.M. Connelly, they have several publications including *Teachers as Curriculum Planners: Narratives of Experience* and *Teachers' Professional Knowledge Landscape*.

F. MICHAEL CONNELLY

F. Michael Connelly is a Professor of Curriculum and Teacher Studies at the Ontario Institute for Studies in Education and the University of Toronto, Canada. He coordinates the Canadian component of the Second International Science Study and is editor of Curriculum Inquiry, and a member of the board of directors of the John Dewey Society for Education and Culture. His research interest is in the study of teaching and has published extensively in teachers' practical knowledge and curriculum practices including books such as the above mentioned with D. Jean Clandinin.

JOYCE E. JAMES

Joyce E. James is the Head of the Specialists Department at the SEAMEO Regional Language Centre, Singapore. She has a Ph.D. from Macquarie University, Sydney. An educationist from Singapore, she has had teaching experiences in secondary schools and colleges in Singapore, the United Kingdom, and Australia prior to joining RELC in 1992. At RELC, Joyce James coordinates and teaches the Diploma in Applied Linguistics course and the Masters in Applied Linguistics Course and other short courses. Joyce James is the Editor of the RELC Journal.

FRED KOFMAN

Fred Kofman is an independent organizational consultant based in Boulder, Colorado. He holds a Ph.D. in economics from the University of California and taught accounting for several years in the Sloan School of Management at M.I.T. where he received the Sloan Teacher of the Year Award in 1992 and wrote a number of cases to improve learning about controversial issues. He is currently involved in corporate sponsored learning and change projects taking place at General Motors, Boeing and Electronic Data Systems.

ORA W. Y. KWO

Ora W. Y. Kwo is Associate Professor in the Department of Curriculum Studies, Faculty of Education, University of Hong Kong. She has conducted a number of research studies in teacher education in Hong Kong and China. She edited the book "Professional Learning Together; Building a Collaborative Culture in Teaching Practicum Supervision" (1998).

CHRISTINE KIM-ENG LEE

Christine Kim-Eng Lee is Associate Professor at the National Institute of Education, Nanyang Technological University, Singapore. She teaches curriculum studies courses at pre-service, in-service and postgraduate levels. She specializes in geography education and social studies and has an active interest in cooperative learning. She trains teachers in cooperative techniques and has published several research studies in the school implementation of cooperative learning, particularly in social studies.

ZIQI LIAO

Ziqi Liao is an Assistant Professor, Nanyang Business School, Nanyang Technological University, Singapore. He specializes in the application of information technology in business and manufacturing areas. More recently, he has been increasingly involved in consulting with China on their online e-commerce mailing systems.

LUM-PENG LIM

Lum-Peng Lim is Associate Professor in the Department of Preventive Dentistry, National University of Singapore, with a keen interest in educational research. Her current focus involves evaluation of problem-based learning and project work in dental education.

SOH-LOI LOI

Soh-Loi Loi is Associate Professor in Division of Actuarial Science & Insurance, School of Accountancy and Business, Nanyang Technological University, Singapore. She is interested in applying statistical methods to business research, comparing East and West education and improving statistical education.

HOWARD MEHLINGER

Howard Mehlinger is Professor of Education and History and Director, Center for Excellence in Education at Indiana University, U.S.A. He also co-directs the Institute for the Study of Russian Education and teaches courses in social studies education and continues to lead in improving higher education through the use of technology.

MOLLIE NEVILLE

Mollie Neville is Senior Lecturer, Massey University, Albany Campus, Auckland, New Zealand. She is the Director of the Masters of Educational Administration Programme at the university and has been a school teacher as well as a university lecturer in Singapore and New Zealand. She has written articles and done a number of research projects on school culture and school leadership.

MAUREEN NG

Maureen Ng is Assistant Professor at the National Institute of Education, Nanyang Technological University, Singapore. She teaches social studies and economic education courses at pre-service and in-service levels. She has been in teacher education for the past 20 years with particular interest in cooperative and collaborative learning. She has also trained teachers in the techniques with Christine Lee and has jointly published several research studies in relation to cooperative learning in Singapore schools.

MARNIE O'NEILL

Marnie O'Neill is Associate Professor and Director of Teaching, Graduate School of Education at the University of Western Australia. She has done extensive research and development in the area of professional development of university teachers including the production of specially designed multimedia packages for use over the Internet. She is the Editor, Education Research and Perspectives, a publication of the University of Western Australia.

RICHARD PRING

Richard Pring is currently Professor and Head, Educational Studies Department at the University of Oxford, UK. He was formerly Dean of Faculty of Education, University of Exeter, a lecturer at the Institute of Education at the University of London and a teacher in two London comprehensive schools. He is a much sought-after international speaker and was the keynote speaker for the Ruth Wong Memorial Lecture in Singapore in 1994. His most recent book *Closing the Gap: Liberal Education and Vocational Preparation*, was highly commended at the Standing Conference on Studies in Education, UK in 1996.

LOUIS SCHMIER

Louis Schmier is a Professor of History at Valdosta University, Georgia, U.S.A. Though his specialization is in Jewish history and the Nazi Movement in German history, his more recent publications are in the areas of teachers' experience and university teaching. Among his recent books is *Random Thoughts: The Humanity of Teaching*.

KIRPAL SINGH

Kirpal Singh is Associate Professor of English Literature and Drama. Kirpal Singh is one of Singapore's best-known writers in English and has been invited to give readings of his works all over the world, including Edinburgh, Toronto, Adelaide, Perth, York, Germany, India, Philippines, Malaysia,

Wellington, Fiji, and Papua New Guinea. As a scholar, he is General Editor of INTERLOGUE: Studies in Singapore Literature and a recognized authority on Aldous Huxley, Indian Literature and Australian Literature. His current research interests include cross-cultural engagements in literature and the ways in which a society treats its more articulate citizens.

JACK TEO CHENG CHUAH

Jack Teo Cheng Chuah is an Assistant Professor at the School of Accountancy and Business, Nanyang Technological University, Singapore. Jack's research interests are in the fields of banking, public international law and the law of international transportation by air.

ALAN J. WATSON

Alan J. Watson is Associate Professor in the School of Teacher Education at the University of New South Wales, Australia. He specializes in the area of Developmental Psychology and its relationship to education. He has published in the areas of child cognition and literacy, teacher knowledge and behaviour, teacher satisfaction and school staffing, and children's concepts of secrecy.